the TRAFFIC OFFICER'S
COMPANION

GORDON WILSON

By the same author:
The Beat Officer's Companion

© Gordon Wilson 1998

7th edition 1992
8th edition 1993
9th edition 1995
10th edition 1998

ISBN 0 85164 083 4

The Police Review
Publishing Co
Celcon House
289-293, High Holborn
London WC1V 7HZ

Illustrations by Rich King, Ashton-Under-Lyne, Lancs
Printed and bound in Great Britain by
the Ashford Colour Press, Gosport, Hampshire.

PREFACE

The present-day police officer engaged in the enforcement of traffic law is faced with the onerous task of interpreting, committing to memory and, whenever the situation demands, instantaneously recalling and making decisions upon, an immense field of technical legislation. This manual attempts to assist in handling the problems encountered, by presenting the more practical aspects of traffic policing in a fashion which facilitates speedy reference and easy interpretation.

In recent years a myriad of text books have been published, many of which contain a comprehensive coverage of traffic legislation. Their authors are to be congratulated in their presentation of a subject which is renowned for its complexity and obscurity. But in the majority of cases such works, whilst ideally suited to the legal practitioner engaged in the wider aspects of the law, are not in keeping with the more urgent demands of the operational policeman dealing with incidents.

The problems experienced in compiling this guidebook have surrounded the need to balance the selection of material thought to be a possible source of assistance, with an easily read and understood format whilst, at the same time, maintaining a system which would facilitate speedy reference. With this in mind material has been presented in almost every case in a diagrammatic or pictorial manner.

Because the book is intended to serve merely as a guide to the operational police officer, the relevant legislation has been subjected to a practical interpretation. It should not, therefore be regarded as a definitive work of reference and specific technical details may require further research.

Gordon Wilson
Former Superintendent
Warwickshire Constabulary

CONTENTS

Part 1: CONSTRUCTION AND USE   1

Part 2: DOCUMENTATION   71

CONTENTS

Part 3: LIGHTING AND MARKING   113

CONTENTS

Part 4: DRIVERS' HOURS AND RECORDS 157

Part 5: MISCELLANEOUS 185

CONTENTS

CONTENTS

PART 1

CONSTRUCTION
AND USE

In Part 1 we will start with relevant vehicle
definitions, and then go on to consider some
of the more complex issues of Construction
and Use (C&U) Regulations in summarised
form, aided by a series of diagrams

VEHICLE DEFINITIONS

Before we go onto consider the main contents of this book, we should consider some of the more important vehicle definitions you are likely to encounter.

MOTOR VEHICLE

Mechanically propelled vehicle intended or adapted for use on the roads.

REG 3 ROAD VEHICLES (CONSTRUCTION AND USE) REGULATIONS 1986

NOTE

The term **'mechanically propelled'** includes all known means of propulsion, eg petrol, diesel, gas, electricity. The test for whether a mechanically propelled vehicle is a motor vehicle is simply that of establishing if the vehicle in question is intended or adapted for use on a road. If the vehicle meets that criteria it is a motor vehicle, if it does not it is a mechanically propelled vehicle.

The Road Traffic Act 1991 made amendments to the Road Traffic Act 1988 which resulted in many (but not all) offences which related to motor vehicles being extended to the wider term of mechanically propelled vehicle.

MOTOR CAR

Under the C&U Regulations a **'motor car'** is a mechanically propelled vehicle, not being a motor tractor, motor cycle or invalid carriage, constructed and adapted for load or passengers, unladen weight (UW) not exceeding:

- if not more than seven passengers and effects, 3,050kg;
- if for goods or burden, 3,050kg; and
- in any other case, 2,450kg.

REG 3 ROAD VEHICLES (CONSTRUCTION AND USE) REGULATIONS 1986

However, under the RTA 1988 a **'motor car'** is a mechanically propelled vehicle, not being a motor cycle or invalid carriage, which is constructed itself to carry a load or passengers and of which the UW:

- does not exceed 3,050kg if constructed solely for the carriage of not more than seven passengers and their effects and is fitted with pneumatic tyres;
- does not exceed 3,050kg (3,500kg if gas propelled) if constructed or adapted for the conveyance of goods or burden of any description;
- does not exceed 2,540kg in cases falling within neither of the above descriptions.

SECTION 185 ROAD TRAFFIC ACT 1988

VEHICLE DEFINITIONS cont

You will have noted that there is little difference between the two definitions. However, you must apply the C&U definition to vehicles coming within the scope of those Regulations and the RTA definition to vehicles coming within the scope of that legislation.

HEAVY MOTOR CAR

Under the C&U Regulations a heavy motor car is a mechanically propelled vehicle, not being a locomotive, motor tractor or motor car, which is constructed itself to carry a load or passengers, UW exceeds 2,540kg.

REG 3 ROAD VEHICLES (CONSTRUCTION AND USE) REGULATIONS 1986

Under the RTA 1988 it is a mechanically propelled vehicle, not being a motor car, which is constructed itself to carry a load or passengers and the UW exceeds 2,540kg.

SECTION 185 ROAD TRAFFIC ACT 1988

MOTOR TRACTOR

Mechanically propelled vehicle not constructed itself to carry a load other than equipment for propulsion, loose tools and loose equipment, UW not exceeding 7,370kg.

SECTION 185 ROAD TRAFFIC ACT 1988

LIGHT LOCOMOTIVE

Mechanically propelled vehicle not itself constructed to carry load other than equipment for propulsion, loose tools and loose equipment, UW exceeding 7,320kg but not exceeding 11,690kg.

SECTION 185(1) ROAD TRAFFIC ACT 1988

HEAVY LOCOMOTIVE

Mechanically propelled vehicle not itself constructed to carry load other than equipment for propulsion, loose tools and loose equipment, uw exceeding 11,690kg.

SECTION 185(1) ROAD TRAFFIC ACT 1988

GOODS VEHICLE

Motor vehicle or trailer constructed or adapted for use for carriage or haulage of goods or burden of any description.

REG 3 ROAD VEHICLES (CONSTRUCTION AND USE) REGULATIONS 1986

(See later for large and medium-sized goods vehicles.)

ARTICULATED VEHICLE

Under the C&U Regulations 1986, an articulated vehicle is a heavy motor car, or motor car not being an articulated bus, with trailer so attached that part of the trailer is superimposed upon the drawing vehicle and not less than 20 per cent of weight of load is borne by drawing vehicle.

REG 3 ROAD VEHICLES (CONSTRUCTION AND USE) REGULATIONS 1986

VEHICLE DEFINITIONS cont

ARTICULATED VEHICLE cont

Under the RTA 1988 an articulated vehicle is:

a) a vehicle so constructed that it can be divided into two parts
- both of which are vehicles, and one of which is a motor vehicle
- and shall (when not so divided) be treated as that motor vehicle with the part attached as a trailer; or

b) a passenger vehicle (ie a vehicle constructed or adapted for use solely or principally for carriage of passengers) so constructed that it can be divided into two parts
- both of which are vehicles and one of which is a motor vehicle
- but cannot be so divided without the use of facilities normally available only at a workshop
- and passengers carried by it, when not so divided can at all times pass from either part to the other, and
- it shall, when not so divided, be treated as a single motor vehicle.

SECTION 187 ROAD TRAFFIC ACT 1988

DUAL PURPOSE VEHICLE

A vehicle constructed and adapted for both the carriage of passengers and goods UW not exceeding 2,040kg and

a) is so constructed or adapted that the driving power of the engine is, or by appropriate use of the controls can be, transmitted to all wheels of the vehicle, or

b) it is constructed so that:
- it has a rigid roof, with or without a sliding roof panel,
- the area of the vehicle to the rear of the driver's seat must have at least one row of properly upholstered transverse seats (fixed or folding) capable of carrying at least two persons,
- the distance between the steering wheel and the backrest of the rear most seats must not be less than one third of the distance between the steering wheel and the rearmost part of the floor, and
- the windows to rear of drivers seat must have an area of not less than 1,850sq cms on either side and not less than 770sq cms at the rear.

REG 3 ROAD VEHICLES (CONSTRUCTION AND USE) REGULATIONS 1986

MEDIUM-SIZED GOODS VEHICLE

A motor vehicle which is constructed or adapted to carry or to haul goods and is not adapted to carry more than nine persons inclusive of the driver and the permissible maximum weight of which exceeds 3.5 but not 7.5 tonnes.

SECTION 108(1) ROAD TRAFFIC ACT 1988

SMALL VEHICLE

NOTE: The terms 'small goods' and 'small passenger vehicles' have now been replaced by the new term 'small vehicle'.

A small vehicle is a motor vehicle, other than an invalid carriage, moped or motor bicycle which:

a) is not constructed to carry more than nine passengers inclusive of the driver; and

b) has a maximum gross weight not exceeding 3.5 tonnes; and includes a combination of such motor vehicle and trailer.

VEHICLE DEFINITIONS cont

INVALID CARRIAGE

A mechanically propelled vehicle, the weight of which unladen does not exceed 254kg and which is specially designed and constructed – not merely adapted – for use of a person suffering from some physical defect or disability and is used solely by such a person.

REG 3 ROAD VEHICLES (CONSTRUCTION AND USE) REGULATIONS 1986
AND SECTION 185(1) ROAD TRAFFIC ACT 1988

LARGE GOODS VEHICLE

A motor vehicle (not being a medium-sized goods vehicle) which is constructed or adapted to carry or to haul goods and the maximum permissible weight of which exceeds 7.5 tonnes.

SECTION 121 ROAD TRAFFIC ACT 1988

MOTOR CYCLE

Mechanically propelled vehicle, not being an invalid carriage, with less than four wheels and the weight unladen does not exceed 410kg.

REG 3(1) ROAD VEHICLES (CONSTRUCTION AND USE) REGULATIONS 1986
AND SECTION 185(1) ROAD TRAFFIC ACT 1988

MOPED

first used on or after 1.8.77

This is a motor cycle, not being a mowing machine or a pedestrian controlled vehicle, which has a maximum design speed which does not exceed 30mph, a kerbside weight which does not exceed 250kg and, if propelled by an internal combustion engine, an engine which does not exceed 50cc. Alternatively;

first used before 1.8.77

A motor cycle which has an engine with a cylinder capacity not exceeding 50cc and is equipped with pedals by means of which the cycle is capable of being propelled.

REG 3 MOTOR VEHICLES (DRIVING LICENCES) REGULATIONS 1987

PASSENGER CARRYING VEHICLE

(a) a **large passenger carrying vehicle**, that is to say, a vehicle used for carrying passengers which is constructed or adapted to carry more than 16 passengers, or
(b) a **small passenger carrying vehicle**, that is to say, a vehicle used for carrying passengers for hire or reward which is constructed or adapted to carry more than 8 but not more than 16 passengers
and includes a combination of such a motor vehicle and a trailer.

SECTION 121 ROAD TRAFFIC ACT 1988

MAXIMUM LENGTH

REG 7 ROAD VEHICLES (CONSTRUCTION AND USE) REGULATIONS 1986

If the maximum is exceeded, refer to 'Special types'.

Rigid vehicles

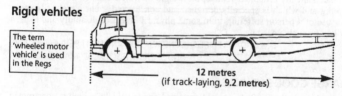

The term 'wheeled motor vehicle' is used in the Regs

12 metres
(if track-laying, **9.2 metres**)

Articulated vehicles

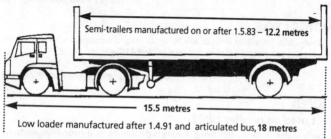

Semi-trailers manufactured on or after 1.5.83 – **12.2 metres**

15.5 metres

Low loader manufactured after 1.4.91 and articulated bus, **18 metres**

Figures shown on above diagram may be increased to **14.04 metres** and **16.5 metres** if distance between rearmost kingpin and front and rear of trailer does not exceed **2.04** metres and **12** metres respectively (**4.19 metres** and **12.5 metres** in the case of a car transporter).

Trailers

(not being a semi-trailer or composite trailer)

Four or more wheels – drawing vehicle not less than 3,500kg (max gross weight) or agricultural trailers.

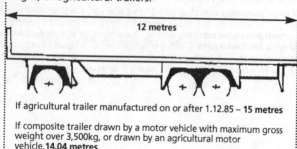

12 metres

If agricultural trailer manufactured on or after 1.12.85 – **15 metres**

If composite trailer drawn by a motor vehicle with maximum gross weight over 3,500kg, or drawn by an agricultural motor vehicle, **14.04 metres**

All other trailers
(not being an agricultural trailed appliance or a semi-trailer)

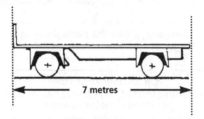

Combinations – 1 trailer (which is not a semi trailer)

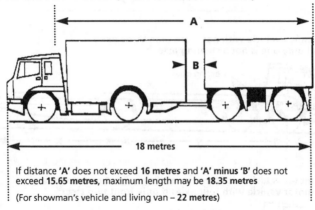

If distance **'A'** does not exceed **16 metres** and **'A' minus 'B'** does not exceed **15.65 metres**, maximum length may be **18.35 metres**

(For showman's vehicle and living van – **22 metres**)

Combinations – two or more trailers or indivisible load

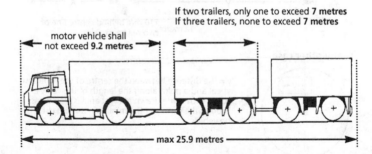

If two trailers, only one to exceed **7 metres**
If three trailers, none to exceed **7 metres**

motor vehicle shall not exceed **9.2 metres**

max 25.9 metres

OVERHANG

REGS 3(1) AND 11(1) ROAD VEHICLES (CONSTRUCTION AND USE) REGS 1986

Overhang 'x' (see diagrams showing categories 1-4 below) must not exceed:

FOR MOTOR TRACTOR
1.83 metres (except track-laying vehicle and agricultural motor vehicle)

FOR HEAVY MOTOR CAR AND MOTOR CAR
60 per cent of 'y'

1. motor vehicle with not more than three axles – and only one is not a steering axle

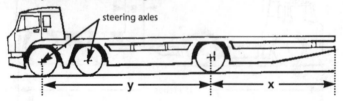

steering axles

2. motor vehicle with three axles if only front one steers, and
3. motor vehicle with four axles if only front two steer:

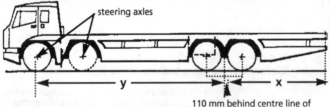

steering axles

110 mm behind centre line of two rearmost axles

4. any other case

'y'= the distance between the centre of the foremost wheel and a point along the length of the vehicle from which a line drawn at right angles would pass through the centre of the minimum turning circle of the vehicle.

MAXIMUM WIDTH

REG 8 ROAD VEHICLES (CONSTRUCTION AND USE) REGULATIONS 1986

If the maximum is exceeded, refer to 'Special types'.

Locomotive		**2.75 m**
Refrigerated vehicle A vehicle specially designed for the carriage of goods at low temperatures and the thickness of each side-wall including insulation is at least 45mm		**2.6 m**
Any other motor vehicle		**2.55 m**
Trailer drawn by a motor vehicle (having max gross weight exceeding 3,500 kg) **Agricultural trailer** **Agricultural trailed appliance,** **or an off-set combination of an agricultural motor vehicle drawing a wheeled trailer**		**2.55 m**
Any other trailer drawn by a vehicle other than a motor cycle		**2.3 m**
Trailer drawn by motor cycle		**1.5 m**

MAXIMUM HEIGHT – BUSES

REG 9 ROAD VEHICLES (CONSTRUCTION AND USE) REGULATIONS 1986

DEFINITION

A bus is a motor vehicle constructed or adapted to carry more than eight seated passengers in addition to the driver.

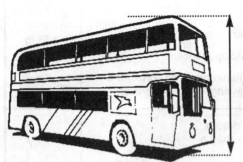

The overall height of a bus shall not exceed **4.57 metres**

NOTE: See later this section for overall travelling heights.

WEIGHT

Regulations prohibiting excess axle weight are designed primarily to prevent damage to the road surfaces and foundations, while those relating to excess overall weight are aimed at ensuring the design limits are not exceeded and that the vehicle can stop within the distance for which its brakes were designed. There are therefore separate offences of:

excess axle weight and
excess overall weight.

All locomotives, motor tractors, and heavy motor cars must have the unladen weight (UW) marked on the near side of the vehicle.

Vehicles should be equipped with a

Manufacturer's plate and a
Ministry plate

containing details of the maximum axle, gross and train weights.

Offences may be committed if the maximum permitted weight contained in C&U Regulations 1986, the manufacturer's plate or the Ministry plate are exceeded. *The following chart may be a guide to procedure:*

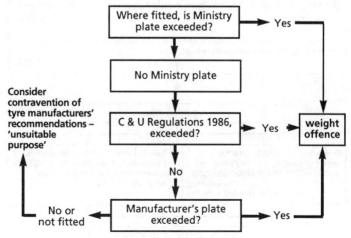

NOTE: For further details see Plating of goods vehicles, in Part 2.

POWER TO WEIGH VEHICLES
ROAD TRAFFIC ACT 1988

Failure to comply or obstructing the exercise of functions is an offence
(S 78(3))

On production of his authority **a constable authorised by the chief constable** may require a person in charge of a motor vehicle to
1. proceed to a weighbridge (or other machine for weighing vehicles)
2. allow the vehicle or trailer to be weighed, either laden or unladen
3. and the weight transmitted to the road by any part of the vehicle or trailer in contact with the road to be tested.

S 78(1)

NOTE: An authorised officer has no power to require the person in charge of a motor vehicle to unload the vehicle or trailer or to cause or allow it to be unloaded in order to have it weighed unladen. S 78(4)

Where a goods vehicle or a motor vehicle adapted to carry more than eight passengers has been weighed under the provision of S 78, and it appears to the authorised officer that the weights imposed by the C&U Regulations 1986 have been exceeded – or would be exceeded were it used on a road – he may give notice* in writing to the person in charge of the vehicle prohibiting it being driven on a road until
(a) the weight is reduced to the limit, and
(b) the person in charge has been notified in writing that it is allowed to proceed. S 70(2)

* This notice may be withheld until the vehicle has been weighed to satisfy the constable that the weight has been sufficiently reduced.

S 70(4)

A person who

drives a goods vehicle on a road, or causes or permits it to be driven, in contravention of a prohibition under S 69 (unfit vehicles) or S 70 (overloaded vehicles)	fails to comply within a reasonable time with a direction under S 70(3) to remove the vehicle to such place specified in writing

shall be guilty of an offence.

S 71(1) (AS SUBSTITUTED BY S 14 RTA 1991)

MAXIMUM OVERALL WEIGHT
ROAD VEHICLES (CONSTRUCTION AND USE) REGULATIONS 1986

If the maximum is exceeded, refer to 'Special types'.

LOCOMOTIVE   REG 75

If fitted with suitable tyres & springs:	
with less than 6 wheels	22,360kg
with 6 wheels	26,420kg
more than 6 wheels	30,490kg
Not conforming as above	20,830kg
Total weight of all trailers laden or unladen, drawn by a locomotive	40,650kg

BUS   REGS 75 & 78

The maximum permitted laden weight is the same as a heavy motor car or motor car but the weight is calculated when the vehicle is complete and fully equipped for service with:

roof luggage space – uniformly distributed load at 75kg per square metre

63.5kg per person who could legally be carried (65kg if bus first used after 1.4.88)

100kg per cubic metre of luggage space or 10kg per person who could legally be carried whichever is less

full supply of water, oil and fuel

MAXIMUM OVERALL WEIGHT cont
ROAD VEHICLES (CONSTRUCTION AND USE) REGULATIONS 1986

If the maximum is exceeded, refer to 'Special types'.

VEHICLE WITH TRAILER (REG 76)

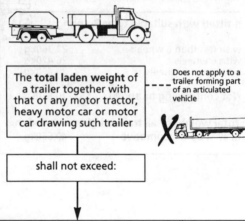

The **total laden weight** of a trailer together with that of any motor tractor, heavy motor car or motor car drawing such trailer

- - - Does not apply to a trailer forming part of an articulated vehicle

shall not exceed:

if trailer and vehicle both have wheels and: combination has total of 4 axles; and drawing vehicle first used on or after 1.4.73 and has relevant brakes	35,000kg
as above but with total of 5 or more axles	38,000kg
if trailer and vehicle are not mentioned above and both have wheels – and brakes as below a) power assisted brakes b) brakes can be operated by driver of drawing vehicle c) brakes will not become ineffective when engine is switched off d) drawing vehicle has warning device, visible to driver, to indicate impending failure of braking system	32,520kg
a wheeled trailer manufactured on or after 27.2.77 and fitted with automatic brakes, drawn by a vehicle first used on or after 1.4.73 and has relevant brakes	29,500kg
if trailer and vehicle are not mentioned above and both have wheels	24,390kg
if trailer or vehicle is track laying	22,360kg

| The sum of the weights transmitted to the road surface by all the wheels of a heavy motor car, motor car or trailer, | in each case not forming part of an articulated vehicle, |

and which:
a) complies with the relevant braking requirements;
b) every driving axle other than a steering axle has twin tyres; and
c) either every driving axle has road-friendly* suspension or does not exceed 9,500kg;

shall not exceed:

*Road-friendly suspension means air suspension or equivalent.

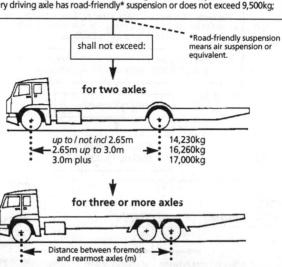

for two axles

up to / not incl 2.65m	14,230kg
2.65m *up to* 3.0m	16,260kg
3.0m plus	17,000kg

for three or more axles

Distance between foremost and rearmost axles (m)

Distance between foremost and rearmost axles (m)	Maximum axle weight	Maximum permitted laden weight
up to but not incl 3.0m	10,170kg	16,260kg
3.0m *up to* 3.2m	10,170kg	18,290kg
3.2m *up to* 3.9m	10,170kg	20,330kg
3.9m *up to* 4.9m	10,170kg	22,360kg
4.9m *up to* 5.2m	10,170kg	25,000kg
5.2m *plus*	10,170kg	26,000kg

for four or more axles

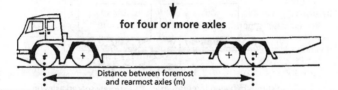

Distance between foremost and rearmost axles (m)

Distance between foremost and rearmost axles (m)	Maximum permitted laden weight
5.2m *up to* / *not incl* 6.4 m	distance (m) x 5,000 rounded up to next 10kg
6.4 m *plus*	32,000kg

MAXIMUM OVERALL WEIGHT cont
ROAD VEHICLES (CONSTRUCTION AND USE) REGULATIONS 1986

If the maximum is exceeded, refer to 'Special types'.

RIGID VEHICLES cont   (REG 75)

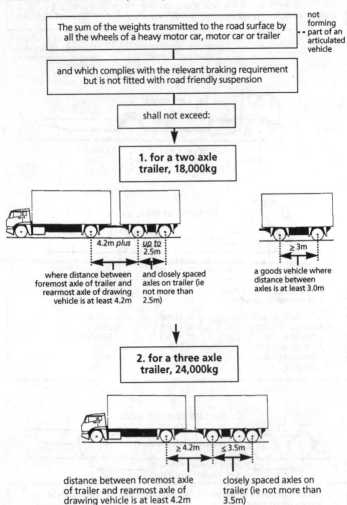

The sum of the weights transmitted to the road surface by all the wheels of a heavy motor car, motor car or trailer — not forming part of an articulated vehicle

and which complies with the relevant braking requirement but is not fitted with road friendly suspension

shall not exceed:

1. for a two axle trailer, 18,000kg

4.2m *plus* | *up to* 2.5m

where distance between foremost axle of trailer and rearmost axle of drawing vehicle is at least 4.2m

and closely spaced axles on trailer (ie not more than 2.5m)

≥ 3m

a goods vehicle where distance between axles is at least 3.0m

2. for a three axle trailer, 24,000kg

≥ 4.2m | ≤ 3.5m

distance between foremost axle of trailer and rearmost axle of drawing vehicle is at least 4.2m

closely spaced axles on trailer (ie not more than 3.5m)

continued on facing page

MAXIMUM OVERALL WEIGHT cont
ROAD VEHICLES (CONSTRUCTION AND USE) REGULATIONS 1986,

If the maximum is exceeded, refer to 'Special types'.

RIGID VEHICLES cont   (REG 75)

continued from previous page

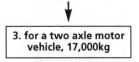

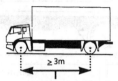

a goods vehicle where distance
between axles is at least 3.0m

If the vehicle is not within the description of the above three categories,
max weight is as follows:

No of axles	Distance between foremost and rearmost axles	Max laden weight
2	*up to/not incl* 2.65m	14,230kg
2	2.65m *plus*	16,260kg
3 or more	*up to* 3.0m	16,260kg
3 or more	3.0m *up to* 3.2m	18,290kg
3 or more	3.2m *up to* 3.9m	20,330kg
3 or more	3.9m *up to* 4.9m	22,360kg
3	4.9m *plus*	25,000kg
4 or more	4.9m *up to* 5.6m	25,000kg
4 or more	5.6m *up to* 5.9m	26,420kg
4 or more	5.9m *up to* 6.3m	28,450kg
4 or more	6.3m *plus*	30,000kg

MAXIMUM OVERALL WEIGHT cont

REGS 75 & 77 & SCHED 11 ROAD VEHICLES (C&U) REGS 1986

If the maximum is exceeded, please refer to 'Special types'.

ARTICULATED

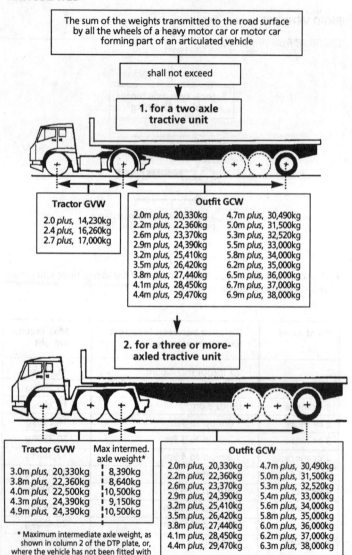

The sum of the weights transmitted to the road surface by all the wheels of a heavy motor car or motor car forming part of an articulated vehicle

shall not exceed

1. for a two axle tractive unit

Tractor GVW	Outfit GCW	
2.0 *plus*, 14,230kg	2.0m *plus*, 20,330kg	4.7m *plus*, 30,490kg
2.4 *plus*, 16,260kg	2.2m *plus*, 22,360kg	5.0m *plus*, 31,500kg
2.7 *plus*, 17,000kg	2.6m *plus*, 23,370kg	5.3m *plus*, 32,520kg
	2.9m *plus*, 24,390kg	5.5m *plus*, 33,000kg
	3.2m *plus*, 25,410kg	5.8m *plus*, 34,000kg
	3.5m *plus*, 26,420kg	6.2m *plus*, 35,000kg
	3.8m *plus*, 27,440kg	6.5m *plus*, 36,000kg
	4.1m *plus*, 28,450kg	6.7m *plus*, 37,000kg
	4.4m *plus*, 29,470kg	6.9m *plus*, 38,000kg

2. for a three or more-axled tractive unit

Tractor GVW	Max intermed. axle weight*	Outfit GCW	
3.0m *plus*, 20,330kg	8,390kg	2.0m *plus*, 20,330kg	4.7m *plus*, 30,490kg
3.8m *plus*, 22,360kg	8,640kg	2.2m *plus*, 22,360kg	5.0m *plus*, 31,500kg
4.0m *plus*, 22,500kg	10,500kg	2.6m *plus*, 23,370kg	5.3m *plus*, 32,520kg
4.3m *plus*, 24,390kg	9,150kg	2.9m *plus*, 24,390kg	5.4m *plus*, 33,000kg
4.9m *plus*, 24,390kg	10,500kg	3.2m *plus*, 25,410kg	5.6m *plus*, 34,000kg
		3.5m *plus*, 26,420kg	5.8m *plus*, 35,000kg
		3.8m *plus*, 27,440kg	6.0m *plus*, 36,000kg
		4.1m *plus*, 28,450kg	6.2m *plus*, 37,000kg
		4.4m *plus*, 29,470kg	6.3m *plus*, 38,000kg

* Maximum intermediate axle weight, as shown in column 2 of the DTP plate or, where the vehicle has not been fitted with a DTP plate, on the manufacturer's plate.

ARTICULATED cont

| HOWEVER |

Articulated vehicles with relevant braking requirements
must comply with whichever is the lower of those
weights listed on the previous page, or those below:

Motor vehicle first used on or after 1.4.73 and semi trailer having total of 5 or more axles:	38,000kg
Motor vehicle with 2 axles first used on or after 1.4.73 and semi trailer with 2 axles used on international transport:	35,000kg
Motor vehicle with 2 axles first used on or after 1.4.73 with driving axles having twin tyres and friendly suspension, and semi trailer with 2 axles:	35,000kg
Motor vehicle and semi trailer not listed above, with 4 or more axles:	32,520kg
Motor vehicle with 2 or more axles first used on or after 1.4.73 with twin tyres and friendly suspension on driving axles, and semi trailer with 1 axle:	26,000kg
Motor vehicle with 2 axles and semi trailer with 1 axle, not described above:	25,000kg

Articulated vehicles not complying with the relevant
braking requirements are permitted the following
maximum laden weight:

less than 4 wheels	20,330kg
4 wheels or more	24,390kg

REG 77

ARTICULATED VEHICLE MATCHING

- Tractive units and semi-trailers are plated separately.
- When loading articulated outfits the plated weights of both the tractive unit and the trailer must be taken into consideration.
- Difficulties may arise where various trailers covering a range of plated weights are used with a tractive unit.
- The same problem arises in relation to excise duty rating where incorrect matching may result in excise offences being committed.

Examples:

Tractive unit plated for operation at 32 tons gross weight when used with a long tandem-axle semi-trailer

For the same tractive unit linked with a short single-axle trailer, a lower weight must be observed, limited by the shorter trailer's gross plated weight.

MAXIMUM GROSS AXLE WEIGHT

REG 78 ROAD VEHICLES (CONSTRUCTION AND USE) REGULATIONS 1986

If the maximum is exceeded, refer to 'Special types'.

For wheeled heavy motor cars, motor cars and trailers, complying with relevant braking requirements, max gross axle weights are as follows:

One wheeled axles	No other wheel in the same line transversely and		
	single tyred not less than 300mm wide	or	double tyred not less than 300mm apart	**5,090kg**
	otherwise			**4,600kg**
More than 2 wheels in line transversely	• Manufactured before 1.5.83 where the wheels are on one axle of a group of closely spaced axles (see later for definition)			**10,170kg**
	• Manufactured on or after 1.5.83			**10,170kg**
	• Any other case			**11,180kg**

Two wheels in line transversely
single tyred not less than 300mm wide
or
double tyred not less than 300mm apart

If wheels are on the sole driving axle	**10,500kg**
Not as above	**10,170kg**
not tyred as above	**9,200kg**

For wheeled heavy motor cars, motor cars and trailers not falling within the above

More than 2 wheels transmitting weight to a strip of road between 2 parallel lines at right angles to the longitudinal axis of the vehicle

up to 1.02m	**11,180kg**
1.02m *up to* 22m	**16,260kg**
1.22m *up to* 2.13m	**18,300kg**

Two wheels in line transversely	**9,200kg**
One wheel, where no other wheel is in the same line transversely	**4,600kg**

For wheeled locomotives

Two wheels in line transversely (except road roller, or vehicle with not more than 4 wheels first used before 1.6.55)	**11,180kg**
Any two wheels of vehicle having not more than 4 wheels first used before 1.6.55 (not being a road roller or agricultural motor vehicle driven at more than 20mph)	**three quarters of total weight of locomotive**

MAX GROSS AXLE WEIGHT cont

REG 79 & SCHED 11 ROAD VEHICLES (CONSTRUCTION AND USE) REGS 1986

This Regulation applies to:

(a) a wheeled motor vehicle which complies with the relevant braking requirements; (b) a wheeled trailer drawn by such a vehicle; and (c) an agricultural motor vehicle, trailer or appliance, as follows

Two closely spaced axles *	**Motor vehicle**	**Trailer**
	up to 1.3m **16,000kg**	*up to* 1.3m **16,000kg**
	1.3m *plus* **18,000kg**	1.3m *up to*1.5m **18,000kg**
	1.3m *plus* and (a) driving axles other than steering axles has twin tyres and (b) either every axle has road friendly suspension or neither has an axle weight over 9,500kg **19,000kg**	Both axles driven from drawing vehicle and fitted with twin tyres; and either have road friendly suspension or neither has axle weight over 9,500kg **19,000kg**
		1.5 *up to* 1.8m **19,320kg**
		1.8m *plus* **20,000kg**

	Three closely spaced axles * Distance between any 2	*up to* 1.3m **21,000kg**
		1.3m *plus* and at least one axle does not have air suspension **22,500kg**
		1.3m plus and all three axles have air suspension **24,000kg**

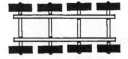 **Four or more closely spaced axles ***

24,000kg

* 'Closely spaced axles' means
(a) 2 axles not falling within (b) or (c) below, spaced not more than 2.5m apart;
(b) 3 axles not falling within (c) below, the outermost placed not more than 3.25m apart; or
(c) 4 or more axles, the outermost placed not more than 4.6m apart.

Exemptions

(a) vehicles first used before 1.6.73 (provided it complies with the requirements of Reg 78 relating to vehicles not complying with braking requirements);
(b) plating certificate issued immediately before 1.1.93 (provided no axle weight exceeds the weight on the certificate) as being the weight not to be exceeded in Great Britain for that axle.

NOTIONAL GROSS WEIGHT

GOODS VEHICLES (ASCERTAINMENT OF MAXIMUM GROSS WEIGHTS)
REGULATIONS 1976

A notional gross weight can be obtained from an unladen weight by multiplying the unladen weight by the following prescribed factor:

This can be used where the appropriate gross weight or train weight is not marked on the vehicle in accordance with C&U Regulations, 1986.

Class of Vehicle	Multiplier	Class of Vehicle	Multiplier
		Trailers	
Motor Vehicles		Engineering plant	1
		Asphalt or tarmac producers	1
Dual Purpose Vehicle	1.5	Agricultural trailer	1
Break-down Vehicle	2	Works trailers	1
Works Trucks	2	Living vans	1.5
Electrically Propelled	2	Any not mentioned above	3
Salt/grit Spreader	2		
Hauling Lifeboats	2		
Living Vans	1.5		
Vehicle with permanently affixed equipment for medical, dental, veterinary, health, display or clerical purposes	1.5		
3 wheeled street cleaners	2		
Steam-propelled vehicles	2		
Aircraft Servicing vehicles	2	**Articulated**	
Permanently attached equipment and not mentioned above	1		
Heavy motor cars and motor cars first used before 1.1.68 and not mentioned above	2	Goods combinations with trailer of a type listed above	1.5
		Any other	2.5
Locomotives and motor tractors first used before 1.4.73	2		
Any motor vehicle not mentioned above	4		

TRAVELLING HEIGHT
DEFINITIONS AND REQUIREMENTS

REGS 10, 10A,10B, 10C ROAD VEHICLES (CONSTRUCTION AND USE) REGS 1986

These Regulations apply to all goods and passenger vehicles over 3 metres high

RELEVANT VEHICLE

A vehicle fitted with equipment which can be raised by means of a power operated device, and when raised or lowered, the overall travelling height is altered.

NON RELEVANT VEHICLE:

A vehicle without high level equipment.

OVERALL TRAVELLING HEIGHT:

The actual height, from the ground, of the vehicles, trailer, load and equipment (when stowed in its normal position)

CAB WARNING DEVICE:

Gives the driver visual warning if the equipment raises through a pre-determined height.

PRE-DETERMINED HEIGHT

Must not exceed the overall travelling height by more than 1 metre.

CAB NOTICE

Positioned where it can be easily read by the driver, the cab notice indicates the overall travelling height to a tolerance of +150 mm in imperial – or both imperial and metric – measurements. The numerals must be at least 40mm high, and no number likely to be confused with the height notice may be displayed.

IMPLEMENTATION DATES

Cab notices – all vehicles, **1.10.97**

Warning devices:

motor vehicles first used on or after 1.4.98, **1.4.98**
trailers manufactured on or after 1.4.98, **1.4.98**
motor vehicles first used on or after 1.4.93 but before 1.4.98, **1.10.98**
trailers manufactured on or after 1.4.93, but before 1.4.98, **1.10.98**

TRAVELLING HEIGHT

REGS 10, 10A,10B, 10C ROAD VEHICLES (CONSTRUCTION AND USE) REGS 1986

See definitions on previous page

Relevant vehicles require	Non-relevant vehicles require
A cab warning device	a cab notice

EXCEPT	EXCEPT
not carrying, its part of the vehicle, high level equipment which is stowed and locked and no-one in the cab can interfere with the locking device	if the driver has documentation which gives information regarding a risk-free route and the driver is following the route or an unforeseen diversion
if unlikely to encounter bridges less than 1 metre higher than the vehicle's maximum travelling height.	if unlikely to encounter bridges less than 1 metre higher than the vehicle's overall travelling height (maximum travelling height in the case of 'relevant' vehicles)
vehicles not over 4 metres overall travelling height, registered in an EEC state (other than UK) or in Norway Iceland or Liechtenstein, and operating in the UK	vehicles not over 4 metres overall travelling height, registered in an EEC state (other than the UK) or in Norway, Iceland or Liechtenstein and operating in the UK
agricultural vehicles, trailers or appliances;	where the driver has bridge height information for a particular route indicating structures under which the vehicle will/will not pass
broken down vehicles being drawn;	
fire brigade vehicles;	
industrial tractors;	
motor vehicles with maximum travelling height not exceeding overall travelling height;	
naval, military or air force vehicles;	
tippers/tipper trailers manufactured before 1.4.98	
vehicle transports/trailers;	
works trucks/trailers;	

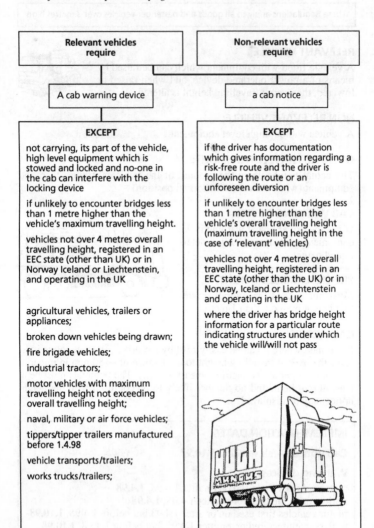

TRAILERS

REG 83 ROAD VEHICLES (CONSTRUCTION AND USE) REGULATIONS 1986

Description of vehicle	Max no of trailers
Motor tractor Laden or unladen See definition at front of book– basically a motor vehicle for Unladen hauling trailers with wide load etc (as a locomotive but lighter)	1 2
Locomotive	3
Motor car or heavy motor car (not being a straddle carrier, articulated bus or a bus) (for buses see following page)	1
If one of the trailers being drawn is a towing implement (ie 'dolly') and the other is an articulated type semi trailer secured to and resting on, or suspended from, the dolly *The following diagram shows a conventional 6-wheel rigid vehicle drawing a dolly mounted semi-trailer.*	2
Agricultural motor vehicle This is a motor vehicle constructed and adapted for use off roads for agricultural, horticultural or forestry and which is primarily used 1. With non- for one or more of those purposes agricultural trailers – not being a dual purpose vehicle or appliances	As for locomotive motor trailer or heavy motor car above
2. With agricultural trailers or trailed appliances An agricultural trailer is a trailer constructed or adapted for the purpose of agriculture, horticulture or forestry and only used for one or more of those purposes An agricultural trailed appliance is trailer which is an implement constructed or adapted for the use off roads for the above purposes	**2** unladen agricultural trailers; or **1** agricultural trailer and **1** agricultural trailed appliance; or **2** agricultural trailed appliances

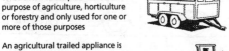

TRAILERS cont

ROAD VEHICLES (CONSTRUCTION AND USE) REGULATIONS 1986

ARTICULATED TRACTIVE UNIT
DRAWING TWO SEMI-TRAILERS   REG 83

An articulated tractive unit drawing two semi-trailers
(a double bottom) will be permitted by the DTP subject
to special ministerial permission

subject to a 30mph limit
(40mph on motorways) and prescribed routes.

Must comply with C&U Regs 1986 but carry additional lights and mirrors.
No maximum weights and lengths are specified.

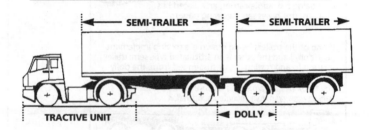

|◄——— SEMI-TRAILER ———►| |◄— SEMI-TRAILER —►|

TRACTIVE UNIT   **◄ DOLLY ►**

NOTES

● *'Trailer' does not include a water carrying vehicle drawn for the purpose of a steam powered drawing vehicle.*

● *A broken down unladen articulated vehicle being towed will be counted as only one trailer.*

MOTOR VEHICLE DRAWING A TRAILER BY ROPE OR CHAIN

REG 86

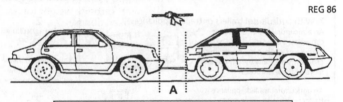

A

'A' must not exceed 4.5m. If it exceeds 1.5m the
rope or chain must be made clearly visible

TRAILERS cont

ROAD VEHICLES (CONSTRUCTION AND USE) REGULATIONS 1986

MOTOR CYCLES   REG 84

A person using, or causing or permitting **ANY MOTOR CYCLE** to be used, on a road, may not:

1. draw more than one trailer;
2. draw a trailer carrying a passenger (unless broken down);
3. draw a trailer with UW over 254kg.

A **TWO-WHEELED MOTOR CYCLE**, (not with a sidecar)

| and engine cc not over 125cc shall not | with engine capacity over 125cc may draw a trailer subject to the following |

draw a trailer except a broken-down motor cycle being ridden.

trailer must not exceed 1 metre wide; distance between rear axle of motor cycle and rear of trailer not to exceed 2.5 metres;
- motor cycle to be marked with kerbside weight (unless broken down);
- trailer to be marked with unladen weight (unless broken down);
- laden weight of trailer not to exceed 150kg or two-thirds kerbside weight of motor cycle, whichever the less (unless broken down).

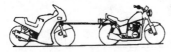

TRAILERS cont

ROAD VEHICLES (CONSTRUCTION AND USE) REGULATIONS 1986

**A WHEELED TRAILER
WHICH IS A LIVING VAN**   REG 90

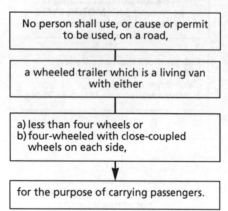

No person shall use, or cause or permit
to be used, on a road,

a wheeled trailer which is a living van
with either

a) less than four wheels or
b) four-wheeled with close-coupled
   wheels on each side,

for the purpose of carrying passengers.

NOTE
*These provisions do not apply when the living van is being tested by its
manufacturers; a person who has been or is repairing it; or a distributor of or dealer in trailers.*

A BUS

A bus – not being an articulated bus or
mini-bus – may draw:

a broken-down bus – where no person
other than the driver is carried on either
vehicle – or

one trailer.

REG 83
BUT REFER TO REG 7 FOR MAXIMUM LENGTH

TRAILERS cont

SECONDARY COUPLING (REG 86A)

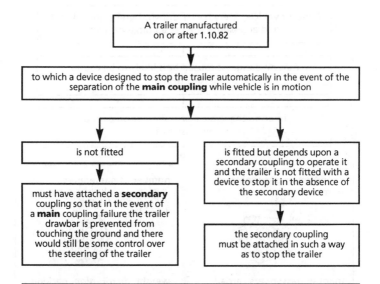

A trailer manufactured
on or after 1.10.82

to which a device designed to stop the trailer automatically in the event of the
separation of the **main coupling** while vehicle is in motion

is not fitted

must have attached a **secondary**
coupling so that in the event of
a **main** coupling failure the trailer
drawbar is prevented from
touching the ground and there
would still be some control over
the steering of the trailer

is fitted but depends upon a
secondary coupling to operate it
and the trailer is not fitted with a
device to stop it in the absence of
the secondary device

the secondary coupling
must be attached in such a way
as to stop the trailer

Except:
Agricultural trailer or appliance not exceeding 20mph. Vehicle with max
speed not over 25km/h. Works trailer. Public works vehicle. Trailer designed,
constructed or adapted to be drawn by a locomotive, motor tractor,
vehicle with max speed not exceeding 25km/h, works truck or public works
vehicle. Street cleansing trailer. Max total design axle weight not
over 750kg. Motor cycle trailer. Broken down vehicle. Gritting trailer
with max gross weight not over 2,000kg.

THESE EXCEPTIONS TO REG 86A CONTAINED WITHIN REG 15 C&U REGS 1986

SIDECARS (REGS 92 & 93)

The sidecar wheel
must not be
wholly outside
this space.

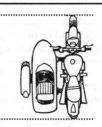

It is an offence to use, cause or permit to be used a 2-wheeled motor
cycle registered on or after 1.8.81 (other than one brought temporarily
into Great Britain by a person resident abroad) if the sidecar is attached
to the right (or offside) of the motor cycle.

DANGEROUS VEHICLES

REG 100 ROAD VEHICLES (CONSTRUCTION AND USE) REGULATIONS 1986
SECTION 40A ROAD TRAFFIC ACT 1988

A motor vehicle, every trailer drawn thereby and all parts
and accessories shall at all times be such

that no danger is caused or is likely to be caused
to any person

in or on the vehicle or trailer, or on a road,
by reason of:

**condition or unsuitable
purpose**

number of passengers
(may not apply to vehicles subject
to PSV (Carrying Capacity)
Regs 1984)

manner passengers carried

**weight, distribution, packing
and adjustment of load**

The load shall be so secured by physical
restraint and be in such a position that

neither danger nor nuisance is likely to
be caused to any person or property

by reason of the load moving or being
blown or falling from the vehicle.

SILENCERS

ROAD VEHICLES (CONSTRUCTION AND USE) REGULATIONS 1986

MOTOR CYCLE SILENCER AND EXHAUST SYSTEM REGS 1995

Every vehicle propelled by an internal combustion engine shall be fitted with an **exhaust system including a silencer**

suitable and sufficient for reducing, as far as may be reasonable, the noise caused by the escape of the exhaust gases from the engine.

No person shall use, cause or permit to be used, a vehicle on a road if exhaust gases from the engine escape into the atmosphere without first passing through the silencer, etc.

The silencer etc shall at all times when the vehicle is used on a road be maintained in good and efficient working order and shall not, after the date of manufacture, have been altered in any way which makes the noise of escaping gases greater.

REG 54 C&U REGS 1986

Motor cycle and moped silencers must now meet requirements of specified EC Directives with a distinction being made between those first used before 1.2.96 and those first used after that date.

A silencer marked 'not for road use' may not be used on a road by such a vehicle.

REG 57A C&U REGS 1986

Using a motor cycle or moped on a road if it does not meet noise limit requirements and it is not in good or efficient working order or has been altered and the noise is therefore greater is an offence

REG 57B C&U REGS 1986

Supply of motor cycle silencers: In the course of a business, no person may supply or offer or agree to supply or expose or have in his possession for the purpose of supplying, an exhaust system, silencer or component for such a system unless it is clearly and indelibly marked with the relevant British Standard Specification or EEC Directive. The above does not apply if the silencer or exhaust system is clearly and indelibly marked 'NOT FOR ROAD USE' or 'PRE-1985 MC ONLY'

S1 MOTOR CYCLE NOISE ACT 1987
AND REGS 3, 4 & 5 MOTOR CYCLE SILENCER AND EXHAUST SYSTEM REGS 1995

As to sound levels generally, see Reg 55, C&U Regulations 1986

No motor vehicle shall be used on a road in a manner which causes any excessive noise which could have been avoided by reasonable care by the driver.

REG 97 C&U REGS 1986

TYRES

REGS 26 AND 27 ROAD VEHICLES (CONSTRUCTION AND USE) REGULATIONS 1986

must

BE SUITABLE having regard to the use to which the vehicle or trailer is being put or to the types of tyres fitted to its other wheels.

BE INFLATED so as to be fit for use to which vehicle is being put

---

Have no portion of the **PLY OR CORD EXPOSED**

---

have **NO LUMP, BULGE OR TEAR** caused by separation or partial failure of its structure.

HAVE THE BASE OF ANY GROOVE which showed in the original tread pattern **CLEARLY VISIBLE**

does not apply to:
1. a 3-wheeled motor cycle UW not over 102kg and incapable of more than 12mph on level; or
2. a pedestrian-controlled works truck

NOT BE A 'TEMPORARY USE SPARE TYRE' (for use only if normal tyre fails and used at lower speed

unless either:
1. a passenger vehicle first used before 1.4.87
2. or complying with ECE Reg 64 or Community Directive 92/93

(REG 24(3))

TYRES cont

REGS 26 AND 27 ROAD VEHICLES (CONSTRUCTION AND USE) REGULATIONS 1986

 **must**

FOR TWO AXLE-VEHICLEs – not have:
1. diagonal ply or bias-belted on rear with radial ply on front;
2. diagonal ply on rear and bias belted on front

NOT BE RECUT TYRES if:
1. ply or cord has been cut or exposed, or
2. wholly or partially different pattern to manufacturer's recut tread pattern

HAVE NO CUT in excess of 25mm or 10 per cent of width, whichever is greater, measured in any direction on outside of tyre, deep enough to reach the ply or cord

HAVE EITHER:
1. depth of groove of tread pattern at least 1mm throughout continuous band of at least three quarters of breadth round entire circumference, or
2. where original tread did not extend beyond three quarters of breadth, whole of original tread to have depth of at least 1mm

does not apply to
1. 3-wheeled motor cycle UW not exceeding 102 kg and incapable of more than 12mph on level:
2. pedestrian controlled works truck; or
3. motor cycle not over 50cc

in the case of
1. passenger vehicles for not more than eight passengers in addition to the driver (other than motor cycles)
2. goods vehicles under 3,500kg,
3. and light trailers,
for 1mm read 1.6mm in the central three quarters of breath and round the entire outer circumference of the tyre.

continued overleaf

TYRES cont

REGS 26 AND 27 ROAD VEHICLES (CONSTRUCTION AND USE) REGULATIONS 1986

must

continued from previous page

BE MAINTAINED in such condition as to be fit for the use to which they are being put and free from any defect which might cause damage to the road surface or danger to persons in or on the vehicle or using the road

---

NOT HAVE DIFFERENT TYPES OF STRUCTURE where fitted to the same axle

---

FOR VEHICLES WITH MORE THAN 1 STEERABLE AXLE – not have different type of structure on different steerable axles; or

FOR VEHICLES WITH MORE THAN 1 DRIVEN AXLE NOT BEING STEERABLE AXLES – not have different type of structure on different non-steerable axles.

SUPPLY OF TYRES
MOTOR VEHICLE TYRES (SAFETY) REGULATIONS 1994

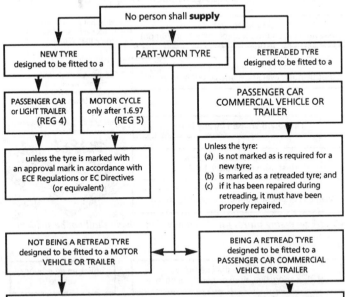

EXEMPTIONS

NEW OR RETREADED TYRES:
- bias belted or diagonal ply for a pre-1.1.49 motor vehicle or trailer
- 'competition' tyres
- 'off-road' tyres
- tyres for pre-1.1.33 vehicles
- tyres for test or trial
- tyres for other than retail supply
- tyre sizes 185R16, 125R400, 135R400 145R400, 155R400, 165R400, 175R400 or 185R400

PART-WORN TYRES:
- where complete vehicle is supplied
- if supplied only for tyre test/trial or other than as a retail transaction, need not bear approval marks etc

Note that this legislation applies throughout Great Britain, but traffic officers in Scotland would leave this matter to the Vehicle Inspectorate.

WARNING INSTRUMENTS

REGS 37 AND 99 ROAD VEHICLES (CONSTRUCTION AND USE) REGULATIONS 1986

Every motor vehicle
(having a maximum speed of more than 20mph)

→ does not apply to agricultural motor vehicle unless driven at more than 20mph

---

shall be fitted with a horn
(not being a reversing alarm or two-tone horn)

→ eg instrument – not being bell, gong, or siren – capable of giving audible and sufficient warning of approach or position of vehicle to which it is fitted

---

The sound emitted by any horn

→ other than a reversing alarm or two-tone horn

---

fitted to a wheeled vehicle
(first used on or after 1.8.73)

BLARE!

---

shall be continuous, uniform, and not strident.

NOTE: *A reversing alarm fitted to a wheeled vehicle shall not be strident.*

No motor vehicle shall be fitted
with a gong, bell, siren or two-tone horn

→ unless an emergency vehicle

Except: A bell, gong or siren may be fitted to prevent theft or to a bus to summon help for driver/conductor/inspector

Every bell, gong or siren fitted to prevent theft – and every device using a vehicle's horn (for vehicles first used on or after 1.10.82) – shall not sound for a continuous period of more than five minutes.

Warning devises may not be sounded
when stationary

→ unless a reversing alarm, but these may only be used on goods vehicles not less than 2,000kg max gross weight, buses, engineering plant, refuse vehicle, or works truck

---

or on a restricted road between 11.30pm and 7am

If carrying goods for sale

An instrument other than a two tone horn may be used to advertise perishable goods, for human consumption, between 12 noon and 7pm

But must not give reasonable cause for annoyance to persons in the vicinity.

S 62(3) CONTROL OF POLLUTION ACT 1974

SPEEDOMETER

REGS 35 AND 36 ROAD VEHICLES (CONSTRUCTION AND USE) REGULATIONS 1986

A speedometer must be fitted to all vehicles,
with the following exceptions

- maximum speed not exceeding 25mph
- unlawful to drive at more than 25mph
- agricultural vehicle not driven at more than 20mph
- motor cycle first used before 1.4.84 not exceeding 100cc
- invalid carriage first used before 1.4.84
- works truck first used before 1.4.84
- vehicle first used before 1.10.37
- vehicle fitted with approved recording equipment indicating the speed.

A speedometer must be fitted in such a position that the driver can see speed of vehicle

---

and if vehicle first used on or after 1.4.84, must be capable of indicating speed in mph and kph

---

Must be maintained in good working order
and must be kept free from any obstruction
which may prevent it being read but:

defence:

- if defect occurred during journey on which contravention detected
- if steps have already been taken to have defect remedied with reasonable expedition.

SEAT BELTS – APPLICATION

REGS 46 AND 47 ROAD VEHICLES (CONSTRUCTION AND USE) REGULATIONS 1986

The Regulations apply to

Every wheeled motor car first used on or after 1.1.65
Every three-wheeled motor cycle with UW exceeding
225kg and first used on or after 1.9.70
Every heavy motor car first used on or after 1.10.88

Anchorage Points

A vehicle first used before 1.4.82
must have anchorage points for the
driver's seat and specified
passenger seat *.

If first used on or after 1.4.82
must have anchorage points
(a) If a minibus, ambulance or
motor caravan, first used before
1.10.88, for the driver's seat and
specified passenger seat. If first
used on or after 1.10.88 for the
driver's seat and any forward-
facing front seat;
(b) Any other passenger or DPV
(Dual-Purpose Vehicle) every
forward-facing adult seat.
(c) Every other case, every forward-
facing front seat and non-
protected seat **and which
comply with EC directives.

**Goods vehicles first used on or
after 1.10.88 with max gross
weight over 3,500kg** need instead
to have two anchorages for lap
belts for driver's seat and each
forward-facing front seat.

Coaches need not comply with the
above if they have anchorage for
each forward-facing exposed seat
and either comply with EC
requirements for such seats or have
anchorages which form part of the
seats and are strongly secured to
them.

The Regulations do not apply to:

Agricultural motor vehicle.
**Electrically propelled goods
vehicles** first used before 1.10.88
Goods vehicles (other than DPVs)
first used
• before 1.4.67;
• or, on or after 1.4.80 and before
1.10.88 if max gross weight
exceeds 3,500kg;
• or, before 1.4.80 and UW over
1,525kg;
• or, if manufactured before
1.10.79 was first used before
1.4.82 and UW over 1,525kg.
Incapable of exceeding 16 mph.
Large bus (other than a coach first
used on or after 1.10.88).
Locomotive.
Minibus first used before 1.10.88
constructed or adapted to carry
more than 12 passengers: or first
used on or after 1.10.80 with max
gross weight over 3,500kg.
Motor cycle equipped with driver's
seat requiring driver to sit astride it,
not constructed by a normal
manufacturer.
Motor tractor.
Pedestrian-controlled vehicle.
Used vehicle imported into GB but
only for transporting to owner's
home or to have seat belts fitted.
Works truck.

NOTE:

* *Specified passenger seat means the forward-facing front seat alongside the
driver or, if there is more than one such seat, the one furthest away. If there
are no seats as above, the foremost forward-facing front passenger seat furthest from the driver (unless there is a fixed partition in front of it)*
** *A non-protected seat is a seat other than a front seat which does not
comply with EC regulations*

SEAT BELTS – FITTING

REG 47

A vehicle to which this Regulation applies (see previous page) must be fitted with seat belts:

Vehicle		Requirement
A: First used before 1.4.81		For driver's seat and any specified passenger seat *(see previous page)*.
B: First used on or after 1.4.81		3-point seat belt for driver's seat and any specified passenger seat *(see previous page)*.
First used on or after 1.4.87, not being a minibus motor ambulance or motor caravan	**Passenger vehicle, DPV or any other case**	In addition to 'B' above, a 3-point seat belt, lap belt or disabled person's belt, for any forward-facing seat alongside the driver's not being a specified passenger's seat.
	Passenger vehicle or DPV with not more than 2 forward-facing seats behind the driver's seat	In addition to 'B' above, either: (a) an inertia reel belt for one of these seats, or (b) a 3-point belt, lap belt, disabled person's belt or child restraint for each of these seats.
	Passenger vehicle or DPV with more than 2 forward-facing seats behind the driver's seat	In addition to 'B' above, either: (a) an inertia reel belt for one of these seats and a 3-point belt, lap belt, disabled person's belt or child restraint for at least one other of these seats, or (b) a 3-point belt for one of these seats, and either a child restraint or disabled person's belt for at least one other of these seats, or (c) a 3-point belt, lap belt, disabled person's belt or child restraint for each of these seats.
Minibus, motor ambulance or motor caravan, first used on or after 1.10.88		(a) For the driver's seat and the specified passenger seat *(see previous page)*, a 3-point belt, and (b) for any forward-facing front seat which is not a specified passenger seat, a 3-point belt or lap belt. (In the latter case, any bar or partition within 1 metre to the front must be padded.)
Coaches which have anchorages for each forward-facing exposed seat *(see previous page)*		3-point belts, lap belts, or disabled person's belts.

SEAT BELTS – MINIBUSES AND COACHES REG 48A

It is an offence to use or cause or permit to be used on a road a

until 10.2.98, does not apply to **a coach** first used before 1.10.98 ───

COACH OR MINIBUS

─── does not apply to the provision of a bus service or public transport service

Pic 3 P.

wholly or mainly for the purpose of carrying a group of

3 OR MORE CHILDREN ─── aged 3 years or more but under 16 years

on an **ORGANISED TRIP** ─── includes being carried to or from their school or from one part of their school premises to another

and the journey is being made for the purposes of the trip

the number of children being carried in the vehicle (excluding disabled children in wheelchairs) ─── unless the **APPROPRIATE NUMBER**

OF FORWARD FACING PASSENGER SEATS ─── does not include the driver's seat

are provided with **SEAT BELTS**

SEAT BELTS – WEARING BY ADULTS

MOTOR VEHICLES (WEARING OF SEAT BELTS) REGULATIONS 1993

**EVERY PERSON
(of 14 years and over)**

| driving a | riding in the front seat of | riding in the rear seat of a |

motor vehicle
(other than a two-wheeled motor cycle with or without a sidecar)

motor car or passenger car
(which is not a motor car) (for definition, see later)

Shall wear an adult belt

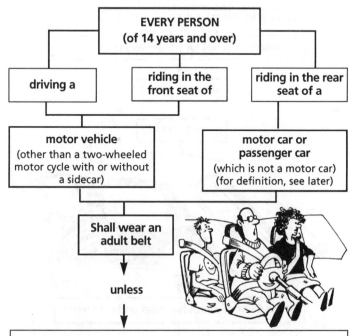

unless

- delivering/collecting mail or goods on local rounds in vehicle constructed/adapted for that purpose
- driving examiner
- fire or police purposes or carrying person in custody
- holding a medical certificate
- no adult belt available
- private hire driver carrying passengers for hire
- procession commonly or customarily held, or notified under Public Order Act *(not applicable in Scotland)*
- procession organised by the Crown
- reversing (includes qualified driver supervising a learner)
- taxi driver while taxi being used as such
- trade licence while vehicle fault being investigated or remedied
- wearing of disabled person's belt by disabled person.

SEAT BELTS – WEARING BY CHILDREN IN FRONT SEATS

MOTOR VEHICLES (WEARING OF SEAT BELTS BY CHILDREN IN FRONT SEATS)
REGULATIONS 1993 AND SECTION 15 ROAD TRAFFIC ACT 1988

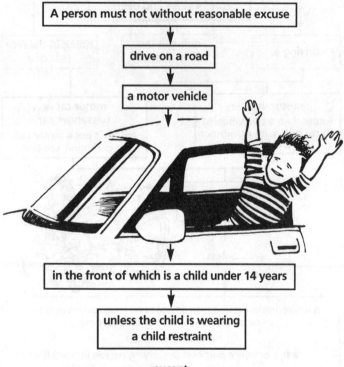

A person must not without reasonable excuse

↓

drive on a road

↓

a motor vehicle

↓

in the front of which is a child under 14 years

↓

unless the child is wearing a child restraint

except

● A child of three years or more where a child restraint is not available in the front or rear and the child is wearing an adult belt.

● Child holding a medical certificate.

● Child under 1 year in a carry cot restrained by the straps.

● Disabled child wearing disabled person's belt.

● Vehicle first used before 1.1.65 if there is no rear seat and no seat other then the driver's is provided with an appropriate belt.

● Vehicle providing a local service and is not a motor car or passenger car *(see previous page)*.

SEAT BELTS – WEARING BY CHILDREN IN REAR SEATS

MOTOR VEHICLES (WEARING OF SEAT BELTS) REGS 1993 AND S 15 RTA 1988

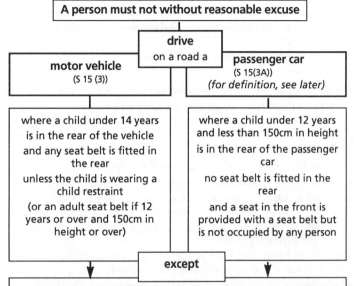

A person must not without reasonable excuse

drive
on a road a

motor vehicle (S 15 (3))	**passenger car** (S 15(3A)) *(for definition, see later)*
where a child under 14 years is in the rear of the vehicle and any seat belt is fitted in the rear unless the child is wearing a child restraint (or an adult seat belt if 12 years or over and 150cm in height or over)	where a child under 12 years and less than 150cm in height is in the rear of the passenger car no seat belt is fitted in the rear and a seat in the front is provided with a seat belt but is not occupied by any person

except

- a child under 1 year in a carry cot restrained by the straps
- a child of 3 years or more for whom a child restraint is not available in the front or rear and who is wearing an adult belt
- disabled child wearing disabled person's belt
- holder of a medical certificate
- licensed taxis and licensed hire cars in which (in each case) the rear seats are separated from the driver, eg fixed partitions
- vehicles which are neither motor cars nor passenger cars

exceptions only applicable to S 15(3)

- a child under 12 years and less than 150cm in height if no appropriate seat belt is available in a passenger car in the front or rear (or in a vehicle other than a passenger car if no appropriate belt is available in the rear)
- a child 12 years or over and 150cm in height or over in any vehicle if no appropriate belt is available in the rear

exception only available to S 15(3A)

- a child for whom no appropriate belt is available in the front

SEAT BELTS – DEFINITIONS

PASSENGER CAR

A passenger car is a motor vehicle which:

- is constructed or adapted for the carriage of passengers and is not a goods vehicle;
- has no more than 8 seats in addition to the driver's;
- has 4 or more wheels;
- has a maximum design speed exceeding 25 km per hour; and
- has a maximum laden weight not exceeding 3.5 tonnes.

SECTION 15 ROAD TRAFFIC ACT 1988

AVAILABLE

A seat belt will be regarded as being available unless:

- another person is wearing the relevant belt;
- a child is occupying the relevant seat and wearing a child restraint which is an appropriate child restraint for that child;
- another person, being a person holding a medical certificate, is occupying the relevant seat;
- a disabled person (not being the person in question) is occupying the relevant seat and wearing a disabled person's belt;
- by reason of his disability, it would not be practicable for the person in question to wear the relevant belt;
- the person in question is prevented from occupying the relevant seat by the presence of a carry cot which is restrained by straps and in which there is a child aged under 1 year, unless the carry cot could reasonably have been carried and restrained in another part of the vehicle;
- the person in question is prevented from occupying the relevant seat by the presence of child restraint which could not readily be removed without the aid of tools; or
- the relevant seat is specially designed so that –
  (i) its configuration can be adjusted in order to increase the space in the vehicle available for goods or personal effects, and
  (ii) when it is so adjusted the seat cannot be used as such, and the configuration is adjusted in the manner described in sub-paragraph (i) and it would not be reasonably practicable for the goods and personal effects being carried in the vehicle to be so carried were configuration not so adjusted.

SCHED 2 MOTOR VEHICLES (WEARING OF SEAT BELTS) REGULATIONS 1993

MIRRORS

REG 33 ROAD VEHICLES (CONSTRUCTION AND USE) REGULATIONS 1986

	Type of vehicle	**Requirement**
1	Motor vehicle drawing a trailer and a person carried thereon has an uninterrupted view to the rear, and can communicate with the driver regarding the signals of other vehicles Works truck Track-laying agricultural vehicle Wheeled agricultural vehicle first used before 1.6.78 } If driver has a view to the rear Pedestrian-controlled vehicle Chassis driven to receive body Agricultural motor vehicle within unladen weight exceeding 7,370kg and is either track-laying or is wheeled and first used before 1.6.78	No requirement
2	Motor vehicle not mentioned in item 1 which is – i. a wheeled locomotive or motor tractor first used on or after 1.6.78 ii. agricultural motor vehicle not being track-laying UW not exceeding 7,370kg (see item 8) or a wheeled agricultural vehicle first used after 1.6.86 which is driven in excess of 20mph (see item 6)	At least one mirror fitted externally on the offside
3	Wheeled motor vehicle not mentioned in item 1 first used on or after 1.4.83 which is – (A) a bus; or (B) a goods vehicle with max gross weight exceeding 3,500kg (not being an agricultural vehicle or one which is driven at more than 20mph) other than a vehicle in item 4	(a) One mirror externally on offside; and (b) one mirror internally, unless not providing rear view; and (c) one mirror externally on nearside unless adequate internal one is fitted
4	Goods vehicle not being an agricultural vehicle with max gross weight exceeding 12,000kg first used on or after 1.10.88	One left and one right main mirror, one wide angle mirror and one close-proximity mirror
5	2-wheeled motor cycle with or without sidecar	No requirement
6	Wheeled motor vehicle not in items 1 - 5 first used on or after 1.6.78 (or if Ford Transit, 10.7.78)	(a) One mirror externally on offside; and (b) one internally, unless not providing rear view; (c) and one externally on nearside unless adequate internal one is fitted
7	Wheeled motor vehicle not in items 1 - 5 first used before 1.6.78 (if ford transit 10.7.78) and track laying not being agricultural first used on or after 1.1.58 which is in either case – i. a bus; ii. DPV; or iii. goods vehicle	One mirror externally on offside and one either internally, or externally on nearside
8	Motor vehicle, wheeled or track-laying not in items 1 - 7 above	One internally or externally

MIRRORS – FITTING AND USE

REG 33 ROAD VEHICLES (CONSTRUCTION AND USE) REGULATIONS 1986

Requirement	Type of vehicle
Each exterior mirror shall, if the vehicle has a maximum permissible weight exceeding 3500kg, be a class 11 mirror and shall in any other case be a class 11 or 111 mirror	Vehicle in item 2 or 6 on preceding page
The edges of any internal mirror shall be surrounded by some material such as will render it unlikely that severe cuts would be caused if the mirror or material were struck by an occupant of the vehicle	Wheeled motor vehicle in item **1, 2, 7 or 8** *(on preceding page)* and first used on or after 1.4.69
Each mirror to be fixed so that it remains steady under normal driving conditions; Each exterior mirror on a vehicle fitted with windows to be visible to the driver through a side window or part of the windscreen swept by the wiper If bottom edge of a mirror is less than 2m above the road surface when the vehicle is laden the mirror shall not project more than 20cm from the side of the vehicle (or trailer, when drawn, if wider) Interior mirrors must be capable of being adjusted from driving position Unless the mirror is of a type which automatically adjusts itself when knocked out of alignment, each exterior mirror shall be capable or being adjusted by the driver from the driving position (but may be of a type which can be locked in position from outside the vehicle)	Wheeled vehicle in item 1 if first used on or after 1.6.78; Vehicle in item 5 if first used on or after 1.10.78; Vehicle in item 6 *(see previous page)*

Instead of complying with these requirements, vehicles may comply with the corresponding EC Directive	'Mirror' means a mirror to assist the driver of a vehicle to become aware of traffic: (a) internal – to the rear; and (b) external – rearwards on that side

VISION

View to the front (REG 30)

Every motor vehicle shall be designed and constructed so that the driver can at all times have a full view of the road and traffic ahead of the vehicle.

All glass or other transparent material shall be maintained in such condition that it does not obscure the vision of the driver while the vehicle is being driven on a road.

Windscreen Wipers and Washers (REG 34)

Every vehicle fitted with a windscreen shall, unless the driver can see to the front without looking through the windscreen, be fitted with one or more efficient **automatic windscreen wipers** capable of clearing the screen so the driver can see the road in front on both sides of the vehicle and the front.

Every wheeled vehicle required to be fitted as above, must also have a windscreen washer capable of clearing mud etc (except agricultural vehicles first used on or after 1.6.86 driven at not more than 20mph; track laying vehicles; vehicles with max speed not over 20mph; or local transport service vehicles).

Glass (REG 32)

Caravans first used on or after 1.9.78 and wheeled motor vehicles and trailers first used on or after 1.6.78 shall have windows as follows:

Windscreens and other windows wholly or partly on either side of the driver's seat.	Glass complying with British Standard Specification or ECE Regulations and bearing the relevant marking.
All other windows, windscreens of motor cycles, temporary replacements for windscreens or windows wholly or partly in front of or on either side of the driver's seat.	Materials other than glass which is so constructed or treated that if fractured it does not fly into fragments likely to cause severe cuts.
Screen or door in interior of a bus first used on or after 1.4.88.	Either of the above.
Police or security vehicles, engineering plant, etc; upper deck of buses; roof windows.	Either of the above or safety glass.

SMOKE

REG 61 ROAD VEHICLES (CONSTRUCTION AND USE) REGULATIONS 1986

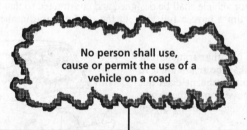

No person shall use, cause or permit the use of a vehicle on a road

if the engine is not so maintained that **vapours or gases** in the engine crank case or in other parts of the engine are prevented from **escaping into the atmosphere** otherwise than through the combustion chamber

if the fuel injection equipment, the engine speed governor or any other parts of the engine have in any way been **altered or adjusted** so as to **increase the emission of smoke**

from which any **smoke**, visible vapour, grit, sparks, ashes, cinders or oily substance is **emitted** if it causes or is likely to cause:

1. Damage to any property; or

2. Injury to any person who is, or may be reasonably expected to be on the road

if a device has been fitted which is designed to facilitate starting by causing the engine to be supplied with excess fuel, and the device is used while the vehicle is in motion – in addition, the device must not be operable by a person inside the vehicle.

SPECIAL TYPES VEHICLES

MOTOR VEHICLES (AUTHORISATION OF SPECIAL TYPES) GENERAL ORDER 1979

Special Types Orders may give exemption for certain vehicles as to compliance with C&U Regulations provided certain conditions are fulfilled.

The specific regulations from which exemption is given, together with the conditions to be met, are referred to in the following sections:

VEHICLE TYPE	SECTION
Naval, military, air force and aviation vehicles	**A**
Grass cutting machines and hedge trimmers	**B**
Track laying vehicles	**C**
Pedestrian controlled road maintenance vehicles	**D**
Vehicles used for experiments or trials	**E**
Straddle carriers	**F**
Wide agricultural vehicles	**G**
Agricultural vehicles with front or rear projections	**H**
Vehicles for moving excavated material	**J**
Vehicles for carrying or drawing abnormal indivisible loads	**K**
Other vehicles carrying loads exceeding 4.3 metres in width	**L**
Engineering plant	**M**

SPECIAL TYPES VEHICLES

NAVAL, MILITARY, AIR FORCE AND AVIATION VEHICLES (ART 6)

Type of vehicle	Exemption	Vehicle belonging to or under the control of
• Combat vehicles or trailers constructed for training in connection with combat. • Constructed for use in connection with instruments of war. • Motor vehicles or trailers constructed for carriage of tanks.	All C&U Regulations	Secretary of State for Defence or Industry, or any contractor or sub contractor making such vehicles for Secretary of State.
Motor vehicles or trailers for search lights and associated equipment.	Springs.	
Motor vehicles or trailers constructed for carriage of aircraft or aircraft parts.	Length, width of HMC, overhang, width of trailer, lateral projection.	
Heavy motor cars and trailers constructed for use, and used only for flying operations, where additional width is necessary for equipment.	Width of heavy motor car and trailer.	
Motor tractors, heavy motor cars and trailers constructed before 1.1.49.	Width, overhang, trailer brakes.	Secretary of State for Defence or Industry.
Aircraft drawn by motor vehicles.	Springs, length, width and trailer brakes.	Secretary of State for Defence.
Motor vehicles and trailers used for generating equipment for military purposes.	Width, length, weight.	Minister of Transport.

SPECIAL TYPES VEHICLES

**GRASS CUTTING MACHINES AND
HEDGE TRIMMERS** (ARTS 7 & 9)

(B)

Motor vehicles constructed or adapted
for use as grass cutters or hedge
trimmers (not pedestrian controlled)

need not comply with Reg 8 of the
C&U Regs (Maximum Width) provided:

- all other relevant C&U requirements are complied with
- overall width of vehicle, together with any equipment mounted on
  it, except when actually operating, shall not exceed 2.55 metres
- except when actually operating, all blades fitted or mounted
  shall be effectively guarded so that no danger is caused or likely
  to be caused to any person.

Trailers constructed or
adapted for use as grass
cutters or hedge trimmers

need not comply with any C&U Regs applicable to
trailers other than Reg 27 (Tyres) provided:

weight	its UW must not exceed 1,020kg if drawn by a locomotive, motor tractor or heavy motor car, or 815kg in any other case;
width	• overall width of the drawing vehicle is not to exceed 2.6 metres, • overall width of the trailer, except when actually cutting grass, is not to exceed 2.6 metres, • overall width of the combination when being towed must not take up more than 2.6 metres of the road;
use	all cutting blades to be guarded so as not to be likely to cause danger, except when cutting grass etc;
speed	restricted to maximum speed of 20mph.

SPECIAL TYPES VEHICLES

TRACK LAYING VEHICLES (ART 5)

Track laying vehicles need not comply
with C&U Regulations provided:

- used only for demonstration or to proceed to a railway station or port for shipment;
- consent in writing is obtained from every Highway Authority (or person responsible for the maintenance or repair) of any road on which it is proposed the vehicle shall be used;
- do not carry goods or burden for hire or reward;
- the drawing or launching of lifeboats is restricted to those owned by the RNLI.

**PEDESTRIAN CONTROLLED ROAD
MAINTENANCE VEHICLES** (ART 10)

Pedestrian controlled road maintenance vehicles
need not comply with the following C&U Regs:

- compensating arrangement for variation in wheel load   REG 23
- parking brake   REG 16
- brakes on motor tractors   REG 16
- brakes on motor cycles   REG 16

provided:

(a) all other C&U Regulations are complied with;
(b) weight of vehicle is not to exceed 410kg;
(c) must be capable of being brought to a standstill and held stationary, by brakes or otherwise.

VEHICLES USED FOR EXPERIMENTS OR TRIALS (ART 11)

If trials conducted under S 283 Highways Act 1980

▼

need not comply with any of the C&U Regulations

STRADDLE CARRIERS (ART 12)

Straddled carriers are defined in C&Use Regulations as:

'a motor vehicle constructed to straddle and lift its load for purpose of transportation'.

They need not comply with the following C&U Regulations:

▼

- springs..REG 22
- direct mechanical brake ....REG 16
- vehicle plate ....REG 66
- power to weight ratio ....REG 45
- width of heavy motor car (2.5 m) ....REG 8
- overhang ....REG 11
- braking efficiencies ....REGS 16, 18
- maintenance of braking efficiencies ...REG 18

Provisions to be complied with:

▼

All other C&U requirements must be complied with.	
use	May only be used for demonstration, delivery following sale or for repairs. When so used, not to carry a load other than necessary gear and equipment.
speed	Speed restricted to 12mph.
width	Overall width not to exceed 2.9 metres.
length	Overall length of vehicle together with any load, if any, shall not exceed 9.2 metres, except with consent of Chief Officer of Police for each area in which it is proposed to be used. (Two days' notice to be given of vehicle, overall length, load carried and route proposed.)

SPECIAL TYPES VEHICLES

WIDE AGRICULTURAL VEHICLES   (ARTS 13 & 13A)

Wide agricultural vehicles, including:

- agricultural motor vehicles;
- agricultural trailers designed to perform functions other than carrying goods and, for the purpose of which, need to be over 2.55 metres wide;
- agricultural trailed appliances; and
- agricultural motor vehicles towing off-set agricultural trailer or trailed appliance which together exceed 2.55 metres wide – if width cannot be reduced without undue expense or risk of damage:

may be use on a road if the following conditions are complied with:

speed	if width exceeds 3.5 metres, maximum speed is 12mph. If width exceeds 2.55 metres maximum speed is 20mph.
notification	24 hours' notice must be given to the chief officer of police if width exceeds 3 metres and either: 1. the journey will be on a road where speed limit is 40mph or less, or 2. the distance to be covered will exceed 5 miles.
trailers	if motor vehicle (or combination of vehicle and trailer/appliance) exceeds 3 metres wide, no trailer (or other trailer) may be drawn except: 1. 2-wheeled trailer carrying equipment used on drawing vehicle; 2. agricultural trailed appliance; 3. harvester used with the drawing vehicle.
warning of danger	if width exceeds 3.5 metres a person other than the driver must warn people of any danger. The extremities of the vehicle shall be clearly visible to other road users in daylight and must be adequately lit in reduced visibility or darkness.
maximum width	in any case the width must not exceed 4.3 metres.

SPECIAL TYPES VEHICLES (H)

AGRICULTURAL VEHICLES WITH FRONT OR REAR PROJECTIONS
(ART 13C)

This category, which includes:

- agricultural motor vehicles;
- agricultural trailers/trailed appliances with an agricultural implement rigidly mounted thereon (need not be permanent)

may be used on roads provided:

projection	condition to be complied with
1 metre	end of projection must be clearly visible to other road users. during the hours of darkness or reduced visibility, the lighting regulations must be complied with.
2 metres	projection markers provided *(see Part 3 later)*.
4 metres	projection markers provided *(see Part 3 later)*. notification to police as above.
6 metres	projection markers provided *(see Part 3 later)*. notification to police as above. person to warn of danger as above.

SPECIAL TYPES VEHICLES

VEHICLES FOR MOVING EXCAVATED MATERIAL (ART 15)

This category, which includes:

heavy motor cars; trailers; or articulated vehicles specially designed and constructed for use on private premises for moving excavated material and fitted with tipping body, moving platform or other similar device;

are exempt from C&U Regs listed oppostite provided:

use	Only used going to and from private premises, or to and from a port, and shall not carry a load other than necessary gear and equipment.
trailer	1. If a heavy motor car not forming part of an articulated vehicle, shall not draw a trailer. 2. Where a trailer is drawn by motor vehicle, no other trailer may be drawn.

width	1. If width exceeds 5 metres, then:
	   a. journey must be in accordance with a written notice of the minister or the directions of the chief officer of police; and
	   b. notice of minister or police must be carried on the vehicle.
	2. if width exceeds 3.5 metres at least one attendant is required to tend the vehicle, load and give warning of danger. If three or more vehicles are travelling in convoy, only the first and last need an attendant.
	3. if width exceeds 2.9 metres, two days' notice is required by chief of police regarding particulars of vehicle, overall width, and time, date and route.

brakes	In the case of a trailer (whether articulated or not), provided an efficient brake or device to hold it stationary is fitted, the braking requirements of regulation 75 need not be complied with.
length	The overall length of a trailer shall not exceed 8.54 metres, and that of an articulated vehicle shall not exceed 13.4 metres.
speed	speed is restricted to 12mph other than on a motorway.
tyres	must have pneumatic tyres.
weight	If any weight regulation is contravened, two days' notice must be given to Highways Authority together with an indemnity. If a heavy motor car not forming part of articulated vehicle, or if an articulated vehicle, max weight transmitted by any 2 wheels in line transversely shall not exceed 22,860kg, and sum of weight transmitted by all wheels shall not exceed 50,800kg.

SPECIAL TYPES VEHICLES

VEHICLES FOR MOVING EXCAVATED MATERIAL –
REGULATIONS FROM WHICH EXEMPT (ART 15)

J
(cont)

A heavy motor car not forming part of articulated vehicle
is exempt from the following Regulations:

- braking efficiencies ....Regs 16,18
- laden weight......................................Regs 75, 76
- maintenance of brakes ....Reg 18 (except (1)(a))
- mechanical brake..Reg 16
- power to weight ratio ....Reg 45
- springs ....Reg 22
- vehicle plate ....Reg 66
- wheel ....Regs 93
- width (2.5 metres)..Reg 8
- wings ....Regs 63

A trailer not forming part of articulated vehicle
is exempt from the following Regulations:

- maintenance of brakes............Reg 18 (except (1)(a))
- overall width ....Reg 8
- springs..Reg 22
- vehicle plate ....Reg 66
- wings..Reg 63

An articulated vehicle
is exempt from the following Regulations:

- Overall length..Reg 7
- Springs..Reg 22
- Mechanical brake..Reg 16
- Vehicle plate..Reg 66
- Power to weight ratio ....Reg 45
- Width (2.5 metres)..Reg 8
- Brake efficiencies.......................................Regs 16, 18
- Wings ....Reg 63
- Overall width..Reg 8
- Wings ....Reg 63
- Laden weight...Regs 75, 77
- Weight ....Reg 79
- Maintenance of brakes Reg18

K SPECIAL TYPES VEHICLES

VEHICLES CARRYING OR DRAWING ABNORMAL LOADS

(ART 18)

Vehicles carrying or drawing an abnormal load are exempt from the below requirements provided the conditions on facing page are met:

- - - ➤ Vehicles must comply with the conditions of an appropriate category:

Total weight of vehicle not exceeding	Category (see table below)
46,000kg	**Category 1**
80,000kg	**Category 2**
150,000kg	**Category 3**

Type of vehicle	Regulations exempt from	
Heavy motor car manufactured before 1.10.89	Springs	REG 22
	Parking brake	REG 16
	Power to weight ratio	REG 45
	Width	REG 8
	Brakes	REGS 15,18 (except 18(1))
	Tyres	REG 24
	Tyre loads and speed ratings	REG 25
	Wings	REG 63
	Weight	REGS 75-80
	Width of load	REG 82
	Number of trailers	REG 83(1)
Locomotive or tractor manufactured before 1.10.89	Springs	REG 22
	Tyre loads and speed ratings	REG 25
	Power to weight ratio	REG 45
	Width	REG 8
	Weight of vehicle & trailer	REGS 75(3), 76
Trailer manufactured before 1.10.89	Length	REG 7
	Springs	REG 22
	Diameter of wheels	REG 21
	Width	REG 8
	Brakes	REGS 15,18 (except 18(1))
	Tyres	REG 24
	Tyre loads and speed ratings	REG 25
	Wings	REG 63
	Spray suppression	REG 64
	Weight	REGS 75-80
	Width of load	REG 82
	Number of trailers	REG 83(1)
Category 1: vehicle or combination of vehicles whenever manufactured	Length	REG 7
	Width	REG 8
	Weight	REG 80
	Width of load	REG 82
Categories 2 and 3: vehicle or combination of vehicles manufactured after 1.10.89	Length	REG 7
	Width	REG 8
	Brakes	REGS 15,16,18 (except 18(1))
	Tyre loads and speed ratings	REG 25
	Power to weight ratio	REG 45
	Spray suppression	REGS 64,65
	Weight	REGS 75-80
	Width of load	REG 82
	Number of trailers	REG 83(1)

K

SPECIAL TYPES VEHICLES

CONDITIONS					
Use	Must not use a bridge if there is another abnormal load using it. Must not remain stationary on a bridge.				
Width	Heavy motor car or trailer, locomotive or motor tractor	*Not to exceed 2.9 metres unless the load can only be safely carried on a vehicle or trailer which exceeds that width*			
	Any vehicle	*Not to exceed 6.1 metres including any projections*			
Length	Not to exceed 27.4 metres.				
Tyres	Must be wheeled vehicle with soft or elastic or pneumatic tyres.				
Max speed			Motorway	Dual Carriageway	Other Roads
	Cat 1 (total weight not exceeding 46,000 kg)		60	50	40
	Cat 2 (total weight not exceeding 80,000kg)		40	35	30
	Cat 3 (total weight not exceeding 150,000kg)		30	25	20
Plate	Category 2 and 3 vehicles manufactured after 1.10.88 must have a plate showing the maximum weights of the vehicle and marked 'SPECIAL TYPES USE'.				
Identif- ication sign	The vehicle (or drawing vehicle in a combination) shall be fitted with a sign to indicate the category. The sign must be fitted vertically on the front facing forwards, in the following form:				
	<div style="text-align:center">400 mm **STGO** **CAT 3** 250 mm 105 mm 70 mm</div>				
	Note: the category number 3 is shown as an example; the number could be 1, 2 or 3 depending upon the category of the vehicle or combination of vehicles.				
weight and general conditions 1 - 5 *see following pages*					

SPECIAL TYPES VEHICLES

MAXIMUM WEIGHT OF ABNORMAL LOADS

REGS 75, 76, 78 AND 79, C&U REGULATIONS APPLY (WEIGHT).
ARTICULATED VEHICLES WITH LESS THAN FIVE AXLES MUST ALSO
COMPLY WITH REG 77 (MAX WEIGHT)

Category 1 (total weight not exceeding 46,000kg)
(maximum permitted laden, wheel and axle weights)

Articulated vehicles with five or more axles:

Distance between rearmost axle on tractive unit and rearmost axle on trailer (metres)	Max weight (kg)
At least 6.5	40,000
" 7.0	42,000
" 7.5	44,000
" 8.0	46,000

Where a semi-trailer has a group of 4 axles, the outermost of which are 3.25 metres apart or less and distance between any two is at least 0.87 metres, then the max weight for any one axle is 6,000kg.

Categories 2 (total weight not exceeding 80,000kg) and 3 (total weight not exceeding 150,000kg)

	Category 2	Category 3
Min number of axles	5	6
Max weight for any one axle	12,500kg	16,500kg
Max weight for any one wheel	6,250kg	8,250kg
Where distance between two adjacent axles is between 1.1m and 1.35m:		
Max weight for any one axle	12,000kg	15,000kg
Max weight for any one wheel	6,000kg	7,500kg
Min distance between two adjacent axles	1.1m	1.1m

SPECIAL TYPES VEHICLES

MAXIMUM WEIGHT OF ABNORMAL LOADS CONT

K

REGS 75, 76, 78 AND 79, CONSTRUCTION AND USE REGS APPLY (WEIGHT). ARTICULATED VEHICLES WITH LESS THAN FIVE AXLES MUST ALSO COMPLY WITH REG 77 (MAX WEIGHT)

Categories 2 and 3 continued from previous page

	Category 2		**Category 3**	
	Distance between foremost and rearmost axles (metres)	**Max weight (kg)**	**Distance between foremost and rearmost axles (metres)**	**Max weight (kg)**
Total max weight	5.07 5.33 6.0 6.67 7.33 8.0 8.67 9.33 10.0 10.67	38,000 40,000 45,000 50,000 55,000 60,000 65,000 70,000 75,000 80,000	5.77 6.23 6.68 7.14 7.59 8.05 8.50 8.95 9.41 9.86 10.32 10.77 11.23 11.68 12.14	80,000 85,000 90,000 95,000 100,000 105,000 110,000 115,000 120,000 125,000 130,000 135,000 140,000 145,000 150,000
Max weight of a group of axles	Adjacent axles in group less than 2 m. and distance between groups is more than 2 metres	50,000	Adjacent axles in group less than 1.5 metres and distance between groups is more than 1.5 metres	100,000
			Distance between 2 axles in a group is less than 1.35 metres	90,000

SPECIAL TYPES VEHICLES
OTHER VEHICLES EXCEEDING 4.3 METRES IN WIDTH
(ART 20)

Vehicles plus any projection may exceed
4.3 metres in width provided:

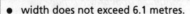

- width does not exceed 6.1 metres.
- speed does not exceed 30mph on
  motorways, 25mph on dual
  carriageways or 20mph on other
  roads.
- conditions 1, 3 and 5 are complied
  with *(see later, General conditions)*
- all C&U Regulations are complied
  with except parts of Reg 82 (length
  of projections).

SPECIAL TYPES VEHICLES

ENGINEERING PLANT (ART 19)

Engineering plant is exempt from C&U Regulations

other than the Regulations shown overleaf

provided the conditions below are applied:

CONDITIONS	
speed	On roads other than motorways – 12mph. However, if the following conditions relating to abnormal loads under Article 18 (see earlier) are complied with, the speed limits are increased to the same as those applicable to abnormal loads under Article 18. The conditions are: weight; all C&U Regulations to be complied with except those from which Category 1, 2 or 3 vehicles are exempt; plate; and identification sign.
brakes	The vehicle and trailer shall be equipped with an efficient brake.
use	Only to proceed to or from, or when actually engaged in, engineering operations, demonstration, testing repair or maintenance.
load	No load except: engineering plant may carry materials for treatment whilst being carried, or which has been excavated by the vehicle's apparatus; and a mobile crane may transport or lift a load.
construction	Either wheeled or track-laying.
trailer	• Mobile cranes not allowed to draw a trailer. • Other engineering plant may draw engineering plant, an office hut or living van, unless vehicle exceeds 7.93 metres in width.
weight	Not to exceed 152,400kg.
length	Not to exceed 27.4 metres.
width	Not to exceed 6.1. metres.
plus	*General conditions, see later*

SPECIAL TYPES VEHICLES

ENGINEERING PLANT cont   (ART 19)

> **C&U Regulations which apply to engineering plant are:**

- Compensating arrangement.................REG 23
- Dangerous parts, accessories and load....REG 100
- Gas containers ....REG 40
- General application ....REG 4
- Glass............................REGS 31, 32
- Maintenance of brakes ......REG 8
- Maintenance of glass........REG 30
- Maintenance of steering gear ....REG 29

- Marking of UW ....REG 10
- Noise ....REG 58
- Radio interference ....REG 60
- Silencer ....REG 54
- Smoke or vapour...............REG 61
- View to front ....REG 30
- Warning instrument ....REG 37
- Washers/wipers ....REGS 27, 28

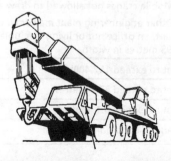

GENERAL CONDITIONS

(ART 22) **CONDITION 1 – attendant to be carried if:**	
width	Of vehicle plus any projection exceeds 3.5 metres.
length	Of vehicle plus any projection exceeds 18.3 metres, or if the combination of vehicle and trailer plus any projection exceeds 25.9 metres.
projection	Exceeds 1.83 metres to the front or 3.5 metres to the rear.

(ART 23) **CONDITION 2 – marking of projections if:**	
Forward or rearward exceeding 1.83 metres.	In accordance with C&U Regulations *(see Projection markers, Part 3, later)*.
Rearward between 1.07 and 1.83 metres.	Rendered clearly visible.

(ART 25) **CONDITION 3 - two days' notice to police if:**	
width	Of vehicle and any projection exceeds 2.9 metres.
length	Of vehicle and any projection exceeds 18.3 metres.
	Of combination of vehicle and trailer plus any projection exceeds 25.9 metres.
projection	Forward or rearward exceeds 3.05 metres.
weight	Of combination of vehicle, trailer (if any) and load exceeds 80,000kg.

(ART 26) **CONDITION 4 – notification to highway authority**	
weights exceeds 80,000kg	Five days' notice, plus an indemnity must be given to Highway Authority.
C&U weight limits exceeded	Two days' notice, plus an indemnity must be given to Highway Authority.

(ART 24) **CONDITION 5 – approval of minister required in writing if width exceeds 5 metres.**

SIDEGUARDS

REG 51 ROAD VEHICLES (CONSTRUCTION AND USE) REGULATIONS 1986

The following vehicles are to be fitted with sideguards to give protection on any side of the vehicle – no sideguard to be outside vehicle's normal width nor more than 30 mm inboard of outer wall of rearmost tyre.

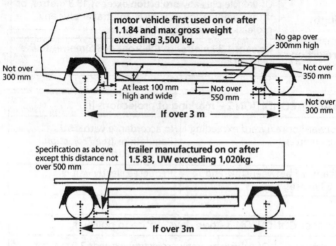

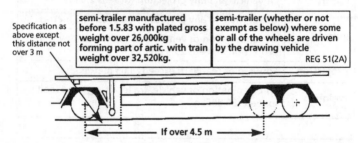

Exemptions

- Incapable of over 15mph on flat
- Agricultural trailer
- Engineering plant
- Fire engine
- Agricultural motor vehicle
- Rear and side tippers
- Defence
- Chassis for testing or fitting

- Used for fitting sideguards
- Street cleaning etc
- Trailer for lengthy beams etc
- Articulated tractive unit
- Trailer for carrying vehicles
- Trailers not over 750mm high
- Trailer temporarily in GB within 12 months of entry

Shall be maintained free from any defect likely to affect effectiveness.
REG 52

REARGUARDS

REG 49 ROAD VEHICLES (CONSTRUCTION AND USE) REGULATIONS 1986

Rearguards generally consists of a cross-member and linking components connected to the chassis side-members or whatever replaces them.

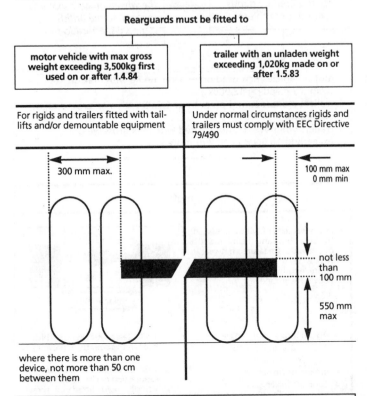

Rearguards must be fitted to

motor vehicle with max gross weight exceeding 3,500kg first used on or after 1.4.84	trailer with an unladen weight exceeding 1,020kg made on or after 1.5.83

For rigids and trailers fitted with tail-lifts and/or demountable equipment

Under normal circumstances rigids and trailers must comply with EEC Directive 79/490

300 mm max.

100 mm max
0 mm min

not less than 100 mm

550 mm max

where there is more than one device, not more than 50 cm between them

Rearguards need not be fitted to

- Incapable of over 15mph on flat
- Articulated tractive unit
- Engineering plant
- Fire engine
- Agricultural motor vehicle
- Agricultural trailer
- Road spreader
- Rear tipper
- Defence
- Chassis for testing or fitting
- For fitting guards
- For carrying other vehicles
- Trailer for lengthy beams etc
- Tail lifts over one metre long
- Concrete carrier/mixer
- Trailer temp. in GB within 12 months of entry

Must be maintained free from any obvious defect which would be likely to adversely affect performance in the event of an impact from the rear.
REG 50

SPRAY SUPPRESSION DEVICES

REG 64 ROAD VEHICLES (CONSTRUCTION AND USE) REGULATIONS 1986

Spray suppression devices are required by goods vehicles which are:

→ *The device must be fitted to the wheels on each axle and conform to the British standard specification.*

↓

1. motor vehicles first used on or after 1.4.86 with max gross weight exceeding 12,000kg
2. trailers manufactured on or after 1.5.85 with max gross weight exceeding 3,500kg
3. trailers whenever manufactured with max gross weight exceeding 16,000kg and 2 or more axles.

Exemptions

- Motor vehicles of which no part in the area consisting the middle 80% of the width (measured between the insides of the wheels) and the entire length is less than 400mm above the ground.

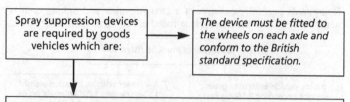

- Agricultural motor vehicle
- Agricultural trailed appliance
- Agricultural trailer
- Broken down vehicles
- Concrete mixer
- Engineering plant
- Fire engine
- Four-wheel drive vehicles
- Max speed not exceeding 30mph
- Military etc vehicles
- Refuse vehicle
- Tipper vehicles (side or rear)

- Trailer leased outside GB which has been in this country in previous 12 months.
- Vehicle being taken for spray suppression device to be fitted. Vehicle already fitted with spray-suppression device in accordance with EC Directive 91/226.
- Vehicle without a body being taken for testing, body fitting or delivery to a dealer.
- Works trailers
- Works trucks

At all times when the vehicle is on a road the device must be maintained free from defects which would adversely affect the efficiency of the device.

REG 65

MISCELLANEOUS CONSTRUCTION AND USE OFFENCES

MASCOTS (REG 53)

No mascot, emblem or other ornamental object shall be carried by a motor vehicle first used on or after 1.10.37 in any position where it is likely to strike any person with whom the vehicle may collide unless the mascot is not liable to cause injury.

MOTOR CYCLE SIDESTANDS (REG 38)

No motorcycle first used on or after 1.4.86 shall be fitted with any sidestand which is capable of:
1. disturbing stability or direction when in motion; or
2. closing automatically if the angle of inclination of the motor cycle is inadvertently altered when it is stationary.

RADIO INTERFERENCE SUPPRESSION (REG 60)

Every wheeled motor vehicle first used on or after 1.4.74 which is propelled by a spark ignition engine shall comply at the time of its first use with EEC or Community Directives relating to suppression. This does not apply to vehicles constructed or assembled by persons not normally in the business of manufacturing such vehicles.

STOPPING OF ENGINE WHEN STATIONARY (REG 98)

The driver of a vehicle shall, when the vehicle is stationary, stop the action of any machinery attached to or forming part of the vehicle so far as may be necessary for the prevention of noise. Does not apply when stationary due to traffic, working of the machinery is necessary for other than driving the vehicle, or gas propelled vehicle producing gas.

AVOIDANCE OF EXCESSIVE NOISE (REG 97)

No motor vehicle shall be used on a road in such a manner as to cause any excessive noise which could have been avoided by the exercise of reasonable care on the part of the driver.

PARKING IN DARKNESS (REG 101)

A motor vehicle must, between sunset and sunrise, when standing on a road, have the nearside of the vehicle as close as may be to the edge of the carriageway. This does not apply with permission of a police officer in uniform; fire, police, ambulance or defence purposes; building, demolition repair of buildings or roads etc; on a one-way street; parking place or taxi or bus stand; or setting down or picking up passengers in accordance with regulations.

MISCELLANEOUS CONSTRUCTION AND USE OFFENCES cont

MOTOR CYCLES – FOOTRESTS (REG 102)

Footrests shall be available for any passenger carried astride a two-wheeled motor cycle (whether a sidecar is attached or not).

OBSTRUCTION (REG 103)

No person in charge of a motor vehicle or trailer shall cause or permit the vehicle to stand on a road so as to cause any unnecessary obstruction of the road.

DRIVER'S CONTROL (REG 104)

No person shall drive or cause or permit any other person to drive, a motor vehicle on a road if he is in such a position that he cannot have proper control of the vehicle or have a full view of the road and traffic ahead.

OPENING OF DOORS (REG 105)

No person shall open, or cause or permit to be opened, any door of a vehicle on a road so as to injure or endanger any person.

REVERSING (REG 106)

No person shall drive, or cause or permit to be driven, a motor vehicle backwards on a road further than may be requisite for the safety or reasonable convenience of the occupants of the vehicle or other traffic, unless for road repairs, etc.

LEAVING VEHICLE UNATTENDED (REG 107)

No person shall leave, or cause or permit to be left, on a road a motor vehicle which is unattended by a licensed driver unless the engine is stopped and the parking brake is set. This does not apply to police, ambulance or fire, or if the engine is needed to drive machinery, etc.

TELEVISION SETS (REG 109)

The driver must not be in a position to see, whether directly or by reflection, any television or other like apparatus used to display anything other than information about the state of the vehicle, location, to assist the driver to see the adjacent road, or to assist the driver to reach his destination.

PART 2

DOCUMENTATION

This part of the book aims to highlight the various types of formal documentation required. Including driving licences, insurance, operators' licences, vehicle excise duty, registration plates, plating and testing, trade licences, the operation of passenger carrying vehicles, and foreign vehicles.

HGV DOCUMENTATION

The following 'check list' may prove to be a guide to the legal requirements for the use of a heavy goods vehicle. Depending on the type of vehicle, reference should be made to the relevant pages as indicated.

DRIVING LICENCES – DEFINITIONS
MOTOR VEHICLES (DRIVING LICENCES) REGULATIONS 1996

LARGE MOTOR BICYCLE
(a) If without sidecar, the bicycle engine has a maximum net power exceeding 25 kilowatts or a power-to-weight ratio exceeding 0.16 kilowatts per kilogram, or
(b) if with sidecar, the combination has a power-to-weight ratio exceeding 0.16 kilowatts per kilogram.

STANDARD MOTOR BICYCLE
Not a large motor bicycle.

PASSENGER CARRYING VEHICLE RECOVERY VEHICLE
A vehicle other than an articulated goods vehicle which:
(a) has unladen weight not exceeding 10.2 tonnes
(b) is being operated by the holder of a PSV Operator's Licence, and
(c) is proceeding to, returning from or giving assistance to, a damaged or disabled passenger-carrying vehicle.

INCOMPLETE LARGE VEHICLE
(a) Typically consisting of a chassis and cab which, when complete, is capable of becoming a medium-sized or large goods vehicle or a passenger-carrying vehicle, or
(b) a vehicle which would be an articulated goods vehicle but for the absence of a 5th wheel coupling.

Continued overleaf

DEFINITIONS cont

MOTOR VEHICLES (DRIVING LICENCES) REGULATIONS 1996

EXEMPTED GOODS VEHICLE

Steam-driven vehicle; road construction vehicle; engineering plant (other than a mobile crane); works truck; industrial tractor; agricultural motor vehicle (not being an agricultural or forestry tractor); digging machine; vehicle not used on public roads for more than 6 miles per week; any vehicle – not being an agricultural motor vehicle – only used for agriculture, horticulture or forestry and used on public roads for not more than 1.5 km to pass between different areas of land; vehicle for hauling lifeboats; unladen vehicle manufactured before 1.1.60 not drawing a trailer; articulated goods vehicle with UW not over 3.05 tonnes; visiting Forces vehicles; vehicle driven by a constable to protect life and property, etc; vehicle with UW not over 3.05 tonnes for raising and drawing disabled vehicles; passenger-carrying vehicle; recovery vehicle; and a mobile project vehicle.

EXEMPTED MILITARY VEHICLE

Defence fire vehicle, urgent national defence work, and defence armoured vehicle not being a tracked vehicle.

MOBILE PROJECT VEHICLE

Vehicle having a maximum authorised mass exceeding 3.5 tonnes, constructed or adapted to carry not more than 8 persons in addition to the driver, carrying play or educational equipment for children, or articles required for an exhibition. Its primary purpose when stationary is recreational, educational or instructional.

QUALIFIED DRIVER

(a) In the case of category B vehicles (other than B1) and where the supervisor has a licence restricted to a particular class because of a disability, the qualified driver is a person who has a full category B (other than B1) licence and who, in an emergency, would be able to take control of the vehicle.

(b) In any other case, a person who holds: (i) a full licence (other than an LGV trainee's licence), (ii) a full Northern Ireland Licence, or (iii) a Community Licence, in each case authorising the driving of that class of vehicle and who is either at least 21 years' old and has held the licence for an aggregate of 3 years, or is acting for naval, military or air force purposes. There is no 3-year requirement in the case of a large goods or passenger-carrying vehicle.

CATEGORIES & SUB-CATEGORIES OF VEHICLE FOR LICENSING PURPOSES

REGS 4 TO 6, 40 AND SCHED 2 MOTOR VEHICLES (DRIVING LICENCES)
REGULATIONS 1996

Category or sub-category	Classes of vehicle included
A	Motor bicycles but excluding any motor vehicle in category K.
A1	A sub-category of category A comprising learner motor bicycles but excluding any motor vehicle in category P.
B	Any motor vehicle, other than a vehicle included in category A, F or P, having a maximum authorised mass not exceeding 3.5 tonnes and not more than 8 seats in addition to the driver's seat, including: (i) a combination of such a vehicle and a trailer where the trailer has a maximum authorised mass not exceeding 750kg, and (ii) a combination of such a vehicle and a trailer where the maximum authorised mass of the combination does not exceed 3.5 tonnes and the maximum authorised mass of the trailer does not exceed the UW of the tractor vehicle.
B1	A sub-category of category B comprising motor vehicles having three or four wheels, UW not exceeding 550kg, a maximum design speed exceeding 50km per hour and, if powered by an internal combustion engine, a cubic capacity exceeding 50cc.
B1 (invalid carriages)	A sub-category of category B comprising motor vehicles which are invalid carriages.
B + E	Combination of a motor vehicle and trailer where the tractor vehicle is in category B but the combination does not fall within that category.
C	Any motor vehicle having a maximum authorised mass exceeding 3.5 tonnes, other than a vehicle falling within category D, F. G or H, including such a vehicle drawing a trailer having a maximum authorised mass not exceeding 750 kilograms.
C1	A sub-category of category C comprising motor vehicles having a maximum authorised mass exceeding 3.5 tonnes but not exceeding 7.5 tonnes, including such a vehicle drawing a trailer having a maximum authorised mass not exceeding 750kg.
D	Any motor vehicle constructed or adapted for the carriage of passengers having more than 8 seats in addition to the driver's seat, including such a vehicle drawing a trailer having a maximum authorised mass not exceeding 750kg.
D1	A sub-category of category D comprising motor vehicles having more than 8 but not more than 16 seats in addition to the driver's seat and including such a vehicle drawing a trailer with a maximum authorised mass not exceeding 750kg.

continued overleaf

CATEGORIES & SUB-CATEGORIES OF VEHICLE FOR LICENSING PURPOSES cont

MOTOR VEHICLES (DRIVING LICENCES) REGULATIONS 1996

Category or sub-category	Classes of vehicle included (CONT FROM PREVIOUS PAGE)
C + E	Combination of a motor vehicle and trailer where the tractor vehicle is in category C but the combination does not fall within that category.
C1 + E	A sub-category of category C + E comprising any combination of a motor vehicle and trailer where: (a) the tractor vehicle is in sub-category C1, (b) the maximum authorised mass of the trailer exceeds 750kg but not the UW of the tractor vehicle, and (c) the maximum authorised mass of the combination does not exceed 12 tonnes.
D + E	Combination of a motor vehicle and trailer where the tractor vehicle is in category D but the combination does not fall within that category.
D1 + E	A sub-category of category D + E comprising any combination of a motor vehicle and trailer where: (a) the tractor vehicle is in sub-category D1, (b) the maximum authorised mass of the trailer exceeds 750 kilograms but not the UW of the tractor vehicle, (c) the maximum authorised mass of the combination does not exceed 12 tonnes, and (d) the trailer is not used for the carriage of passengers.
F	Agricultural or forestry tractor, but excluding any motor vehicle included in category H.
G	Road roller.
H	Track-laying vehicle steered by its tracks.
K	Mowing machine or vehicle controlled by a pedestrian excluding any motor vehicle included in category B.
P	Moped.
C1 + E (8.25 tonnes)	A sub-category of category C + E comprising any combination of a motor vehicle and trailer in sub-category C1 + E the maximum authorised mass of which does not exceed 8.25 tonnes.
D1 (not for hire or reward)	A sub-category of category D comprising motor vehicles in sub-category D1 driven otherwise than for hire or reward.
D1 + E (not for hire or reward)	A sub-category of category D + E comprising motor vehicles in sub-category D1 + E driven otherwise than for hire or reward.
L	Motor vehicle propelled by electrical power.

LICENCES – LGV/PCV EXEMPTIONS

REG 47 MOTOR VEHICLES (DRIVING LICENCE) REGULATIONS 1996

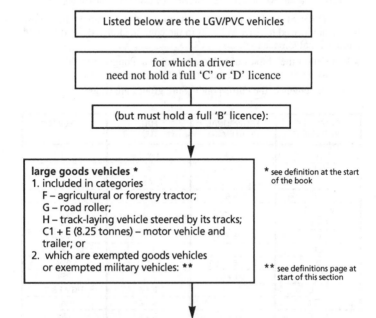

Listed below are the LGV/PVC vehicles

for which a driver
need not hold a full 'C' or 'D' licence

(but must hold a full 'B' licence):

large goods vehicles *
1. included in categories
   F – agricultural or forestry tractor;
   G – road roller;
   H – track-laying vehicle steered by its tracks;
   C1 + E (8.25 tonnes) – motor vehicle and trailer; or
2. which are exempted goods vehicles or exempted military vehicles: ******

* see definition at the start of the book

** see definitions page at start of this section

passenger-carrying vehicles *
1. manufactured more than 30 years before the date when driven and not used for hire or reward or for the carriage of more than 8 passengers;
2. driven by a constable for the purpose of removing or avoiding obstructions, or protecting life or property, etc.

* see definition at the start of the book

DRIVING LICENCES – ADDITIONAL ENTITLEMENTS

REGS 17 & 40 MOTOR VEHICLES (DRIVING LICENCES) REGULATIONS 1996

● The holder of a full licence for a category specified in the table below is also authorised to drive vehicles in the column alongside as if he held a provisional licence to do so.

● In addition the classes of vehicle mentioned alongside in the 3rd column may be driven as if a full licence for that category was held.

● For convenience, the corresponding old groups are shown.

CATEGORY ENTITLEMENT	PROVISIONAL ENTITLEMENT	FULL ENTITLEMENT	OLD GROUP
A	B & F	B1, K & P	D
A1	A, B, F & K	P	
B	A, B + E, G & H	F, K & P	A
B1	A, B & F	K & P	C, J
B1 (inv.)			
B + E			A
C	C1 + E, C + E		HGV 2 & 3
C1			A
D	D1 + E, D + E		PSV
D1	D1 + E		PSV
C + E		B + E	HGV 1 & 2
C1 + E		B + E	A
D + E		B + E	PSV
D1 + E		B + E	PSV
F	B & P	K	F
G	H		G
H	G		H
K			K
P			E
L			L

● Where a full licence authorises only vehicles with automatic transmission, it will act as a provisional licence for manual vehicles in that category.

● If a licence authorises only A1 category motor cycles or standard motor cycles, large motor cycles may not be driven by a person under 21.

ADDITIONAL CLASSES COVERED BY EXISTING LICENCE

REG 6 MOTOR VEHICLES (DRIVING LICENCES) REGULATIONS 1996

Licence Held	Additional Classes Covered
'C' for at least 2 years	Vehicles in Category 'D' (a) not operated by a PSV Operator's licence; or (b) not carrying any person not connected with the operator; and in either case the vehicle is being taken for repair or being tested after repair.
'C'	Dual Purpose Vehicle if (a) a member of the Armed Forces; and (b) the vehicle is adapted to carry not more than 24 persons in addition to the driver, and being used for naval, military or air force purposes.
Full passenger-carrying licence	Passenger-carrying vehicle recovery vehicle. (But if licence is restricted to automatic vehicles then recovery vehicle must be automatic.)
'B' except if restricted to B1 and B1 (invalid carriages)	Incomplete large vehicle. Exempted goods vehicle other than a passenger-carrying vehicle recovery vehicle. Exempted military vehicle. B + E where (a) the trailer is a damaged or defective vehicle likely to be a road safety hazard or obstruction, and (b) driven only so far as is reasonably necessary. (Unless licence is restricted to automatic transmission, in which case the above vehicles must also be automatic.)
'B' except if restricted to B1 and B1 (invalid carriages), has held the licence for not less than 2 years and aged 21 or over	Mobile project vehicle for a non-commercial body: (a) to or from a place where the equipment, display or exhibition is used, or (b) to or from a place where a defect is being remedied, or (c) vehicle is exempt from excise duty due to it being subject to a compulsory test or weight test. (Unless licence is restricted to automatic transmission, in which case above vehicles must also be automatic.)
'B' except if restricted to B1 and B1 (invalid carriages), and has held the licence for not less than 2 years, aged 21 or over, and receives no payment except expenses.	D1 without trailer and maximum authorised mass not exceeding: (a) 3.5 tonnes (excluding specialised equipment for disabled passengers), and (b) 4.25 tonnes otherwise. (But if licence is restricted to automatic transmission, the above vehicles must also be automatic.) Vehicles must be driven for a non-commercial body for social purposes but not for hire or reward.

NOTE:

If a test is passed,
(a) on a vehicle with automatic transmission, only classes of vehicle with automatic transmission are authorised to be driven;
(b) on an invalid carriage, only they are authorised; and
(c) on a vehicle adapted for a disabled person, only vehicles so adapted are authorised.

PROVISIONAL LICENCES – CONDITIONS

REG 15 MOTOR VEHICLES (DRIVING LICENCES) REGULATIONS 1996

Provisional licence-holders must comply with the following conditions:

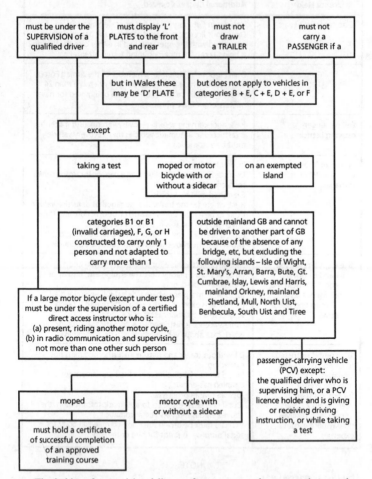

- The holder of a provisional licence for a motor cycle or moped must take Compulsory Basic Training before they may ride on a road. Upon successful completion, a certificate will be issued and must be produced to the police if requested. (S 164(4A) RTA 1988)
- When motor cyclists pass their test, they are restricted to standard motor cycles for the first 2 years unless, if over 21 years, they take a further test.

PROVISIONAL LICENCES – PREREQUISITES FOR ISSUE

REG 9 MOTOR VEHICLES (DRIVING LICENCES) REGS 1996

● Before a provisional licence for a particular category of vehicle can be issued, a relevant full licence must be held in the appropriate category.

● The table below shows the category of full licence needed for a particular provisional licence.

CATEGORY OF LICENCE APPLIED FOR	FULL LICENCE NEEDED
B + E	B
C	B
C1	B
D	B
D1	B
C1 + E	C1
C + E	C
D1 + E	D1
D + E	D
G	B
H	B

NOTE: The above provisions do not apply to full-time members of the armed forces.

LARGE GOODS VEHICLE LICENCES – TRAINEE DRIVERS

REG 51 MOTOR VEHICLES (DRIVING LICENCES) REGULATIONS 1996.

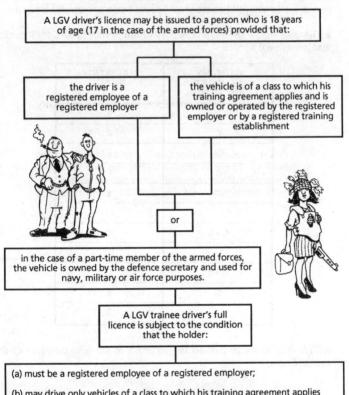

A LGV driver's licence may be issued to a person who is 18 years of age (17 in the case of the armed forces) provided that:

the driver is a registered employee of a registered employer

the vehicle is of a class to which his training agreement applies and is owned or operated by the registered employer or by a registered training establishment

or

in the case of a part-time member of the armed forces, the vehicle is owned by the defence secretary and used for navy, military or air force purposes.

A LGV trainee driver's full licence is subject to the condition that the holder:

(a) must be a registered employee of a registered employer;

(b) may drive only vehicles of a class to which his training agreement applies and which is owned by that registered employee or registered training establishment;

(c) may not draw a trailer otherwise than under the supervision of the holder of a full LGV licence for that class of vehicle; and

(d) may only drive C + E as a provisional licence holder after 2 years from passing the category C test.

LICENCES –
NEWLY QUALIFIED DRIVER

ROAD TRAFFIC (NEW DRIVERS) ACT 1995

- A driver who acquires 6 or more penalty points within two years of passing his test may have his driving licence revoked and will then have to take another driving test. Newly qualified drivers are on a 2-year probationary period starting from the day on which the driving test is passed.

  SECTION 1

- If a newly qualified driver acquires 6 or more penalty points, the Secretary of State will be informed by the convicting court and must revoke the licence by notice to the driver which will state the date of revocation (cannot be earlier than the date of service of the notice). There is provision for the licence to be restored without re-testing where the driver successfully appeals against the conviction and where he gives notice of appeal.

  SECTION 5

- Until the driver passes a driving test he is in the position of a learner driver, and he must apply for a provisional licence.

LICENCES – MINIMUM AGES

REG 7 MOTOR VEHICLES (DRIVING LICENCES) REGULATIONS 1996
AND SECTION 101 ROAD TRAFFIC ACT 1988

CATEGORY	AGE	REMARKS
A	21 (17)	Large motor bicycle, 21 years. But will not apply if: (a) test for category 'A' licence (but not 'A1') passed 2 years ago (b) large motor bicycle owned by defence secretary or being driven subject to the orders of the armed forces, and being used for naval, military or air force purposes,17 years.
A1	17	Other motor cycles, 17 years.
B	17 (16)	Generally 17 but if in receipt of a disability living allowance and no trailer drawn, then16.
B + E	17	
B1	17	
B1 (invalid carriages)	16	
C1, C1 + E and C1 + E (8.25 tonnes)	21 (17, 18)	Generally 21 years except: (a) max authorised mass not over 7.5 tonnes (18 years), or (b) owned by defence secretary or being driven under orders of the armed forces (17 years).
C and C + E	21 (17, 18)	Generally 21 but if on LGV training scheme,18 years. If owned by defence secretary and driven under orders of the armed forces, 17 years.
D1 (not for hire or reward)	21 (18)	Generally 21 but if an ambulance,18 years
D1 + E (not for hire or reward)	21	
D1, D1 + E, D and D + E	21 (17, 18)	Generally 21 except: (a) provisional licence and not carrying passengers except supervisor and other trainees,18 years. (b) used under PSV operator's licence or community bus permit and (i) carrying passengers on a regular service with route not over 50km, or (ii) where not carrying passengers as aforementioned and the vehicle is in category D1,18 years, or (c) vehicle owned by defence secretary and driven subject to orders of the armed forces, 17 years.
F	17 (16)	Generally 17 but if a wheeled vehicle with overall width not over 2.45 metres and not drawing a trailer other than one which is either 2-wheeled or close-coupled 4 wheeled in either case with width not over 2.45 metres; and a cat F test has been passed or being used to take such a test.
G H K L P	17 - 21 17 - 21 16 - 21 16 - 21 16	Refer to specific category

LICENCES – UNDER AGE
ROAD TRAFFIC ACT 1988

● A person is disqualified from holding or obtaining a licence if he is under the age specified *(see previous page)*   S 101 RTA 1988

● A person who drives under age may be prosecuted for driving without a licence.   S 87 RTA 1988

NOTE:
Where an under-age driver has been disqualified from driving by a court order for a previous driving offence, he may be prosecuted for disqualified driving   S 103 RTA 1988
and may be arrested without warrant by a constable in uniform if he is found driving or attempting to drive a motor vehicle on a road.

DRIVING LICENCES – MISCELLANEOUS

RENEWAL
A person may drive even when he has not received his licence provided that a valid application for the grant or renewal of the licence has been received by the driving licence computer centre at Swansea, except where the application relates to:
(a) the first provisional licence
(b) further classes of vehicle not covered in existing licence
(c) a replacement more than 10 years after the expiry of the previous one
(d) an applicant suffering from a relevant disability and this is declared in the application
(e) an applicant disqualified until he passes a test of competence
                                                                        S 88 (1) - (2) RTA 1988

FOREIGNERS

● A person resident outside the UK and here temporarily is allowed to drive without a licence for 12 months from his last arrival here, while his international driving licence or foreign licence remains valid, provided he is within the UK age limits (see later).

● A person who becomes resident in Great Britain shall during the period of one year after he becomes resident be treated as the holder of a driving licence for those classes which he is authorised to drive by any permit he may hold provided that permit is valid and he is not disqualified from holding a GB Licence.   REG 74 MV (DL) REGS 1996

SIGNATURE
Every person to whom a licence is granted shall forthwith sign it in ink with his usual signature.   REG 18 MV (DL) REGS 1996

PRODUCTION OF DRIVING LICENCE etc

SECTION 164 ROAD TRAFFIC ACT 1988

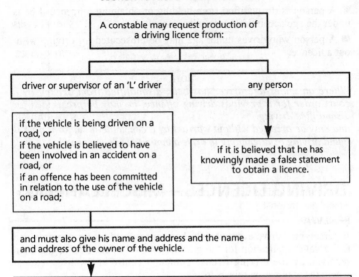

A constable may request production of a driving licence from:

driver or supervisor of an 'L' driver

if the vehicle is being driven on a road, or
if the vehicle is believed to have been involved in an accident on a road, or
if an offence has been committed in relation to the use of the vehicle on a road;

any person

if it is believed that he has knowingly made a false statement to obtain a licence.

and must also give his name and address and the name and address of the owner of the vehicle.

If a driving licence is not produced; suspected not to be granted to him; granted in error; or altered with intent to deceive, where the driver number has been altered, removed or defaced; or (if supervising a provisional licence holder) he is suspected to be under 21 years of age, he must also give his date of birth

(MV (DL) REGS 1996 (REG 77)

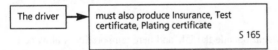

The driver → must also produce Insurance, Test certificate, Plating certificate

S 165

NOTE:

- If licence not produced at the time, may be at a police station within seven days   S 164(8)

- Upon a licence being granted it must be signed in ink forthwith

- The owner of a mechanically propelled vehicle shall produce the registration document when requested by a constable at any reasonable time

INSURANCE

SECTION 143 ROAD TRAFFIC ACT 1988

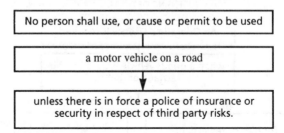

No person shall use, or cause or permit to be used

a motor vehicle on a road

unless there is in force a police of insurance or security in respect of third party risks.

Defence

It shall be a defence if a person proves that he was not the owner of the vehicle, nor had he hired the vehicle and it was used in the course of his employment and he did not know or have reason to believe there was no insurance in force.

Exemptions:

The following vehicles are exempt from the requirements of section 143 above:

S 144 RTA 1988

- Vehicles where owner has deposited £500,000 with Supreme Court
  Note – vehicle only exempted when being driven under owner's control.
- Invalid carriages not exceeding 254kg
- Local authority vehicles
- Police authority vehicles
- Vehicles owned by official receiver of Metropolitan Police
- Vehicles being driven for police purposes or under the direction of PC for police purposes
- Crown vehicles
- Vehicles being used for salvage purposes under Merchant Shipping Act 1894
- Vehicles requisitioned by army or air force
- London Transport Executive Vehicles
- Tramcars and trolley vehicles
- Visiting Forces Vehicles
- Vehicles made available under National Health Service Acts when used for NHS purposes
- Vehicles owned by health service body when driven under owner's control
- Ambulances owned by NHS Trust when driven under owner's control

---

Green card

Vehicles temporarily in Great Britain for which a Green Card has been issued may use the card the same as insurance. Insurance certificates issued in Community Member States (Austria, Belgium, Denmark, France, Finland, Germany, Greece, Ireland, Italy, Luxembourg, Netherlands, Portugal, Spain, Sweden, UK) provide third-party cover throughout all other Member States – there is no need for a Green Card.

S 143 RTA 1988

OPERATORS' LICENCES

GOODS VEHICLES (LICENSING OF OPERATORS) ACT 1995
GOODS VEHICLES (LICENSING OF OPERATORS) REGULATIONS 1995

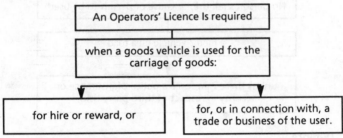

An Operators' Licence Is required

when a goods vehicle is used for the carriage of goods:

for hire or reward, or

for, or in connection with, a trade or business of the user.

S2 G V (L OF O) ACT 1995

Vehicles covered

Any vehicle or trailer in the lawful possession of the licence-holder (whether that motor vehicle is specified or not). However a licence may impose maximum weights for motor vehicles and trailers, may prohibit the use of trailers, or may prohibit the use of motor vehicles which are not specified in the licence.

S 5 GV (L OF O) ACT 1995

To avoid making application for the authorisation of motor vehicles temporarily in the operator's possession, the original licence may authorise the use of additional vehicles. If such vehicles are acquired, the Licensing Authority must be notified within one month of acquisition of the vehicle.

S 5(6) GV (L OF O) ACT 1995

TYPE	S 3 GOODS VEHICLES (LICENSING OF OPERATORS) ACT 1995	
I	**Standard (International)**	For hire or reward or in connection with any trade or business carried on by the holder in both national and international transport.
N	**Standard (National)**	For hire or reward etc in UK.
R	**Restricted**	For carrying goods only in connection with operator's trade or business, other than carrying goods for hire or reward.

Displaying operator's disc

All motor vehicles used under a licence must display a disc in a waterproof container on the nearside near the lower edge of the windscreen with the obverse side facing forwards (or, if not fitted with a windscreen, in a conspicuous position on the front or nearside of the vehicle)

REG 23 GV (L OF O) REGULATIONS 1995

OPERATORS' LICENCES – EXEMPTIONS

GOODS VEHICLES (LICENSING OF OPERATORS) ACT 1995
GOODS VEHICLES (LICENSING OF OPERATORS) REGULATIONS 1995

> A Goods Vehicle Operators' licence is
> not required for the following

small goods vehicles:

rigid vehicles not forming part of a combination

1. with relevant **plated** weight of not more than 3.5 tonnes, or
2. if **unplated**, an unladen weight of not more than 1,525kg;

rigid vehicles forming part of a combination

1. if all the vehicles (except any small trailer with unladen weight not exceeding 1,020 kg) **have relevant plated weights** the aggregate of which does not exceed 3.5 tonnes
2. if any are **not plated**, the aggregate of the unladen weight (excluding and small trailer with unladen weight not exceeding 1,020kg) does not exceed 1,525kg;

articulated vehicles

1. if the aggregate of the unladen weight of the tractive unit, together with the **plated weight** of semi-trailer is not more than 3.5 tonnes
2. if semi-trailer unplated, the aggregate unladen weight of tractive unit and semi-trailer is not more than 1,525kg;

goods vehicle used for international carriage

1. a goods vehicle for international carriage by a haulier established in a member State other than the UK and not established in the UK;
2. a goods vehicle for international carriage by a haulier established in Northern Ireland and not established in Great Britain.

continued overleaf

OPERATORS' LICENCES
– EXEMPTIONS cont

GOODS VEHICLES (LICENSING OF OPERATORS) ACT 1995
GOODS VEHICLES (LICENSING OF OPERATORS) REGULATIONS 1995

cont from previous page

> A Goods Vehicle Operators' licence is
> not required for the following

*For fuller details consult
Sched 3 to the Regulations.*

agricultural machinery and trailers taxed at the concessionary excise rate and being used for an authorised purpose

civil defence vehicles

dual-purpose vehicles (such as Land Rovers) and trailers

electric vehicles

fire-fighting and rescue vehicles used in mines

hearses and other vehicles used for funerals

local authority vehicles for weights & measures etc enactments

pre-1977 vehicles not over 1,525kg unladen, plated between 3.5 tonnes and 3.5 tons

police, fire brigade and ambulance vehicles

RNLI and Coastguard vehicles

recovery vehicles

road maintenance trailers

road rollers and trailers

showmen's goods vehicles and trailers

snow clearing vehicles and gritters etc

steam-propelled vehicles

tower wagons and trailers carrying only goods used in connection with its work

uncompleted vehicles on test or trial

vehicle allowed to carry out cabotage in the UK under EEC Regs

vehicles and their trailers using the roads for less than six miles a week while moving between parts of private premises

vehicles carrying a load for the purposes of the examination of that vehicle

vehicles constructed or adapted primarily for the carriage of passengers and their effects, and trailers drawn thereby

vehicles used by highway authorities for weighing vehicles

vehicles used by or under the control of HM UK Forces

vehicles used solely on aerodromes

vehicles with special fixed equipment (such as road sweepers and feedmobiles)

vehicles with trade plates

visiting Forces' vehicles

water, electricity, gas or telephone vehicles held ready for use in emergencies.

OPERATORS' LICENCES cont

GOODS VEHICLES (LICENSING OF OPERATORS) ACT 1995
GOODS VEHICLES (LICENSING OF OPERATORS) REGULATIONS 1995

FORGERY (S 38)

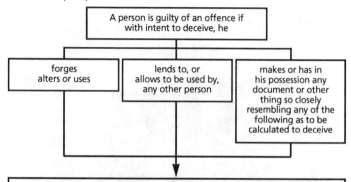

A person is guilty of an offence if with intent to deceive, he

- forges alters or uses
- lends to, or allows to be used by, any other person
- makes or has in his possession any document or other thing so closely resembling any of the following as to be calculated to deceive

any operators' licence; any document, plate, mark or other thing by which a vehicle is to be identified as being authorised to be used under an operators' licence; any document evidencing the authorisation of any person for the purpose of inspecting maintenance facilities or the seizure or disposal of documents etc.; any certificate of qualification to be engaged in road transport undertakings; or any certificate or diploma of professional competence.

PRODUCTION OF LICENCE   (REG 26)

An officer or police constable may require the production of an operator's licence by the holder of such within 14 days at an operating centre or (in the case of the requirement being made by a police officer) at a police station chosen by the licence holder.

Failure to comply is an offence.   (REG 32)

POWER TO INSPECT   (S 40)

An officer or police constable may, at any reasonable time, enter the premises of an applicant for, or holder of, an operator's licence and inspect any facilities on those premises for maintaining vehicles in a fit and serviceable condition. Any obstruction in the exercise of these powers constitutes an offence.

POWER TO SEIZE DOCUMENTS ETC   (S 41)

If an officer or police constable has reason to believe that:
a. a document or article carried on or by the driver of a vehicle, or
b. a document produced to him in pursuance of this Act, is a document or article in relation to which an offence under S 38 (forgery etc) or S 39 (false statement to obtain) relates, he may seize that document or article.

EXCISE LICENCES

VEHICLE EXCISE AND REGISTRATION ACT 1994

Excise licences are required by all mechanically propelled vehicles used

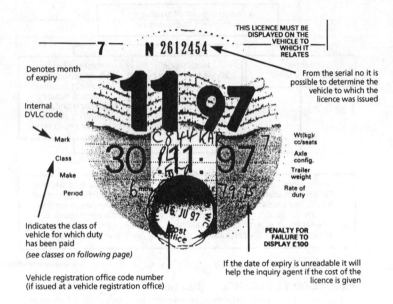

THIS LICENCE MUST BE DISPLAYED ON THE VEHICLE TO WHICH IT RELATES

Denotes month of expiry

From the serial no it is possible to determine the vehicle to which the licence was issued

Internal DVLC code

Mark

Class

Make

Period

Wt(kg)/ cc/seats

Axle config.

Trailer weight

Rate of duty

Indicates the class of vehicle for which duty has been paid
(see classes on following page)

PENALTY FOR FAILURE TO DISPLAY £100

Vehicle registration office code number (if issued at a vehicle registration office)

If the date of expiry is unreadable it will help the inquiry agent if the cost of the licence is given

---

Exemptions

Electrically propelled vehicles	Vehicles for export
Fire and ambulance vehicles and health service vehicles	Vehicles carrying disabled persons and registered in name of disabled driver
Grit spreaders	
Invalid carriages weighing less than 508kg	Vehicles owned or operated by the Crown
Lifeboat haulage vehicles	Vehicles travelling less than six miles per week between premises owned by the registered owner of the vehicle
Mine rescue vehicles	
Road construction and maintenance vehicles	Veterinary ambulances
Road rollers	Vehicles not constructed, adapted or used to carry any person
Trams	
Vehicles being taken for annual test by prior appointment	SECTION 5 AND SCHED 2

EXCISE DUTY CLASSES

SCHED 1 VEHICLES EXCISE AND REGISTRATION ACT 1994

The following details the classes of vehicle as described in the above-mentioned Act and Schedule

GENERAL
Applies to vehicle not otherwise mentioned in Schedule 1

Motor bicycles and tricycles

Buses *

Recovery vehicles.

Vehicles used for exceptional loads

Haulage vehicles

Goods vehicles
Including farmers' goods vehicles and showmens' goods vehicles; rigid goods vehicles exceeding 7,500kg plated gw; and tractive units exceeding 7,500kg tw, vehicles for conveying machines

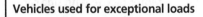

Special vehicles
Agricultural machines, digging machines, mobile cranes, works trucks, mowing machines, road roller.

* NOTE: When the 1994 Act was amended by the Finance Act 1996, the term 'Hackney Carriage' was dropped from Part III of Schedule 1 and replaced by the term 'Buses' (a bus being a PSV under the Public Passenger Vehicles Act 1981, and is not an excepted vehicle or a special concessionary vehicle).

EXHIBITION OF EXCISE LICENCES

VEHICLE EXCISE AND REGISTRATION ACT 1994
ROAD VEHICLES (REGISTRATION AND LICENSING) REGULATIONS 1971

> **Excise licences must be fixed to and exhibited on vehicle in a manner prescribed by the regulations**
>
> S 33

Separate offences exist of:

> using or keeping an unlicensed vehicle on a public road   S 29

> contravening terms of trade licence.   S 34

> and must be displayed in a holder to protect it from the weather and must be clearly visible from the nearside in daylight.

Motor bicycle, tricycle or invalid carriage

Position: nearside of vehicle in front of driver's seat

Motor bicycle with side car

Position: nearside of handlebars or nearside of sidecar in front of driving seat

Any vehicle fitted with glass windscreen extending to the nearside

Position: nearside lower corner of windscreen

Any other vehicle

- If fitted with cab having nearside window – on that window; or,
- on nearside of vehicle in front of driver's seat; or,
- if pedestrian controlled towards the front of the vehicle

REGISTRATION MARKS

VEHICLE EXCISE AND REGISTRATION ACT 1994
ROAD VEHICLES (REGISTRATION AND LICENSING) REGULATIONS 1971

When the Secretary of State registers a vehicle under the Vehicle Excise and Registration Act 1994, he assigns a registration mark to the vehicle which indicates its registered number.

Motor vehicles first registered on or after 1.1.73 must carry a registration mark which conforms with the following:

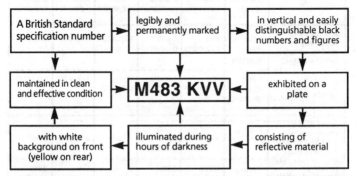

NOTE: *Bicycles and invalid carriages only require one plate to the rear (yellow background).*

Exceptions:
vehicles with UW exceeding 3 tons and having rear marker boards; stage carriage; works truck; agricultural machines

---

Exemptions and motor vehicles first registered before 1.1.73:

1. May carry white, silver or light grey letters or figures on a black surface indelibly inscribed or permanently attached.
2. If on a plate with cast or pressed metal, may have raised letters.
3. May use the reflex reflecting type in accordance with rules applying to post 1.1.73 vehicles.
4. May be displayed on a flat rectangular plate, or on a flat rectangular and unbroken area on the surface of the vehicle.

SCHEDS 2 AND 3 ROAD VEHICLES (REGISTRATION AND LICENSING) REGULATIONS 1971

OFFENCES   VEHICLE EXCISE AND REGISTRATION ACT 1994

Not fixing registration mark   S 42
Obscured registration mark   S 43

REGISTRATION MARKS – SIZE

REG 17 AND SCHED 2 ROAD VEHICLES (REGISTRATION AND LICENSING) REGS 1971

CLASS OF VEHICLE	Height of letters or figures	Breadth of every part	Width of letters or figures	Space between letters	Margin top and bottom	Margin side
General *or*	3 and a half	five eighths	2 and a half	a half	a half	1
	3 and an eighth	nine sixteenths	2 and a quarter	seven sixteenths	seven sixteenths	seven sixteenths
Alternative to above may be used by a bicycle, invalid carriage or *or* pedestrian controlled vehicle (front)	1 and three quarters	five sixteenths	1 and a quarter	a quarter	a quarter	a half
	1 and three quarters	five sixteenths	1 and a quarter	three sixteenths	a quarter	a quarter
Alternative to above may be used by a bicycle, invalid carriage or *or* pedestrian controlled vehicle (rear)	2 and a half	three eighths	1 and three quarters	a half	a half	a half
	2 and a half	three eighths	1 and three quarters	three eighths	three eighths	three eighths

all measurements shown in inches

The space between letters and figures should be 1 and a half inches except where embossed or pressed. These may be up to 2 and seven sixteenths.

TRAILERS

REG 22 ROAD VEHICLES (REGISTRATION AND LICENSING) REGULATIONS 1971

The towing vehicle need not display a registration mark on the rear –

– the trailer (or rearmost trailer) must display the registration mark of the towing vehicle –

– the mark on the rear of the trailer need not comply with the requirement of post 1.1.73 vehicles.

Except: agricultural machines, and vehicles exempt from Excise duty, which may display the registration mark of another vehicle belonging to the owner.

PLATING AND TESTING OF GOODS VEHICLES

GOODS VEHICLES (PLATING AND TESTING) REGULATIONS 1988

The following goods vehicles are required to be tested annually, the first examination being not later than the end of the calender month in which falls the first anniversary of the date of registration (or, in the case of a trailer, the date of being sold or supplied by retail).

REG 9

Heavy motor cars and motor cars constructed or adapted for the purpose of forming part of an articulated vehicle

Other motor cars the design gross weight of which exceeds 3,500kg

Other heavy motor cars semi trailers; converter dollies manufactured or or after 1.1.79

Other trailers, the weight of which, unladen exceeds 1,020kg

REG 4

● A test certificate is issued and, in the case of a trailer, a test disc is also issued. The disc must be displayed on the trailer in a position where it is conspicuous, readily accessible and clearly visible from the nearside.

Light vehicles

● Goods vehicles under the above weights, private cars and dual-purpose vehicles under 2,040kg must be submitted for an annual test to an approved garage, starting on the third anniversary of first registration.

● However, certain vehicles have to be tested by the time they are **one year old**: taxies, ambulances, minibuses and other passenger vehicles with more than 8 seats (excluding the driver's).

S 47 ROAD TRAFFIC ACT 1988

PLATING OF GOODS VEHICLES

REGS 66, 70 AND 70A ROAD VEHICLES (CONSTRUCTION AND USE) REGULATIONS 1986
GOODS VEHICLES (PLATING AND TESTING) REGULATIONS 1988

There are two basic types of plate:

Manufacturer's Plate
and Ministry Plate

MANUFACTURER'S PLATE   REG 66 OF THE 1986 REGS

Contains details of maximum permitted weights. Must be fitted to:

heavy motor cars and motor cars first used on or after 1.1.68.

> **Exceptions:** dual-purpose vehicles, agricultural vehicles, works trucks, pedestrian controlled, or passenger vehicles.

buses first used on or after 1.4.82.
wheeled locomotives and motor tractors first used on or after 1.4.73.

> **Exceptions:** agricultural vehicles, industrial tractors, works trucks, engineering plant, or pedestrian controlled vehicles.

wheeled trailers manufactured after 1.1.68 exceeding 1,020kg UW

> **Exceptions:** those not constructed or adapted to carry a load other than permanent or essentially permanent fixtures – and not exceeding 2,290kg in total; living van not exceeding 2,040kg UW; works trailer; trailers for street cleaning or agricultural purposes; broken down vehicle; gritting trailer, trailers manufactured and used initially outside GB; converter dolly manufactured on or after 1.1.79.

MINISTRY PLATE   REGS 17-22 OF THE 1988 REGS
Purpose of examination

Upon submission of the vehicle for its first Goods Vehicle test, the vehicle is also examined for plating. The examination seeks to determine whether:
(a) the vehicle is of a make, model and type to which the standard lists apply. These lists are published by the Goods Vehicle Centre and show, in relation to vehicles of certain constructional particulars, the gross weight, axle weight, and train weight for that type of vehicle;
(b) the constructional particulars relating to that type of vehicle are substantially complied with; and
(c) the weights shown in the standard lists are applicable to the vehicle.

PLATING OF GOODS VEHICLES cont

Production of evidence of conformity

In conjunction with the plating examination, the driver must produce either a certificate of conformity issued by the manufacturer or a Minister's approval certificate as required under the National Type Approval for Goods Vehicles Regulations. This certificate is treated as a plating certificate.

The examination

The examiner ensures that the particulars on the certificate are appropriate for the vehicle; and the vehicle has not been altered. If the examiner is satisfied, that certificate is then deemed to be the plating certificate issued for the purposes of these Regulations.

If the examiner is not so satisfied the vehicle must be subject to a full examination and determination of the various weights.

Plating certificate

The plating certificate contains the maximum weights permissible for the vehicle. Once a plating certificate has been issued, a Ministry Plate must be securely affixed, so as to be legible at all times, in a conspicuous and readily accessible position, and in the cab of the vehicle if it has one. The certificate is retained by the operator.

REG 70 OF THE 1986 REGS

Test certificate

Following the plating examination, the vehicle may undergo a goods vehicle test. Vehicles submitted for test are examined by a goods vehicle examiner for compliance with C&U Regulations. Following successful test, a goods vehicle test certificate is issued in relation to the vehicle.

SPEED LIMITER PLATE

Coaches, buses and goods vehicles which must be fitted with speed limiters must also have speed limiter plates fitted in a conspicuous position in the driver's cab, clearly and indelibly marked with the relevant limited speed.

REGS 36A, 36B AND 70A OF THE 1986 REGS

PLATING & TESTING EXEMPTIONS

SCHED 2 GOODS VEHICLES (PLATING & TESTING) REGULATIONS 1988

> The following are exempt from the requirements of the regulations:

breakdown vehicles

cranes (mobile)

dual purpose vehicles

electrically or steam propelled vehicles

engineering plant (not being moveable plant – being part of motor vehicle or trailer (not constructed to carry load)) designed and constructed for the special purposes of engineering operations

export – vehicles going to a port for export

funeral vehicles used solely for that purpose

land tractors and implements and agricultural trailers

licenced taxis

lifeboat vehicles

living vans not exceeding 3,500kg

police and fire vehicles

public service vehicles

road construction vehicles

road rollers

snow ploughs and gritters

tower wagons

three-wheeled cleansing vehicles

track-laying vehicles

trailers designed for the production of tar-macadam etc

trailers with only over-run brakes

vehicles for servicing or controlling aircraft

vehicles manufactured before 1.1.60 used unladen

vehicles temporarily in GB, including vehicles licensed in Northern Ireland and those based on certain specified Scottish Islands

vehicles travelling no more than 6 miles per week and exempt from duty

vehicles used for medical, dental, veterinary, health, education, display or clerical purposes but not for sale, hire or loading goods

vehicles used for test or trial of new vehicles or equipment

visiting Forces

works trucks

MOTORCYCLE PLATES

REG.69 AND SCHED 9 ROAD VEHICLES (CONSTRUCTION AND USE) REGULATIONS 1986

Every motor cycle first used on or after 1.8.77

which is not

a. propelled by an internal combustion
   engine with a cylinder capacity exceeding:
   i) 150cc if first used before 1.1.82, or
   ii) 125cc if first used on or after 1.1.82, or

b. a mowing machine; or

c. a pedestrian-controlled vehicle

must have a conspicuous and readily
accessible plate securely fixed to the vehicle
stating whether the machine is a

standard motor cycle	**moped**

means a motor cycle which is not a moped.	means a motorcycle which has: (a) maximum design speed not in excess of 30mph (b) kerbside weight not exceeding 250kg (c) engine not exceeding 50cc

The plate must also include:

- manufacturer's name
- engine capacity
- kerbside weight (mopeds only)
- maximum design speed (mopeds only)
- manufacturer's vehicle identification number
- power to weight ratio (standard motor cycle)
- maximum engine power (standard motor cycle).

TRADE LICENCES

SECTION 11 VEHICLES EXCISE AND REGISTRATION ACT 1994
REGS 28-40 ROAD VEHICLES (REGISTRATION AND LICENSING) REGULATIONS 1971

> Trade Licences are issued under section 11 of the Vehicle Excise and Registration Act 1994, by the Secretary of State, to persons who are

Motor Traders	Vehicle Testers

and persons intending to commence business as same

a) a manufacturer or repairer of, or dealer in, mechanically propelled vehicles or
b) any person not falling within a) above who carries on a business of such description as may be prescribed in regulations, ie a dealer in mechanically propelled vehicles if he carries on business consisting wholly or mainly of delivering such vehicle and not including any other activities, except as a manufacturer or repairer, of or dealer in such vehicles

a person other than a motor trader, who regularly, in the course of business, engages in testing of mechanically propelled vehicles belonging to other persons.

- When used with trade plates, the vehicle need not be taxed.

- Where the vehicle is drawing a trailer it is deemed to constitute a single vehicle. REG 35(2)

- The vehicle must be temporarily in his possession in the course of his business. REG 35(3)

Who is the passenger?
REG 40

> No person may be carried on the vehicle or trailer unless carried in connection with a purpose for which the holder may use the vehicle.

Purpose? REGS 35-37

Restricted to the following

1. Test or trial following construction, modification or repair or, for a prospective purchaser, or for vehicle's promotion;
2. Weighing, registration or inspection, breaking or dismantling;
3. Delivery to, or demonstration for, purchaser;
4. Delivery between his own or another trader's premises;
5. Fitting, painting, valeting or repairing;
6. To and from place of sale or storage;
7. Manufacturers engaged in research and development may only use it for such purposes;
8. Vehicle testers may only use it for such purposes.

TRADE LICENCES cont

ROAD VEHICLES (REGISTRATION AND LICENSING) REGULATIONS 1971

Carrying goods? REGS 38-39)
Restricted to the following

1. Goods carried for testing or demonstrating the vehicle or equipment. They must be returned to the place of loading without being removed from the vehicle, unless water, fertiliser or refuse.
2. Where a vehicle is being delivered or collected, a load consisting of another vehicle used for travel to or from the place of delivery or collection.
3. Loads permanently attached to the vehicle.
4. A load consisting of a trailer.
5. Equipment designed to be fitted to the vehicle.

PUBLIC SERVICE VEHICLES

PUBLIC PASSENGER VEHICLES ACT 1981

Definition
A public service vehicle is a motor vehicle (other than a tram car) which is either:

adapted to carry more than eight passengers and used for carrying passengers for hire or reward

not adapted to carry more than eight passengers and used for carrying passengers at separate fares in the course of a business of carrying passengers

See over for fuller explanation

For 'Minibuses', see later this section

PUBLIC SERVICE VEHICLES – DEFINITIONS

PUBLIC PASSENGER VEHICLES ACT 1981

Adapted

There must be sufficient seating for more than eight passengers.

Used

Includes periods when temporarily used without passengers, but its use for such purpose has not been permanently discontinued.

Hire or reward

Would not cover an isolated occasion, nor a social arrangement between friends where contributions are made towards the expenses of the journey. There must be a systematic carrying of passengers beyond the bounds of mere social kindness.

But it would cover the case of payments made by members of an association in respect of a vehicle owned by that association.

Separate fares

Will not be treated as being a PSV (unless adapted to carry more than 8 passengers) if:
(a) the agreement to pay separately must not have been initiated by the driver, owner, person making the vehicle available, or receiving remuneration;
(b) no previous advertisement of separate fares (except under local authority approval);
(c) all passengers going to same destination;
(d) no differentiation of fares on the basis of distance or time.
Bearing in mind the exceptions already mentioned, it includes the case where a number of passengers are carried and one of them pays the total cost of the journey to the driver and then collects a share from the other passengers.

In the course of a business

Where passengers are carried at separate fares it shall not be in the course of a business of carrying a passenger if:
• the total fare for the journey does not exceed the running costs of the vehicle for that journey (including depreciation and general wear); and
• the arrangement for the payment of the fares was made before the journey began.

Terminology (PSVs/PCVs)

The change in terminology from PSV to PCV only relates to new issues of driving licences. Old driving licences still refer to a PSV and for other purposes the term PSV remains valid.

Taxis

TRANSPORT ACT 1985

A licensed taxi may carry passengers at separate fares without becoming a PSV if hired in an area where the licensing authority has made a scheme under this section, provided the hiring falls within the terms of the scheme.   S 10

Similarly, a licensed taxi or licensed hire car may carry passengers at separate fares without becoming a PSV if all passengers booked their journeys in advance and each consented, when booking, to share the use of the vehicle.

PSVs – LOCAL SERVICES

SECTIONS 3 AND 6 TRANSPORT ACT 1985

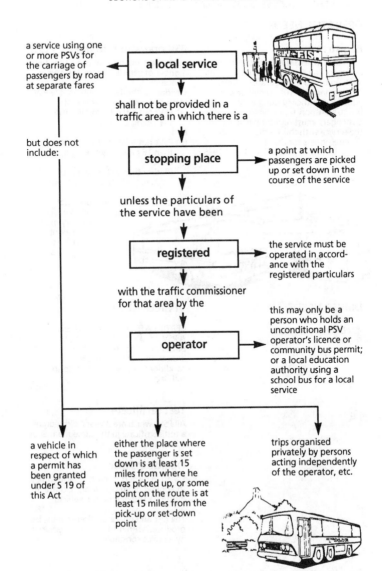

a service using one or more PSVs for the carriage of passengers by road at separate fares

a local service

shall not be provided in a traffic area in which there is a

but does not include:

stopping place

a point at which passengers are picked up or set down in the course of the service

unless the particulars of the service have been

registered

the service must be operated in accordance with the registered particulars

with the traffic commissioner for that area by the

operator

this may only be a person who holds an unconditional PSV operator's licence or community bus permit; or a local education authority using a school bus for a local service

a vehicle in respect of which a permit has been granted under S 19 of this Act

either the place where the passenger is set down is at least 15 miles from where he was picked up, or some point on the route is at least 15 miles from the pick-up or set-down point

trips organised privately by persons acting independently of the operator, etc.

PSV DOCUMENTATION

PUBLIC PASSENGER VEHICLES ACT 1981
PUBLIC SERVICE VEHICLES (OPERATOR'S LICENCE) REGULATIONS 1995

OPERATOR NEEDS:

Registration

In an area where there are stopping places for the services, the holder of an 'unconditional PSV operator's licence' or a 'community bus permit' or an education authority using a free school bus to transport fare-paying passengers, must register particulars of the service with the Traffic Commissioners for that area.

S 6 TRANSPORT ACT 1985

PSV operator's licence   S 12(1)

Permits the operator to run a specified number of vehicles. There are 2 types of licence:
standard authorises the use of any PSV;
restricted authorises the use of
(a) PSVs not adapted to carry more than eight passengers
and
(b) PSVs not adapted to carry more than 16 passengers being operated either
(i) other than in the course of a business of carrying passengers, or
(ii) by a person who does not normally operate PSVs adapted to carry more than eight passengers.

S 13(1)

DRIVER NEEDS:

PSV DRIVER'S LICENCE
See section on 'Driving Licences'

VEHICLE NEEDS:

CERTIFICATE OF INITIAL FITNESS
A PSV adapted to carry more than 8 passengers requires a certificate indicating that the prescribed conditions as to vehicle fitness are fulfilled.

S 6(1)

Test certificate

All PSVs which are 3 years' old require a test certificate in the same manner as a car.

Operator's disc

Issued in respect of each vehicle run by the holder of an Operators' Licence. It must be exhibited on the vehicle

S 18(1)

The disc and operators licence must be produced within 14 days if so required by a police constable.

REG 1

See also 'Passenger carrying vehicle licences' early in this section

MINIBUSES

S19 MINIBUS AND OTHER SECTION 19 PERMIT BUSES REGULATIONS 1987
TRANSPORT ACT 1985

Exempt from being classified as PSVs, therefore do not need PCV operator's or driver's licence, if:

- adapted to carry more than eight and not more than 16 passengers
- specified in the permit
- not used for members of the public
- not used for profit
- used only by permit holder
- used in accordance with permit conditions.
- comply with the conditions of fitness:

    a. first used on or after 1.4.88

    REGS 41-43 ROAD VEHICLES (C&U) REGULATIONS 1986
    (locks, doors, seats, fire extinguishers, first aid kit etc)

    b. before 1.4.88, either as (a) above, or

REGS 5 -28 MINIBUS (CONDITIONS OF FITNESS, EQUIPMENT AND USE) REGULATIONS 1977

- Permits are granted to bodies concerned with
    - activities for the benefit of the community
    - education
    - recreation
    - religion
    - social welfare.

- Every authorised minibus shall carry a disc and a driver's notice setting out the conditions which have been imposed. Drivers must be over 21.

HACKNEY CARRIAGES

VEHICLES EXCISE AND REGISTRATION ACT 1994

A hackney carriage is a mechanically propelled vehicle standing or plying for hire, or let for hire by a seller or hirer, other than a community bus.

The rate of duty for a hackney carriage now varies according to the seating capacity.

TRANSPORT ACT 1980

LOCAL AUTHORITY LICENCE

If the vehicle stands or plies for hire in an area to which the Town Police Clauses Act, 1847 applies, a local authority licence is required.

PRIVATE HIRE

If the vehicle does not stand or ply for hire a local authority licence is not required, but the vehicle must still display the hackney carriage plate.

TAXI ROOF SIGNS – VEHICLES OTHER THAN TAXIS

Taxis are defined as vehicles which are licensed as such by the local authority.

If carrying passengers for hire or reward, vehicles other than taxis must **not display** on or above the roof any sign which consists of or includes the word *Taxi* or *Cab* or any word of similar meaning or appearance; or any sign, notice, mark, illumination or other feature which may suggest that the vehicle is a taxi.   S64

NOTE: (England and Wales only) the 1980 Act does not apply in Scotland

SIGNS ON BUSES CARRYING CHILDREN

REGS 11, 17A AND SCHED 21A ROAD VEHICLES LIGHTING REGULATIONS 1989

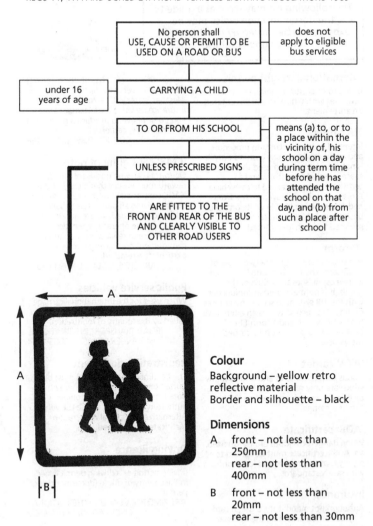

No person shall
USE, CAUSE OR PERMIT TO BE
USED ON A ROAD OR BUS

does not
apply to eligible
bus services

under 16
years of age

CARRYING A CHILD

TO OR FROM HIS SCHOOL

means (a) to, or to
a place within the
vicinity of, his
school on a day
during term time
before he has
attended the
school on that
day, and (b) from
such a place after
school

UNLESS PRESCRIBED SIGNS

ARE FITTED TO THE
FRONT AND REAR OF THE BUS
AND CLEARLY VISIBLE TO
OTHER ROAD USERS

Colour

Background – yellow retro
reflective material
Border and silhouette – black

Dimensions

A   front – not less than
    250mm
    rear – not less than
    400mm

B   front – not less than
    20mm
    rear – not less than 30mm

SCHEDULE 21A

FOREIGN VEHICLES TEMPORARILY IN GB

The following list may serve as a guide to the documentation which may be expected to be carried by the driver of a foreign goods vehicle.

International freight permit

Issued to operators running services from countries with which Britain has entered an agreement.

TIR carnet

Intended to simplify customs procedures and avoid liability to pay customs duty. It is not mandatory but if used the carrying space is sealed by customs and a certificate must be carried in the vehicle. A plate must be displayed on the front and rear showing 'TIR' in white on a blue background. A separate carnet is required for each load carried.

'T' form

Not mandatory. There are two types of certificate. The first is a form T2L which merely establishes the origin of the goods. It is normally used in conjunction with the TIR system to secure lower rates of duty. The second type is an alternative to the TIR system and a form T1 or T2, certified by customs must be carried on the vehicle.

'ATA' carnet

Goods such as samples and display items which are only temporarily imported can receive customs clearance if an 'ATA' carnet is carried.

'ADR' certificate

When dangerous goods are transported, an 'ADR' certificate must be carried to signify that the vehicle and load conform with safety standards.

Insurance

Although not mandatory, a green card may be carried providing the necessary evidence of cover. In the event of an accident, the police may retain the duplicate page, endorsing the front cover accordingly.
REG 5 MOTOR VEHICLES (INTERNATIONAL MOTOR INSURANCE CARD) REGS 1971

Insurance (cont)

Note that drivers of vehicles from EC Member States will be covered by the insurance issued in that Member State and do not have to produce a green card (see Insurance, earlier).
COUNCIL DIRECTIVE 72/166

'CMR' consignment note

Operators carrying goods for hire or reward must ensure that a copy of the 'CMR' consignment note is carried on the vehicle, giving all particulars of sender, addressee and load, where goods are carried on the operator's own account (not for hire or reward) only a simple consignment note giving brief particulars is required.
ARTICLE 6, COUNCIL REG 11/1960

Public service vehicles

When used for the international carriage of passengers must carry an authorisation issued by the country of registration.
(ROAD TRANSPORT INTERNATIONAL PASSENGER SERVICES) REGS 1984

Registration document

The document (or copy of it) must be carried on the vehicle, together with a note from the employer or owner authorising the driver to use the vehicle. Alternatively, a special registration certificate may be used.

Driving licence

This may be either an international driving permit or a driving permit issued in the country of origin (domestic driving permit).
ART 2 MOTOR VEHICLES (INTERNATIONAL CIRCULATION) ORDER 1955

Excise Form 115E

This is the authorisation for the vehicle to be in this country. It gives the date by which the vehicle should have returned to its place of origin.

COMMUNITY DRIVING LICENCES

DRIVING LICENCES (COMMUNITY DRIVING LICENCE) REGS 1996

Exchange for British Licence

The holder of a licence issued within the European Economic Area (EEA) – a 'Community Licence', who become resident in G.B. need not now exchange it for a British one within 12 months. There remains, however, a right to exchange. But exchange of licences is mandatory for the purpose of periods of validity, health standards and disqualification, where applicable.

Period of Validity of licence held by British residents

Community licences held by Britons are valid for the same period as a British licence unless it would have expired earlier had the holder remained in the State of issue or would otherwise have become invalid in that State.

Health and Fitness

Community licence holders resident in G.B. are subject to the same health and fitness standards and medical checks as persons holding British licences.

LGV and PCV Licences

Resident community licence holders who are entitled to drive large goods and passenger carrying vehicles are subject to the requirements of Part IV of the Road Traffic Act (hours of work and records, etc.) For certain classes, details must be submitted to the Secretary of State within 1 year of becoming resident.

Endorsements

Counterpart licences will be issued to provide evidence of convictions and fixed penalties.

Modification of Vehicle Categories and Ages

Provision is made in the Road Traffic Act for the re-categorisation of vehicles for licensing purposes and for changes to the minimum age for driving motor cycles.

Right to Issue of British Licence

This is restricted to persons normally resident in G.B. or the U.K.

Other Benefits

Certain statutory benefits such as taxi and community bus licences are extended to the holders of community motor car licences.

PART 3

LIGHTING
AND MARKING

This section looks at obligatory lights,
directional indicators and reflectors, the
use and movement of lamps. It then
moves on to consider the requirement for
fog lights, reversing lights, warning lights
and beacons. Finally it considers their
aspects applicable to goods vehicles, eg,
marker lamps and reflectors, and the
marking of projecting loads.

OBLIGATORY LAMPS ETC DEFINITIONS

REG 13 ROAD VEHICLES LIGHTING REGULATIONS 1989

POSITION LAMP – FRONT OR REAR

A lamp used to indicate the presence and width of a vehicle when viewed from the front or rear.

HEADLAMP

A lamp used to illuminate the road in front of a vehicle and which is not a front fog lamp.

HOURS OF DARKNESS

Means the time between half an hour after sunset and half an hour before sunrise.

MAINTENANCE
REG 23

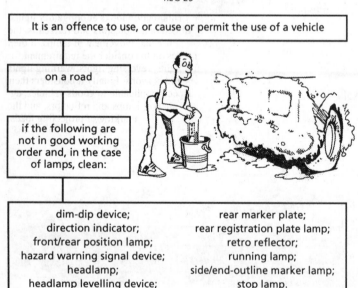

It is an offence to use, or cause or permit the use of a vehicle

on a road

if the following are not in good working order and, in the case of lamps, clean:

dim-dip device;	rear marker plate;
direction indicator;	rear registration plate lamp;
front/rear position lamp;	retro reflector;
hazard warning signal device;	running lamp;
headlamp;	side/end-outline marker lamp;
headlamp levelling device;	stop lamp.
rear fog lamp;	

OBLIGATORY LAMPS ETC cont

REG 18 AND SCHED 1 ROAD VEHICLES LIGHTING REGULATIONS 1989

A SOLO MOTOR BICYCLE OR COMBINATION	

Type	Vehicle exemptions
Front position lamp	Solo m/cycle fitted with headlamp
Dipped beam headlamp	First used before 1.1.31
Main beam headlamp	1. Max speed n/e 25mph. 2. Less than 50cc and first used before 1.1.72 3. First used before 1.1.31. 4. Constructed or adapted for use off roads and can carry only 1 person (If combination, 1 person plus 1 in sidecar)
Direction indicator	1. Max speed n/e 25mph 2. First used before 1.4.86 3. Constructed or adapted for use off roads and can carry only 1 person. (If combination, 1 person plus 1 in sidecar)
Rear position lamp	None
Stop lamp	1. Max speed n/e 25mph 2. Less than 50cc and first used before 1.4.86 3. First used before 1.1.36
Rear reg plate lamp	Vehicle not required to have reg plate
Rear retro reflector	None

A PEDAL CYCLE

Type	exemptions
Front position lamp	None
Rear position lamp	None
Rear retro reflector	None
Pedal retro reflector	Manufactured before 1.10.85

OBLIGATORY LAMPS ETC

REG 18 AND SCHED 1 ROAD VEHICLES LIGHTING REGULATIONS 1989

A MOTOR VEHICLE, HAVING 3 OR MORE WHEELS

not being
a motor cycle (or combination), pedal cycle,
pedestrian-controlled vehicle, horse-drawn
vehicle, track-laying vehicle, or trailer drawn by a
motor vehicle

shall be fitted with lamps, reflectors, rear
markings and devices which are stated below
unless exempted:

- - - ▶ Exemptions are
shown in the
following tables

Type	Vehicle exemptions
Front position lamp	none
Dim-dip or running lamp device	1. Max speed n/e 40mph 2. First used before 1.4.87 3. Home Forces vehicle 4. Vehicles in respect of certain conditions being satisfied re the fitting of lighting and light-signalling devices as per requirements of EEC Directive 76/756 as amended, and alignment of dipped beam headlamps
Dipped beam headlamps	1. Max speed n/e 15mph 2. Agricultural vehicle or works truck first used before 1.4.86 3. First used before 1.1.31
Main beam headlamp	1. Max speed n/e 25mph 2. Agricultural vehicle or works truck first used before 1.4.86 3. First used before 1.1.31
Direction indicator	1. Max speed n/e 15mph 2. Invalid carriage n/e 4mph 3. Agricultural vehicle, industrial tractor or works truck first used before 1.4.86 4. First used before 1.1.36.
Hazard warning signal device	1. As for 'direction indicators' above 2. First used before 1.4.86
Rear position	None
Rear fog lamp	1. Max speed n/e 25 mph 2. Agricultural vehicle or works truck first used before 1.4.86 3. First used before 1.4.80 4. Width n/e 1,300mm

OBLIGATORY LAMPS ETC cont

REG 18 AND SCHED 1 ROAD VEHICLES LIGHTING REGULATIONS 1989

Continued from previous page

Type	Vehicle exemptions cont...
Stop lamp	1. Max speed n/e 25mph 2. Agricultural vehicle or works truck first used before 1.4.86 3. First used before 1.1.36
Rear reg plate lamp	1. Vehicle not requiring reg plate 2. Works truck
Side retro reflector	1. Max speed n/e 25mph 2. Goods vehicle: length n/e 6 metres and first used on or after 1.4.86; or length n/e 8 metres and first used before 1.4.86 3. Passenger vehicle 4. Incomplete vehicle going for completion, storage or display 5. Excavator (special types vehicle) 6. Mobile crane or engineering plant
Rear retro reflector	None
Rear marking	1. Max speed n/e 25mph 2. UW n/e 3,050kg and first used before 1.8.82 3. Max gross weight n/e 7,500kg 4. Passenger vehicle not being articulated bus 5. Articulated tractive unit 6. Incomplete vehicle going for completion, storage or display for sale 7. Agricultural vehicle, works truck or engineering plant first used before 1.4.86 8. First used before 1.1.40 9. Home forces' vehicle 10.Vehicle constructed or adapted for: fire fighting or salvage; or aircraft servicing or controlling; or road maintenance, dispensing tar etc; or transporter for 2 or more vehicles or boats
Side marker lamp	1. Max speed n/e 25mph 2. Passenger vehicles 3. Incomplete vehicle going for completion, storage or display for sale. 4. overall length n/e 6 metres 5. vehicle first used before 1.4.91 6. vehicle first used after 1.4.96 in respect of which certain conditions are satisfied re fitting of lighting and light signalling devices as per EEC Directive 76/756 as amended, and alignment of dipped beam headlamps

OBLIGATORY LAMPS ETC cont

REG 18 AND SCHED 1 ROAD VEHICLES LIGHTING REGULATIONS 1989

TRAILER DRAWN BY A MOTOR VEHICLE

shall be fitted with lamps, reflectors, rear markings and devices which are stated below unless exempted

Exemptions are shown in the following tables

Type	Vehicle exemptions
Front position lamp	1. Trailers for carrying or launching boats 2. Width n/e 1,600mm 3. Length n/e 2,300mm and manufactured before 1.10.85
Direction indicator	1. Manufactured before 1.9.65 2. Agricultural vehicle or works trailer manufactured before 1.10.90
Side marker lamp	1. Excluding any drawbar and any fitting, length n/e 6 metres or 9.15 metres, manufactured before 1.10.90 2 Incomplete trailer going for completion, storage or display for sale 3. Agricultural vehicle or works truck 4. Caravan 5. Trailer for carriage and launching boat 6. Trailer manufactured before 1.10.95 in respect of which certain conditions are satisfied re fitting of lighting and light signalling devices as per EEC Directive 76/756 as amended, and are installed and maintained as per requirements
Rear position lamp	None
Rear fog lamp	1. Manufactured before 1.4.80 2. Width n/e 1,300mm 3. Agricultural vehicle or works trailer
Stop lamp	Agricultural vehicle or works trailer.

OBLIGATORY LAMPS ETC cont

REG 18 AND SCHED 1 ROAD VEHICLES LIGHTING REGULATIONS 1989

Continued from previous page

Type	Vehicle exemptions cont...
End-outline marker lamp	1. Width n/e 2,100mm 2. Incomplete trailer going for completion, storage or display for sale 3. Agricultural vehicle or works trailer 4. Manufactured before 1.10.90
Rear reg plate lamp	Trailer not required to have a registration plate
Side retro reflector	1. Length n/e 5 metres excluding drawbar 2. Incomplete trailer going for completion, storage or display for sale 3. Engineering plant 4. Excavator trailer (Special types vehicle)
Front retro reflector	1. Manufactured before 1.10.90 2. Agricultural vehicle or works trailer
Rear retro reflector	None
Rear marking	1. UW n/e 1,020kg and manufactured before 1.8.82 2. Max gross weight n/e 3,500kg 3. Incomplete trailer going for completion storage or display 4. Agricultural vehicle, works trailer or engineering plant 5. Drawn by a bus 6. Home Forces' vehicle 7. Constructed or adapted for fire fighting; aircraft servicing etc; dispensing tar etc; carrying asphalt or macadam, being mixing or drying plant; transporting 2 or more vehicles or boats

LAMPS ETC – GENERAL EXEMPTIONS

ROAD VEHICLES LIGHTING REGULATIONS 1989

TOWING REG 6

Type of Vehicle	Exemption
Motor vehicle first used before 1.4.86 and pedal cycle or trailer manufactured before 1.10.85.	Rear position lamp, stop lamp, rear direction indicator, rear fog lamp or rear reflector while a trailer fitted with such is attached to the rear.
Trailer manufactured before 1.10.85.	Front position lamp while being drawn by passenger vehicle.
Trailer manufactured on or after 1.10.85.	Stop lamp, rear fog lamp or rear direction indicator while being drawn by vehicle not requiring them.
Trailer manufactured before 1.10.90.	Stop lamp or direction indicator if towing vehicle is fitted with such and dimensions of trailer allow them to be seen from a point 6 metres behind the trailer (does not apply to trailers manufactured on or after 1.10.90).
Vehicle in combination	Rear marking if another vehicle in combination would obscure it.
Broken down vehicle being drawn.	Lamp, reflector or rear marking (except rear position lamps, and rear reflectors between sunset and sunrise).

LAMPS ETC – GENERAL EXEMPTIONS cont

ROAD VEHICLES LIGHTING REGULATIONS 1989

MASKING, ETC

A lamp shall not be treated as a lamp if:

1. Painted over or marked, so as not capable of immediate use or of readily being put to use; or
2. No wiring system to electrical source.

REG 4(4)

DURING DAYTIME

Lamps and reflectors need not be fitted during the daytime to:

1. Vehicle not fitted with any position lamps
2. Incomplete vehicle going for completion
3. Pedal cycle
3. Pedestrian-controlled vehicle
4. Horse-drawn vehicle
5. Vehicle drawn or propelled by hand, or
6. Combat vehicle.

REG 4 (3)

USE OF LAMPS

REGS 24 AND 25 ROAD VEHICLES LIGHTING REGULATIONS 1989

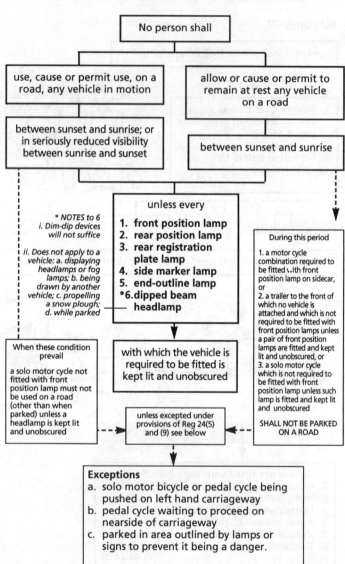

No person shall

use, cause or permit use, on a road, any vehicle in motion

allow or cause or permit to remain at rest any vehicle on a road

between sunset and sunrise; or in seriously reduced visibility between sunrise and sunset

between sunset and sunrise

* NOTES to 6
i. Dim-dip devices will not suffice

ii. Does not apply to a vehicle: a. displaying headlamps or fog lamps; b. being drawn by another vehicle; c. propelling a snow plough; d. while parked

unless every
1. **front position lamp**
2. **rear position lamp**
3. **rear registration plate lamp**
4. **side marker lamp**
5. **end-outline lamp**
*6.**dipped beam — headlamp**

During this period

1. a motor cycle combination required to be fitted with front position lamp on sidecar, or
2. a trailer to the front of which no vehicle is attached and which is not required to be fitted with front position lamps unless a pair of front position lamps are fitted and kept lit and unobscured, or
3. a solo motor cycle which is not required to be fitted with front position lamp unless such lamp is fitted and kept lit and unobscured

SHALL NOT BE PARKED ON A ROAD

When these condition prevail

a solo motor cycle not fitted with front position lamp must not be used on a road (other than when parked) unless a headlamp is kept lit and unobscured

with which the vehicle is required to be fitted is kept lit and unobscured

unless excepted under provisions of Reg 24(5) and (9) see below

Exceptions
a. solo motor bicycle or pedal cycle being pushed on left hand carriageway
b. pedal cycle waiting to proceed on nearside of carriageway
c. parked in area outlined by lamps or signs to prevent it being a danger.

USE OF LAMPS cont

REG 24(5) ROAD VEHICLES LIGHTING REGULATIONS 1989

Lamps 1. - 5. on previous page must also remain lit when the vehicle remains at rest

except when any of the following

1 Goods vehicle UW n/e 1,525kg
2. Passenger vehicle other than large passenger vehicle
3. Invalid carriage
4. Motor cycle or pedal cycle with or without sidecar

provided no trailer attached and projection lamps not required

are parked

| on a road where the speed limit is 30mph or less | as near as possible to the nearside of the road or either side of a one-way street | in a place which is set aside as a parking place | in a lay-by which is indicated by prescribed road markings or a different colour or texture from the carriageway |

AND
not less than 10 metres from a junction

10 metres

10 metres

10 metres

OBSTRUCTION OF LIGHTS   REG 19

At least part of the surface of any obligatory front and rear position lamp, front and rear direction indicator and rear reflector, must be visible when every door, boot or other movable part of the vehicle is in a fixed open position.

COLOUR OF LIGHT SHOWN BY LAMPS AND RETRO REFLECTORS

REG 11 ROAD VEHICLES LIGHTING REGULATIONS 1989

It is an offence to use, cause or permit use on a road a vehicle readily capable of showing a — **red light to the front**

except

1. Red and white chequered domed lamp or a red and white segmented mast mounted warning beacon fitted to a fire control vehicle, intended for use at scene of an emergency
2. Prescribed traffic sign attached to a vehicle; or side marker lamp, or side retro reflector;
3. Retro reflective material or reflector in wheels or tyres of
   a. pedal cycle and any sidecar attached
   b. solo motor bicycle or combination
   c. invalid carriage.

NOTE: For police control vehicle, read blue light from chequered domed lamp fitted to vehicle; and in case of ambulance control vehicle, a green light and white light from chequered domed lamp fitted to vehicle

It is an offence to use, cause or permit use on a road a vehicle readily capable of showing a — **any light to the rear, other than a red light**

except

airport vehicle (yellow)
ambulance service control (green & white)
breakdown vehicle;
Customs and Excise fuel testing vehicle, surveying purposes, statutory removal or immobilisation of vehicles, escort purposes under 25 mph,
direction indicator and side marker lamp (amber)
emergency vehicle (blue)
fire service control vehicle (red & white)
illuminated rear registration plate
illumination of bus route indication
interior illumination
medical practitioner (green)
pedal reflectors (amber)
police control vehicle (blue & white)
prescribed traffic sign attached to vehicle (any colour)
rear markers reflex reflective (yellow)

reflective material incorporated in prescribed sign and fitted to the rear of a bus
reflected orange light to rear of vehicle carrying dangerous substances
registration plates reflex reflective (yellow)
retro reflective material as above (any col)
retro reflective (amber)
reversing lamp (white)
road clearance vehicle
taxi meter illumination
vehicle having max speed of 25mph,
vehicle over 2.9 metres wide,
warning beacon (amber) fitted to: refuse collection vehicle; road clearance vehicle; road cleansing etc vehicle; road apparatus cleansing etc vehicle, special types vehicles etc – S 44 RTA 1988,
work lamp (white)

FITTING BEACONS

Other than vehicles mentioned above, it is an offence to a fit warning beacon/special warning light – whether working or not – or device resembling such.

REG 16

MOVEMENT OF LAMPS

ROAD VEHICLE LIGHTING REGULATIONS 1989

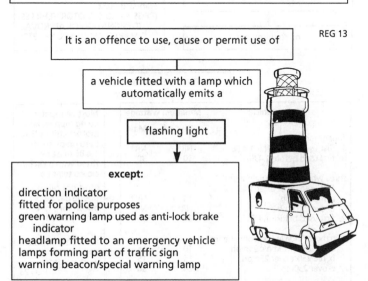

REG 12

It is an offence to use, cause or permit use, on a road

a vehicle fitted with a

lamp , reflector or marking capable of being moved by swivelling, deflecting or otherwise while the vehicle is in motion

except:

amber pedal reflex indicator
direction indicator on vehicle first used before 1.4.86
headlamps adjustable to compensate for load
lamps/reflectors turning with steering wheels
movable dipping headlamps
reflex reflective material/reflector fitted to wheel or tyre of pedal
   cycle/sidecar solo motor bicycle/combination invalid carriage
retractable headlamps/front fog lights
warning beacon
work lamp

REG 13

It is an offence to use, cause or permit use of

a vehicle fitted with a lamp which automatically emits a

flashing light

except:

direction indicator
fitted for police purposes
green warning lamp used as anti-lock brake
   indicator
headlamp fitted to an emergency vehicle
lamps forming part of traffic sign
warning beacon/special warning lamp

HEADLAMPS

REG 18 AND SCHEDS 1, 4 AND 5 ROAD VEHICLES LIGHTING REGULATIONS 1989

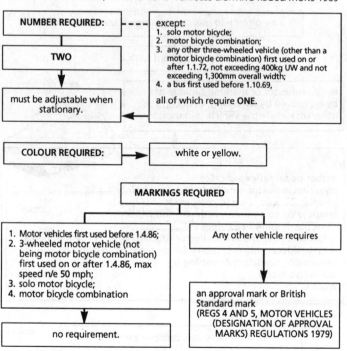

NUMBER REQUIRED:

→ **TWO**

→ must be adjustable when stationary.

except:
1. solo motor bicycle;
2. motor bicycle combination;
3. any other three-wheeled vehicle (other than a motor bicycle combination) first used on or after 1.1.72, not exceeding 400kg UW and not exceeding 1,300mm overall width;
4. a bus first used before 1.10.69,

all of which require **ONE**.

COLOUR REQUIRED: → white or yellow.

MARKINGS REQUIRED

1. Motor vehicles first used before 1.4.86;
2. 3-wheeled motor vehicle (not being motor bicycle combination) first used on or after 1.4.86, max speed n/e 50 mph;
3. solo motor bicycle;
4. motor bicycle combination

→ no requirement.

Any other vehicle requires

→ an approval mark or British Standard mark
(REGS 4 AND 5, MOTOR VEHICLES (DESIGNATION OF APPROVAL MARKS) REGULATIONS 1979)

WATTAGE REQUIRED

Motor vehicle	Minimum wattage	
	Dipped	Main
four or more wheels		
1. first used on or after 1.4.86	NR*	NR*
2. first used before 1.4.86	30	30
three wheels (not combination)		
1. first used on or after 1.4.86		
a. max 50mph	15	NR*
b. over 50 mph	NR*	NR*
2. first used before 1.4.86	24	30
solo motor bicycle (incl combination)		
a. n/e 250cc and n/e 25mph	10	15
b. n/e 250cc over 25mph	15	15
c. over 250cc	24	30

Must be capable of being dipped, and motor vehicles first used on or after 1.4.86 must be fitted with a circuit-closed tell-tale.

Must not cause undue dazzle or discomfort, or be lit while parked
REG 27

Must be kept clean and in good working order
REG 23

HEADLAMPS cont

REG 18 AND SCHEDS 1, 4 AND 5 ROAD VEHICLES LIGHTING REGULATIONS 1989

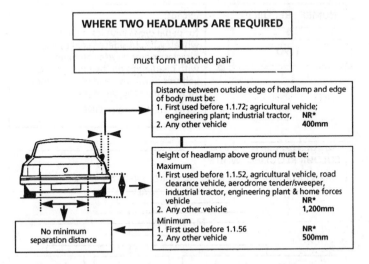

WHERE TWO HEADLAMPS ARE REQUIRED

must form matched pair

Distance between outside edge of headlamp and edge of body must be:
1. First used before 1.1.72; agricultural vehicle; engineering plant; industrial tractor,   **NR***
2. Any other vehicle   **400mm**

height of headlamp above ground must be:
Maximum
1. First used before 1.1.52, agricultural vehicle, road clearance vehicle, aerodrome tender/sweeper, industrial tractor, engineering plant & home forces vehicle   **NR***
2. Any other vehicle   **1,200mm**
Minimum
1. First used before 1.1.56   **NR***
2. Any other vehicle   **500mm**

No minimum separation distance

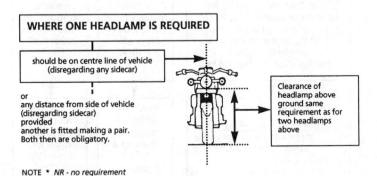

WHERE ONE HEADLAMP IS REQUIRED

should be on centre line of vehicle (disregarding any sidecar)

or
any distance from side of vehicle (disregarding sidecar)
provided
another is fitted making a pair. Both then are obligatory.

Clearance of headlamp above ground same requirement as for two headlamps above

NOTE * *NR - no requirement*

OPTIONAL LAMPS.

● Any number may be fitted but must comply with vertical fitting and colour requirements.

NOTE: If first used after 1.4.91 only one pair of dipped headlamps may be shown at a time. Two pairs may be fitted only if one pair is for driving in other countries on the right of the road.

FRONT POSITION LAMPS

REG 18 AND SCHEDS 1 AND 2 ROAD VEHICLES LIGHTING REGULATIONS 1989

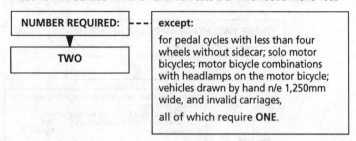

NUMBER REQUIRED: – – – **except:**

for pedal cycles with less than four wheels without sidecar; solo motor bicycles; motor bicycle combinations with headlamps on the motor bicycle; vehicles drawn by hand n/e 1,250mm wide, and invalid carriages,

all of which require **ONE**.

TWO

COLOUR REQUIRED: WHITE

unless incorporated in headlamp which is yellow.

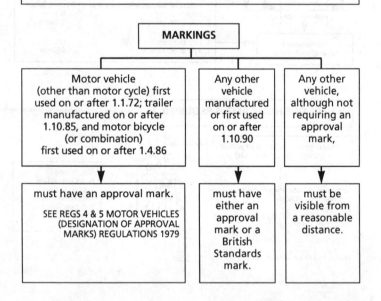

MARKINGS

Motor vehicle (other than motor cycle) first used on or after 1.1.72; trailer manufactured on or after 1.10.85, and motor bicycle (or combination) first used on or after 1.4.86	Any other vehicle manufactured or first used on or after 1.10.90	Any other vehicle, although not requiring an approval mark,
must have an approval mark. SEE REGS 4 & 5 MOTOR VEHICLES (DESIGNATION OF APPROVAL MARKS) REGULATIONS 1979	must have either an approval mark or a British Standards mark.	must be visible from a reasonable distance.

Must be kept clean and in good working order.   REG 23

Optional Lamps

Any number may be fitted – apart from for solo motor bicycles first used after 1.4.91, with can have a maximum of two.   SCHED 2

FRONT POSITION LAMPS cont

REG 18 AND SCHEDS 1 AND 2 ROAD VEHICLES LIGHTING REGULATIONS 1989

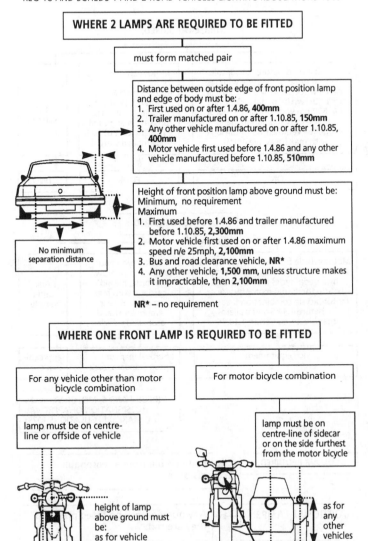

WHERE 2 LAMPS ARE REQUIRED TO BE FITTED

must form matched pair

Distance between outside edge of front position lamp and edge of body must be:
1. First used on or after 1.4.86, **400mm**
2. Trailer manufactured on or after 1.10.85, **150mm**
3. Any other vehicle manufactured on or after 1.10.85, **400mm**
4. Motor vehicle first used before 1.4.86 and any other vehicle manufactured before 1.10.85, **510mm**

Height of front position lamp above ground must be:
Minimum, no requirement
Maximum
1. First used before 1.4.86 and trailer manufactured before 1.10.85, **2,300mm**
2. Motor vehicle first used on or after 1.4.86 maximum speed n/e 25mph, **2,100mm**
3. Bus and road clearance vehicle, **NR***
4. Any other vehicle, **1,500 mm**, unless structure makes it impracticable, then **2,100mm**

No minimum separation distance

NR* – no requirement

WHERE ONE FRONT LAMP IS REQUIRED TO BE FITTED

For any vehicle other than motor bicycle combination

For motor bicycle combination

lamp must be on centre-line or offside of vehicle

lamp must be on centre-line of sidecar or on the side furthest from the motor bicycle

height of lamp above ground must be:
as for vehicle requiring 2 lamps (see above)

as for any other vehicles

MOTOR BICYCLE MUST HAVE HEADLAMP

REAR POSITION LAMPS

REG 18 AND SCHEDS 1 AND 10 ROAD VEHICLES LIGHTING REGULATIONS 1989

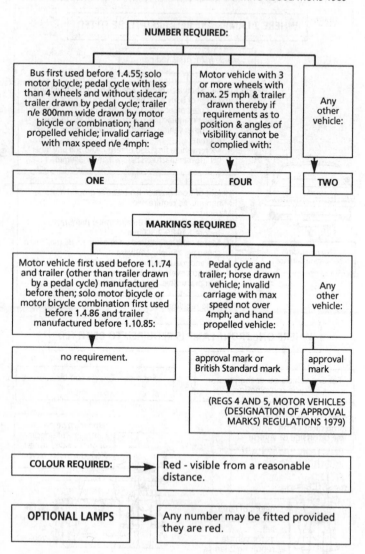

NUMBER REQUIRED:

Bus first used before 1.4.55; solo motor bicycle; pedal cycle with less than 4 wheels and without sidecar; trailer drawn by pedal cycle; trailer n/e 800mm wide drawn by motor bicycle or combination; hand propelled vehicle; invalid carriage with max speed n/e 4mph:	Motor vehicle with 3 or more wheels with max. 25 mph & trailer drawn thereby if requirements as to position & angles of visibility cannot be complied with:	Any other vehicle:
ONE	**FOUR**	**TWO**

MARKINGS REQUIRED

Motor vehicle first used before 1.1.74 and trailer (other than trailer drawn by a pedal cycle) manufactured before then; solo motor bicycle or motor bicycle combination first used before 1.4.86 and trailer manufactured before 1.10.85:	Pedal cycle and trailer; horse drawn vehicle; invalid carriage with max speed not over 4mph; and hand propelled vehicle:	Any other vehicle:
no requirement.	approval mark or British Standard mark	approval mark
	(REGS 4 AND 5, MOTOR VEHICLES (DESIGNATION OF APPROVAL MARKS) REGULATIONS 1979)	

COLOUR REQUIRED: → Red - visible from a reasonable distance.

OPTIONAL LAMPS → Any number may be fitted provided they are red.

- Must be kept clean and in good working order   REG 23

REAR POSITION LAMPS cont

REG 18 AND SCHEDS 1 AND 10 ROAD VEHICLES LIGHTING REGULATIONS 1989

WHERE TWO REAR POSITION LAMPS ARE REQUIRED TO BE FITTED

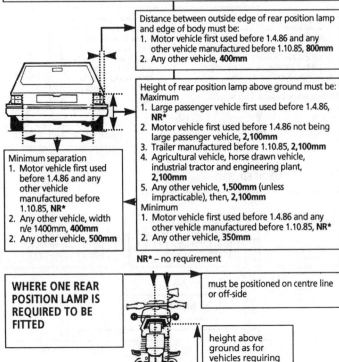

Distance between outside edge of rear position lamp and edge of body must be:
1. Motor vehicle first used before 1.4.86 and any other vehicle manufactured before 1.10.85, **800mm**
2. Any other vehicle, **400mm**

Height of rear position lamp above ground must be:
Maximum
1. Large passenger vehicle first used before 1.4.86, **NR***
2. Motor vehicle first used before 1.4.86 not being large passenger vehicle, **2,100mm**
3. Trailer manufactured before 1.10.85, **2,100mm**
4. Agricultural vehicle, horse drawn vehicle, industrial tractor and engineering plant, **2,100mm**
5. Any other vehicle, **1,500mm** (unless impracticable), then, **2,100mm**
Minimum
1. Motor vehicle first used before 1.4.86 and any other vehicle manufactured before 1.10.85, **NR***
2. Any other vehicle, **350mm**

Minimum separation
1. Motor vehicle first used before 1.4.86 and any other vehicle manufactured before 1.10.85, **NR***
2. Any other vehicle, width n/e 1400mm, **400mm**
2. Any other vehicle, **500mm**

NR* – no requirement

WHERE ONE REAR POSITION LAMP IS REQUIRED TO BE FITTED

must be positioned on centre line or off-side

height above ground as for vehicles requiring 2 lamps (above)

WHERE FOUR REAR POSITION LAMPS ARE REQUIRED TO BE FITTED

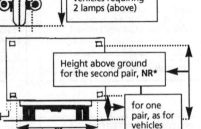

Height above ground for the second pair, **NR***

Max distance from side of vehicle:

one pair must satisfy the requirements above as for 2 lamps, the other pair, **NR***

Minimum separation

for one pair, as for vehicles requiring two lamps

REAR RETRO REFLECTORS

REG 18 AND SCHEDS 1 AND 18 ROAD VEHICLES LIGHTING REGULATIONS 1989

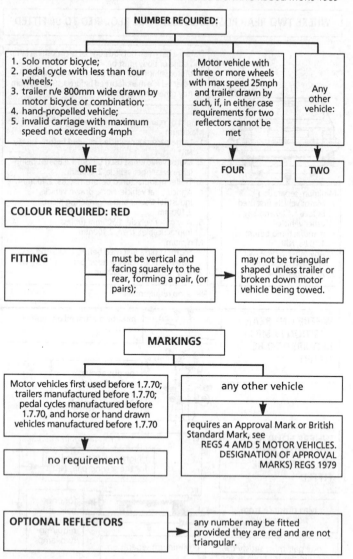

NUMBER REQUIRED:

1. Solo motor bicycle;
2. pedal cycle with less than four wheels;
3. trailer n/e 800mm wide drawn by motor bicycle or combination;
4. hand-propelled vehicle;
5. invalid carriage with maximum speed not exceeding 4mph

ONE

Motor vehicle with three or more wheels with max speed 25mph and trailer drawn by such, if, in either case requirements for two reflectors cannot be met

FOUR

Any other vehicle:

TWO

COLOUR REQUIRED: RED

FITTING | must be vertical and facing squarely to the rear, forming a pair, (or pairs); | may not be triangular shaped unless trailer or broken down motor vehicle being towed.

MARKINGS

Motor vehicles first used before 1.7.70; trailers manufactured before 1.7.70; pedal cycles manufactured before 1.7.70, and horse or hand drawn vehicles manufactured before 1.7.70

no requirement

any other vehicle

requires an Approval Mark or British Standard Mark, see
REGS 4 AMD 5 MOTOR VEHICLES. DESIGNATION OF APPROVAL MARKS) REGS 1979

OPTIONAL REFLECTORS | any number may be fitted provided they are red and are not triangular.

- Must be kept clean and in good working order   REG 23

REAR RETRO REFLECTORS cont

REG 18 AND SCHEDS 1 AND 18 ROAD VEHICLES LIGHTING REGULATIONS 1989

WHERE TWO RETRO REFLECTORS ARE REQUIRED TO BE FITTED

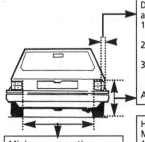

Distance between outside edge of retro reflectors and edge of body must be:
1. Bus first used before 1.10.54 and horse-drawn vehicle manufactured before 1.10.85, **NR***
2. Vehicle constructed or adapted to carry round timber, **765mm**
3. Any other motor vehicle first used before 1.4.86 and any other vehicle manufactured before 1.10.85, **610mm**
Any other vehicle, **400mm**

Height of retro reflectors above ground must be:
Maximum
1. Motor vehicle first used before 1.4.86 and any other vehicle manufactured before 1.10.85, **1,525mm**
2. Any other vehicle, **900mm**, (unless impracticable), then **1,200mm**
Minimum
1. Motor vehicle first used before 1.4.86 and any other vehicle manufactured before 1.10.85, **NR***
2. Any other vehicle, **350mm**

Minimum separation
1. Motor vehicle first used before 1.4.86 and any other vehicle manufactured before 1.10.85, **NR***
2. Any other vehicle n/e 1,300mm wide, **400mm**
3. Any other vehicle, **600mm**

NR* – no requirement

WHERE ONE REAR RETRO REFLECTOR IS REQUIRED TO BE FITTED

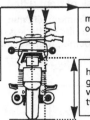

must be positioned on centre line or off-side

height above ground as for vehicles requiring two (above)

WHERE FOUR REAR RETRO REFLECTORS ARE REQUIRED TO BE FITTED

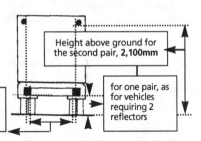

Height above ground for the second pair, **2,100mm**

for one pair, as for vehicles requiring 2 reflectors

Minimum separation one pair as per vehicle requiring two, the other pair, no requirement.

FRONT RETRO REFLECTORS

REG 18 AND SCHEDS 1 AND 21 ROAD VEHICLES LIGHTING REGULATIONS 1989

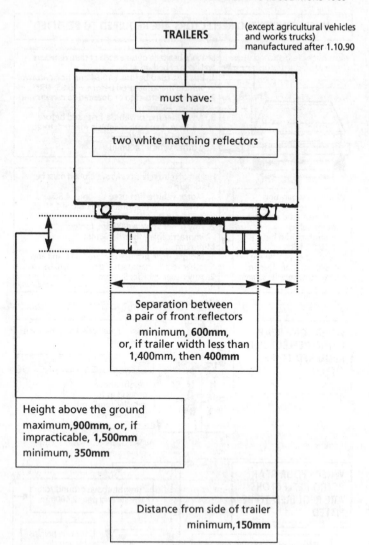

TRAILERS (except agricultural vehicles and works trucks) manufactured after 1.10.90

must have:

two white matching reflectors

Separation between a pair of front reflectors

minimum, **600mm**, or, if trailer width less than 1,400mm, then **400mm**

Height above the ground

maximum, **900mm**, or, if impracticable, **1,500mm**

minimum, **350mm**

Distance from side of trailer minimum, **150mm**

SIDE RETRO REFLECTORS

REG 18 AND SCHEDS 1 AND 17 ROAD VEHICLES LIGHTING REGULATIONS 1989

```
                    ┌─────────────────────────┐
                    │    NUMBER REQUIRED:      │
                    └─────────────────────────┘
```

Motor vehicle first used on or after 1.4.86 and trailer manufactured on or after 1.10.85:	any other vehicle:
two on each side and as many more as required.	two on each side.

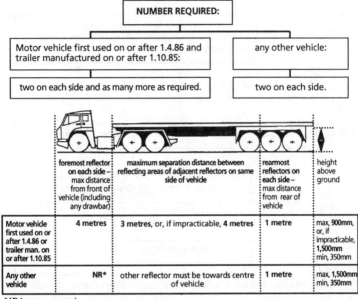

	foremost reflector on each side – max distance from front of vehicle (including any drawbar)	maximum separation distance between reflecting areas of adjacent reflectors on same side of vehicle	rearmost reflectors on each side – max distance from rear of vehicle	height above ground
Motor vehicle first used on or after 1.4.86 or trailer man. on or after 1.10.85	4 metres	3 metres, or, if impracticable, 4 metres	1 metre	max, 900mm, or, if impracticable, 1,500mm min, 350mm
Any other vehicle	NR*	other reflector must be towards centre of vehicle	1 metre	max, 1,500mm min, 350mm

NR* = no requirement

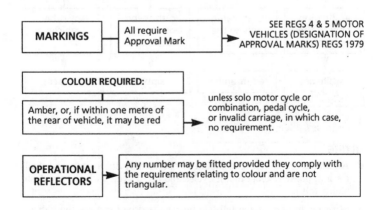

MARKINGS	All require Approval Mark	SEE REGS 4 & 5 MOTOR VEHICLES (DESIGNATION OF APPROVAL MARKS) REGS 1979

COLOUR REQUIRED:	
Amber, or, if within one metre of the rear of vehicle, it may be red	→ unless solo motor cycle or combination, pedal cycle, or invalid carriage, in which case, no requirement.

OPERATIONAL REFLECTORS	→ Any number may be fitted provided they comply with the requirements relating to colour and are not triangular.

- Must be kept clean and in good working order.   REG 23
- Must be vertical and facing squarely to the side.
- May not be triangular.

DIRECTION INDICATORS

REG 18 AND SCHEDS 1 AND 7 ROAD VEHICLES LIGHTING REGULATIONS 1989

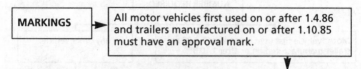

| MARKINGS | → | All motor vehicles first used on or after 1.4.86 and trailers manufactured on or after 1.10.85 must have an approval mark. |

SEE REGS 4 AND 5 MOTOR VEHICLES (DESIGNATION OF APPROVAL MARKS) REGS 1979

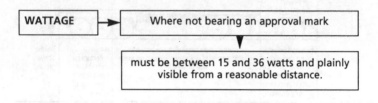

| WATTAGE | → | Where not bearing an approval mark |

must be between 15 and 36 watts and plainly visible from a reasonable distance.

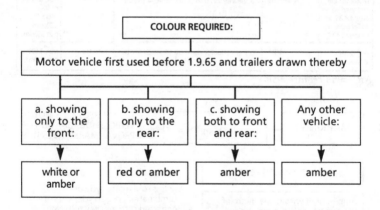

COLOUR REQUIRED:

Motor vehicle first used before 1.9.65 and trailers drawn thereby

a. showing only to the front:	b. showing only to the rear:	c. showing both to front and rear:	Any other vehicle:
white or amber	red or amber	amber	amber

FITTING

- All indicators on one side should be operated by one switch, and shall flash in phase (except motor cycles and pedal cycles which may flash alternately).
- Must be an operational tell-tale unless the driver can see the indicators from the driving position.
- Must flash between 60 and 120 flashes per minute. Must form a pair (or if more than 2 – 2 pairs).

DIRECTION INDICATORS cont

REG 18 AND SCHEDS 1 AND 7 ROAD VEHICLES LIGHTING REGULATIONS 1989

Minimum separation distance between indicators on opposite sides of vehicle

A motor vehicle (other than solo motor bicycle or motor bicycle combination or invalid carriage having maximum speed not exceeding 8mph) first used on or after 1.4.86; a trailer manufactured on or after 1.10.85; a horse-drawn vehicle, pedestrian controlled vehicle and vehicle drawn or propelled by hand, **500mm**

or, if the overall width of vehicle is less than 1,400mm, **400mm**

Before above date, **NR***

Height above ground

Maximum
motor vehicle first used before 1.4.86 & trailer manufactured before 1.10.85, NR* maximum speed n/e 25mph , NR* any other vehicle, **1,500mm** unless impracticable, then, **2,300mm**

Minimum, **350mm**

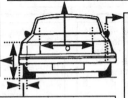

Minimum separation distance between front indicator and any headlamp or front fog lamp

Motor vehicle not being solo motor bicycle or motor bicycle combination first used on or after 1.4.95
CAT 1 indicator, **40mm**;
CAT 1a indicator, **20mm**;
CAT 1b indicator, **NR***

Before above date, **NR***

Maximum distance from side of vehicle

Motor vehicle first used before 1.4.86; trailer manufactured before 1.10.85; solo motor bicycle, pedal cycle, horse-drawn vehicle or vehicle drawn by hand, **NR***

Before the above dates, **NR***

Any other vehicle, **400mm**

Minimum separation distance between front indicator and headlamp or foglamp

for solo motor bicycles or motor bicycle combination first used on or after 1.4.86 (includes combinations), **100mm**

before above date, **NR***

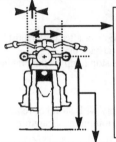

Minimum separation distance between indicators on opposite sides of vehicle

over 50cc and first used on or after 1.4.86:
front, **300mm**; rear, **240mm**; Side, **NR***

n/e 50 cc and first used on or after 1.4.86 and pedal cycle:
front, **240mm**; rear, **180mm**; side, **NR***

Combination first used on or after 1.4.86, **400mm**

Invalid carriage maximum speed n/e 8mph:
front, **240mm**; rear, **300mm**

Before the above dates – **NR***

Height above ground as shown for above

* NR = no requirement

● Must be kept clean and in good working order. REG 23

STOP LAMPS

REG 18 AND SCHEDS 1 AND 12 ROAD VEHICLES LIGHTING REGULATIONS 1989

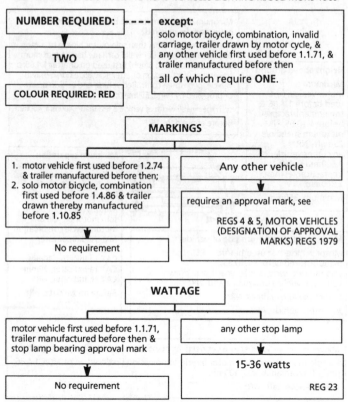

NUMBER REQUIRED: - - - - **except:**
solo motor bicycle, combination, invalid carriage, trailer drawn by motor cycle, & any other vehicle first used before 1.1.71, & trailer manufactured before then

TWO

all of which require **ONE**.

COLOUR REQUIRED: RED

MARKINGS

1. motor vehicle first used before 1.2.74 & trailer manufactured before then;
2. solo motor bicycle, combination first used before 1.4.86 & trailer thereby manufactured before 1.10.85

Any other vehicle

requires an approval mark, see

REGS 4 & 5, MOTOR VEHICLES (DESIGNATION OF APPROVAL MARKS) REGS 1979

No requirement

WATTAGE

motor vehicle first used before 1.1.71, trailer manufactured before then & stop lamp bearing approval mark

any other stop lamp

15-36 watts

REG 23

No requirement

ELECTRICAL CONNECTIONS

A motor bicycle (including combination) first used on or after 1.4.86 must be capable of operating the stop lamp by both front and back brakes.
Every other vehicle and trailer must operate the stop lamp by the braking system.

OPTIONAL LAMPS

Any number may be fitted but they must comply with all other requirements relating to obligatory stop lamps except minimum separation distance between 2 stop lamps.

Must be kept clean & in good working order   Reg 23

STOP LAMPS cont

REG 18 AND SCHEDS 1 AND 12 ROAD VEHICLES LIGHTING REGULATIONS 1989

WHERE TWO STOP LAMPS ARE FITTED

↓

must be at least one on each side must form matched pairs

If also fitted in rear window
of vehicle first used after
1.4.91, must be between 20
and 60 candelas

↓

Clearance of headlamp above ground must be:

maximum:
motor vehicle first used before 1.1.71, trailer
manufactured before then & motor vehicle
with max speed r/e 25 mph, **NR ***;

any other vehicle, **1,500mm**
and (unless impracticable) **2,100mm**;

minimum
motor vehicle first used before 1.1.71. & trailer
manufactured before then, **NR***;

any other vehicle, **350mm**

Minimum separation **400 mm**

WHERE ONE IS FITTED

↓

to be fitted on centre line or offside (disregarding the combination).

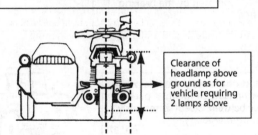

Clearance of
headlamp above
ground as for
vehicle requiring
2 lamps above

* NR - no requirement

REAR FOG LAMPS

REG 18 SCHEDS 1 AND 11

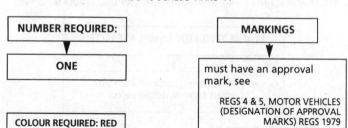

NUMBER REQUIRED:

ONE

COLOUR REQUIRED: RED

MARKINGS

must have an approval mark, see

REGS 4 & 5, MOTOR VEHICLES (DESIGNATION OF APPROVAL MARKS) REGS 1979

ELECTRICAL CONNECTIONS
Must not be capable of being operated by braking systems. A circuit-closed tell-tale must be fitted.

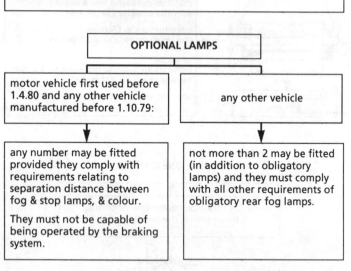

OPTIONAL LAMPS

motor vehicle first used before 1.4.80 and any other vehicle manufactured before 1.10.79:

any number may be fitted provided they comply with requirements relating to separation distance between fog & stop lamps, & colour.

They must not be capable of being operated by the braking system.

any other vehicle

not more than 2 may be fitted (in addition to obligatory lamps) and they must comply with all other requirements of obligatory rear fog lamps.

Must not cause undue dazzle or discomfort, be lit when parked, nor be used except in seriously reduced visibility

REG 27

REAR FOG LAMPS cont

REG 18 SCHEDS 1 AND 11

WHERE TWO REAR FOG LAMPS ARE FITTED

↓

Laterally there is no fitting requirement, but

must form a matching pair if vehicle first used on or after 1.4.86, or trailer manufactured on or after 1.10.85.

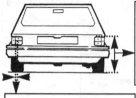

Height of fog lamp above ground must be:

maximum
1. agricultural vehicle, engineering plant and motor tractor, **2,100mm;**
2. any other vehicle, **1,000mm;**

minimum, **250mm.**

Minimum separation distance between fog lamp and stop lamp, **100mm**

WHERE ONE REAR FOG LAMP IS FITTED

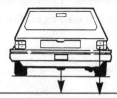

Fitted on centre line or offside of the vehicle (disregarding any sidecar forming part of motor bicycle combination)

Must be kept clean, in good working order and maintained so as not to cause undue dazzle or inconvenience

REG 23

REVERSING LIGHTS

REG 20 AND SCHED 14

These lamps are not obligatory, but must comply with the following:

NUMBER: not more than two

COLOUR: white

POSITION: no requirement

MARKINGS

Motor vehicle first used on or after 1.4.86 and trailer manufactured on or after 1.10.85 requires an approval mark. See
REGS 4 AND 5 OF THE MOTOR VEHICLES (DESIGNATION OF APPROVAL MARKS) REGS 1979

Any other vehicle, no requirement

WATTAGE

Lamp bearing approval mark, no requirement

All other lamps n/e 24 watts each.

TELL-TALE

Motor vehicle first used on or after 1.7.54 with automatic switching of lamp upon selection of reverse gear, no requirement

A motor vehicle first used before 1.7.54, no requirement

Any other motor vehicle first used on or after 1.7.54 requires a circuit-closed tell-tale.

A vehicle which is not a motor vehicle, no requirement

● Must be kept clean, in good working order and maintained so as not to cause undue dazzle or inconvenience
REG 23

● Must only be lit for reversing.
REG 27

FRONT FOG LAMPS

REG 20 AND SCHED 6

**These lamps are not obligatory, but must
comply with the following:**

NUMBER:

motor vehicles (other than motor bicycle or motor bicycle combination) first used on or after 1.4.91 – not more than two.

Any other vehicle, no requirement

COLOUR: white or yellow

POSITION: no requirement

MARKINGS:

first used before 1.4.86, no requirement

any other vehicle needs an approval mark, see:
REGS 4 & 5, MOTOR VEHICLES (DESIGNATION OF APPROVAL MARKS)
REGULATIONS 1979

When used as a pair in seriously reduced visibility in place of obligatory head lights, **400 mm**

Any other case, **no requirement**

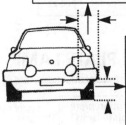

Maximum height above the ground:
1. agricultural vehicle, road clearance vehicle aerodrome fire tender or runway sweeper, industrial tractor, engineering plant & home forces vehicle, **no requirement**
2. any other vehicle, **1,200 metres**

Minimum height above the ground, **no requirement**

● Must not cause undue dazzle or discomfort, be lit when parked, nor be used except in seriously reduced visibility

REG 27

● Must be kept clean, in good working order and maintained so as not to cause undue dazzle or inconvenience

REG 23

HAZARD WARNING

REG 18 AND SCHEDS 1 AND 8 ROAD VEHICLES LIGHTING REGULATIONS 1989

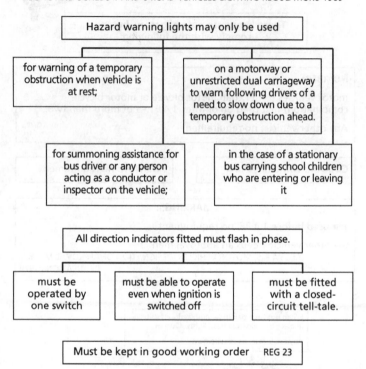

Hazard warning lights may only be used

for warning of a temporary obstruction when vehicle is at rest;

on a motorway or unrestricted dual carriageway to warn following drivers of a need to slow down due to a temporary obstruction ahead.

for summoning assistance for bus driver or any person acting as a conductor or inspector on the vehicle;

in the case of a stationary bus carrying school children who are entering or leaving it

All direction indicators fitted must flash in phase.

must be operated by one switch

must be able to operate even when ignition is switched off

must be fitted with a closed-circuit tell-tale.

Must be kept in good working order   REG 23

REAR REGISTRATION PLATE LAMP

REG 18 AND SCHED 1 ROAD VEHICLES LIGHTING REGULATIONS 1989

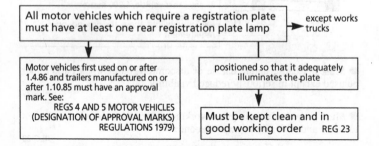

All motor vehicles which require a registration plate must have at least one rear registration plate lamp   → except works trucks

Motor vehicles first used on or after 1.4.86 and trailers manufactured on or after 1.10.85 must have an approval mark. See:
REGS 4 AND 5 MOTOR VEHICLES (DESIGNATION OF APPROVAL MARKS) REGULATIONS 1979)

positioned so that it adequately illuminates the plate

Must be kept clean and in good working order   REG 23

WARNING BEACONS

ROAD VEHICLES LIGHTING REGULATIONS 1989

Except for emergency vehicles

REG 16 AND
SCHED 16

it is an offence to fit a blue warning beacon or special warning lamp or device resembling such

whether working or not

- *For improper use of beacons see Reg 27*
- *See also Reg 11 (colour of light)*

Must be visible from any point a reasonable distance from the vehicle.

May be blue, amber green or yellow   IN ACCORDANCE WITH REG 11.

Light to be displayed between 60 and 240 equal times per minute at constant intervals.

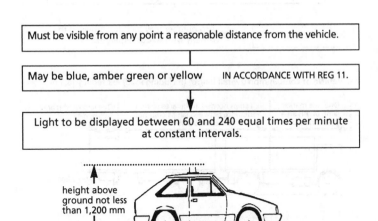

height above ground not less than 1,200 mm

OBLIGATORY WARNING BEAKON

It is an offence to use on an unrestricted dual carriageway

REG 17

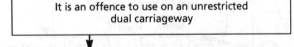

a motor vehicle with four or more wheels, having max. speed not exceeding 25mph	→	unless it has at least one amber warning beacon.

SIDE MARKER LAMPS

REGS 18, 20, 22 AND SCHEDS 1 AND 9 ROAD VEHICLES LIGHTING REGS 1989

> It is an offence to use, cause or permit to be used, on a road

> during the hours of darkness
> or in seriously reduced visibility, in the daytime

> any vehicle | or combination of vehicles

> unless fitted with side marker lamps as detailed in the
> following diagrams

OPTIONAL LAMPS: ----▶ Any number may be fitted provided they
comply with colour requirements.

1. Vehicle or combination overall length (including load) exceeding 18.3 m

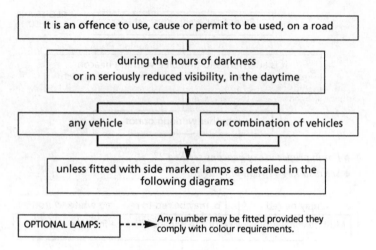

One side marker lamp in this area 9.15 m max

Lamps needed in this area so that distance between lamps **does not exceed 3.05 m**

One lamp in this area 3.05 m max

Max 2,300 mm
Min NR*

2. Combination of vehicles overall length (including load) exceeding 12.2 m but not exceeding 18.3 m and carrying a load supported by any two of the vehicles but not including a load carried by an articulated vehicle.

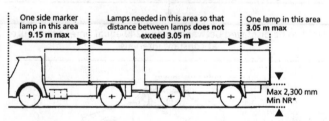

One side marker lamp within 1,530 mm of rear of towing vehicle.

1,530mm

1,530mm max

Max. 2,300mm
Min. no req.

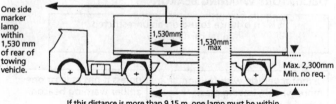

If this distance is more than 9.15 m, one lamp must be within 1,530 mm behind centre point of overall length of load. This also applies to any other trailer.

SIDE MARKER LAMPS cont

REGS 18, 20, 22 AND SCHEDS 1 AND 9 ROAD VEHICLES LIGHTING REGS 1989

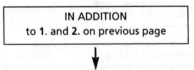

IN ADDITION
to **1.** and **2.** on previous page

3. **Motor vehicles first used after 1.4.91 and trailers manufactured after 1.10.90 must also comply with the following:**

Lamps must be amber,

OR

| a. may be red if within 1m of rear | b. may be red to rear and white to front if on a trailer manufactured before 1.10.90. |

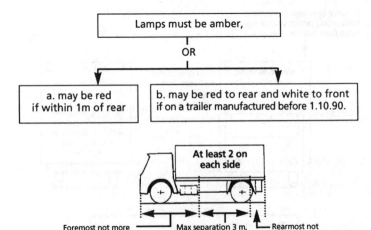

At least 2 on each side

Foremost not more than 4 m from front

Max separation 3 m, unless not practicable, then 4 m.

Rearmost not more than 1 m from rear

Exceptions:

1. Agricultural or works trailers;
2. caravan;
3. length n/e 6 metres and first used before 1.4.91. (but if trailer manufactured before 1.10.90 n/e 9.15 metres);
4. max speed n/e 25mph;
5. passenger vehicle;
6. proceeding for completion or sale;
7. vehicle for carrying or launching boat.

END-OUTLINE MARKER LAMPS

REGS 18, 20 AND SCHEDS 13 ROAD VEHICLES LIGHTING REGULATIONS 1989

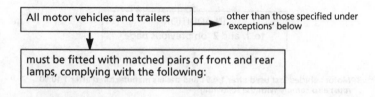

All motor vehicles and trailers → other than those specified under 'exceptions' below

must be fitted with matched pairs of front and rear lamps, complying with the following:

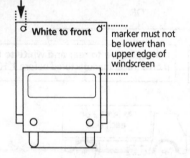

Distance between end-outline marker and side of vehicle not more than **400mm**

White to front — marker must not be lower than upper edge of windscreen

Red to rear — At the front of a trailer and the rear of any vehicle, must be at the maximum height compatible with lateral position and use of the vehicle

The white front and rear red lamps may be combined to form a single lamp.

OPTIONAL LAMPS: → Any number of optional lamps may be fitted but must comply with colour requirements.

Exceptions

Motor vehicles
1. First used before 1.4.91.
2. Incomplete vehicle going for completion, storage or display for sale.
3. Maximum speed n/e 25mph.
4. Overall width n/e 2,100mm.

Trailers
1. Agricultural vehicle.
2. Incomplete trailer going for completion, storage or display for sale.
3. Manufactured before 1.10.90.
4. Overall width n/e 2,100 mm.
5. Works trailer.

REAR REFLECTIVE MARKERS – REQUIREMENTS

The following vehicles are required to be fitted with the type of reflector indicated (and illustrated on the following pages).

	Motor vehicles first used before 1.4.96 and trailers manufactured before 1.10.95	Any motor vehicles regardless of date of first use, and any trailer regardless of date of manufacture
	TYPE	TYPE
motor vehicle n/e 13 m long	1, 2 or 3	A, B, C or D
motor vehicle over 13 m long	4 or 5	E, F, G or H
trailer forming part of a combination of vehicles n/e 11 m overall length	1, 2 or 3	A, B, C or D
trailer forming part of a combination of vehicles over 11 m but n/e 13 m overall length	1, 2, 3, 4 or 5	Any of types A – H
trailer forming part a combination of vehicles over 13 m overall length	4 or 5	E, F, G or H

REAR REFLECTIVE MARKERS – TYPES

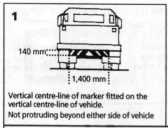

1

140 mm

1,400 mm

Vertical centre-line of marker fitted on the vertical centre-line of vehicle.
Not protruding beyond either side of vehicle

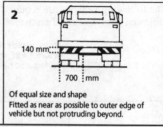

2

140 mm

700 mm

Of equal size and shape
Fitted as near as possible to outer edge of vehicle but not protruding beyond.

For **1** and **2**: angle of bars, **46°**
width and distance apart of bar, **140mm**

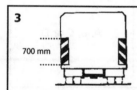

3

700 mm

Equal size and shape
Fitted as near as possible to outer edge of vehicle but not protruding beyond.

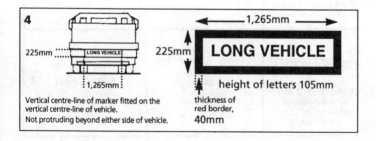

4

225mm

1,265mm

1,265mm

225mm

LONG VEHICLE

height of letters 105mm

Vertical centre-line of marker fitted on the vertical centre-line of vehicle.
Not protruding beyond either side of vehicle.

thickness of
red border,
40mm

REAR REFLECTIVE MARKERS
– TYPES cont

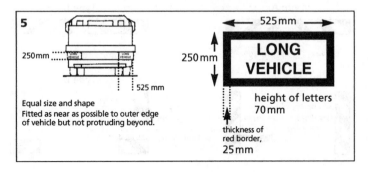

5

250 mm

525 mm

Equal size and shape
Fitted as near as possible to outer edge
of vehicle but not protruding beyond.

◄── 525 mm ──►

250 mm

LONG VEHICLE

height of letters
70 mm

thickness of
red border,
25 mm

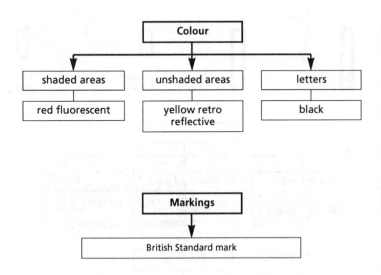

Colour		
shaded areas	unshaded areas	letters
red fluorescent	yellow retro reflective	black

Markings
British Standard mark

Must be kept clean and in good working order   REG 23

REAR REFLECTIVE MARKERS – TYPES cont

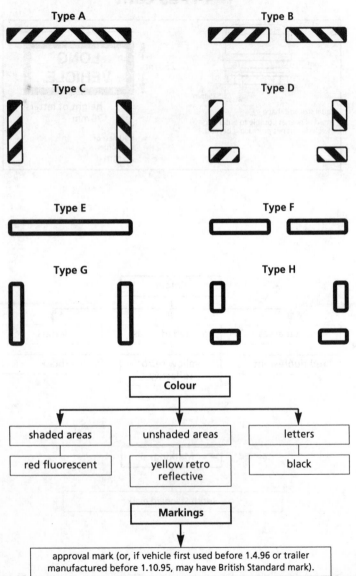

Type A

Type B

Type C

Type D

Type E

Type F

Type G

Type H

Colour		
shaded areas	unshaded areas	letters
red fluorescent	yellow retro reflective	black

Markings
approval mark (or, if vehicle first used before 1.4.96 or trailer manufactured before 1.10.95, may have British Standard mark).

REAR REFLECTIVE MARKERS
– OPTIONAL

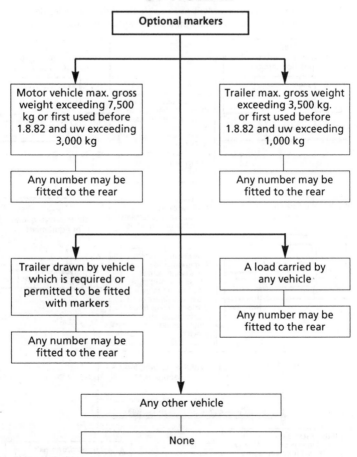

Optional markers

Motor vehicle max. gross weight exceeding 7,500 kg or first used before 1.8.82 and uw exceeding 3,000 kg

Any number may be fitted to the rear

Trailer max. gross weight exceeding 3,500 kg. or first used before 1.8.82 and uw exceeding 1,000 kg

Any number may be fitted to the rear

Trailer drawn by vehicle which is required or permitted to be fitted with markers

Any number may be fitted to the rear

A load carried by any vehicle

Any number may be fitted to the rear

Any other vehicle

None

LAMPS ON PROJECTING LOADS
REG 21 ROAD VEHICLES LIGHTING REGULATIONS 1989

Offence to use, cause or permit use of vehicle during hours of darkness or in seriously reduced visibility unless it complies with the following:

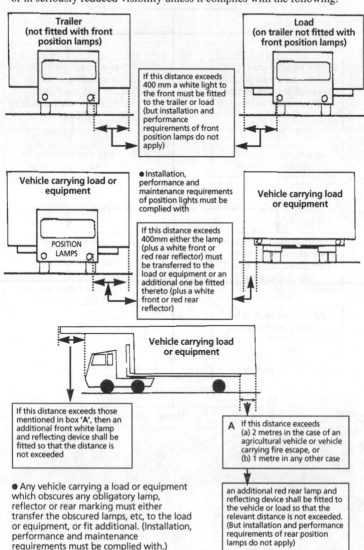

PROJECTION MARKERS

ART 23 MOTOR VEHICLES (AUTHORISATION OF SPECIAL TYPES) GENERAL ORDER 1979

SCHED 12 ROAD VEHICLES (CONSTRUCTION AND USE) REGULATIONS 1986

Projection	Requirement
Forward or rearward projection exceeding 1.83m	End markers unless rear marking is in accordance with the Lighting Regs
Forward projection exceeds 2m or rearward exceeds 3m	One side marker on each side
Forward projection exceeds 4.5m that or rearward exceeds 5m	Extra side markers on each side so that horizontal distance between marker and end of projection or between adjacent markers on the same side, does not exceed: forward projection - 2.5m rearward projection - 3.5m

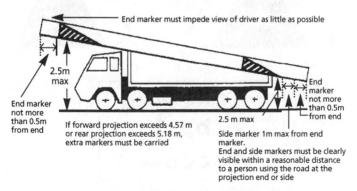

End marker must impede view of driver as little as possible

2.5m max

End marker not more than 0.5m from end

If forward projection exceeds 4.57 m or rear projection exceeds 5.18 m, extra markers must be carried

2.5 m max

End marker not more than 0.5m from end

Side marker 1m max from end marker.
End and side markers must be clearly visible within a reasonable distance to a person using the road at the projection end or side

Markers must have alternating red and white stripes 100 mm wide, with 50 mm wide red border. Each not less than 610 mm high

not less than 1,520 mm

side marker

front or rear end marker

- Must be kept illuminated between sunset and sunrise.
- End projection markers are not required if reflective rear markings are carried on the load.

TRAILER PLATES – REAR REFLECTORS

REG 18 AND SCHEDS 1 AND 18 ROAD VEHICLES LIGHTING REGULATIONS 1989

REG 3 EEC DIRECTIVE 76/757

A trailer (other than a broken down motor vehicle) manufactured on or after 1.7.70 must have a pair of reflex reflectors of one of the following types:

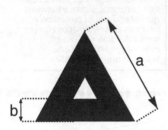

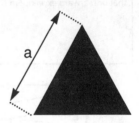

$$150mm \leqslant a \leqslant 200 \text{ mm}$$

$$b \geqslant \frac{a}{5}$$

$$c \leqslant 15 \text{ mm}$$

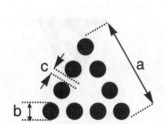

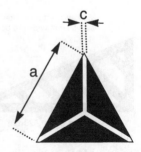

PART 4

DRIVERS' HOURS

AND RECORDS

Here we discuss the need to comply with
drivers' hours and the keeping of records.
The use of the tachograph and possible
malpractices are then considered. Both
community and domestic rules are explained.

DRIVERS' HOURS AND RECORDS (GENERAL)

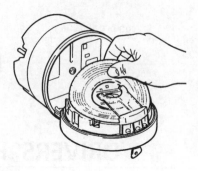

The set of rules to be followed depends upon the type of vehicle and the work being carried out. Unless totally exempt, vehicles will have to comply with:

- **Community Rules**

   (COUNCIL REGULATIONS (EEC) 3820/85 AND 3821/85)

   or

- **Domestic Rules**   (TRANSPORT ACT 1968)

(1) These rules apply to journeys made by vehicles, whether laden or not, used for the carriage of passengers or goods within the Community.

(2) The same rules relating to hours apply to operations to, from or through countries which are not in the European Union but which have entered an agreement to comply. The rules also apply to operations to or from countries which are not party to the AETR agreement where the journey is made within the European Union by a vehicle registered in one of those countries.

(3) However, certain types of operation within the UK are exempt from the EC rules but may be required to comply with domestic rules.

To decide which type of rule is applicable follow the flow chart opposite:

DRIVERS' HOURS AND RECORDS

SELECTOR

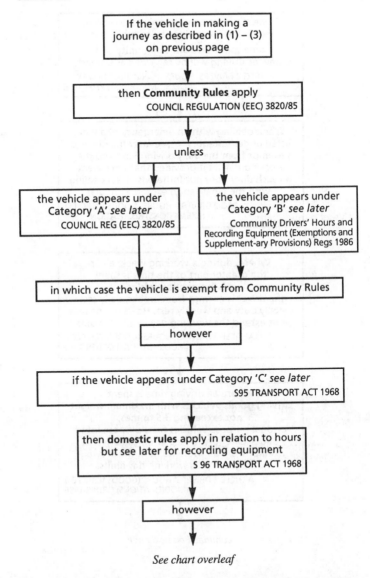

If the vehicle in making a journey as described in (1) – (3) on previous page

↓

then **Community Rules** apply
COUNCIL REGULATION (EEC) 3820/85

↓

unless

↓

the vehicle appears under Category 'A' *see later*
COUNCIL REG (EEC) 3820/85

the vehicle appears under Category 'B' *see later*
Community Drivers' Hours and Recording Equipment (Exemptions and Supplement-ary Provisions) Regs 1986

↓

in which case the vehicle is exempt from Community Rules

↓

however

↓

if the vehicle appears under Category 'C' *see later*
S95 TRANSPORT ACT 1968

↓

then **domestic rules** apply in relation to hours but see later for recording equipment
S 96 TRANSPORT ACT 1968

↓

however

↓

See chart overleaf

DRIVERS' HOURS AND RECORDS cont

SELECTOR cont

Domestic rules do not apply to driving to which the Community rules apply, but:

time spent on both **community** and **domestic driving** will be regarded as Domestic

REG 2 DRIVERS' HOURS (HARMONISATION WITH COMMUNITY RULES) REGS 1986

↓

When dealing with an **emergency** of a type listed under Category 'E' *see later* the driver is exempt from the daily driving limit and the working day limit provided that time spent on such duty does not (otherwise than dealing with the emergency) exceed 11 hours

REG 2 DRIVERS' HOURS (GOODS VEHICLES) (EXEMPTIONS) REGULATIONS 1986

↓

Where, during a working week, all or the greater part of the time is spent **driving goods vehicles,** the driver is exempt from breaks, daily rest, weekly duty and weekly rest. However, he may not extend the working day to 12 1/2 hours

ARTICLE 2 DRIVERS' HOURS (GOODS VEHICLES) (MODIFICATIONS) ORDER 1986

↓

Where all driving time is spent **driving goods vehicles with maximum weight not exceeding 3.5 tonnes,** or dual purpose vehicles for a purpose listed under Category 'D' *see later*, the driver is exempt from all those items in the previous paragraph plus working day limits.

ARTICLE 3 DRIVERS' HOURS (GOODS VEHICLES) (MODIFICATIONS) ORDER 1986

↓

continued on next page

DRIVERS' HOURS AND RECORDS cont

SELECTOR cont

Drivers are exempt from the daily
driving limit when driving elsewhere than
on a road in the course of
**agriculture, forestry, quarrying,
construction etc. of buildings, or construction
or civil engineering (including roads)**

TRANSPORT ACT 1968 AND DRIVERS' HOURS
(GOODS VEHICLES) (MODIFICATIONS) ORDER 1970

Where a driver spends all or the greater part of
a working day **driving passenger vehicles**,
the following modifications will take effect:

(a) within any continuous period of 8 and a
half hours he may drive for periods
amounting to not more than 7.75 hours
if, during which, he has a break of three
quarters of an hour.

(b) the working day may be extended to 16
hours if all or the greater part of the time
is spent driving passenger vehicles.

(c) daily rest shall not be less than 10 hours
but for not more than 3 occasions in any
working week it may be reduced to not
less than 8 1/2 hours.

(d) exempt from weekly duty restrictions.

(e) weekly rest periods reduced to 24 hours
in 2 weeks.

ARTICLE 4 DRIVERS' HOURS (PASSENGER AND GOODS
VEHICLES) (MODIFICATIONS) ORDER 1971

VEHICLE CATEGORIES

Category A (Exemptions from Community rules)
ARTICLE 4 COUNCIL REGULATION (EEC) 3820/85

Goods vehicle not exceeding 3.5 tonnes maximum permissible weight (including trailer or semi-trailer).

Passenger vehicle constructed and intended for not more than nine persons including driver.

Carrying passengers on scheduled services and route not exceeding 50 km.

Max authorised speed not exceeding 30 kph.

Armed services, civil defence, fire service and forces responsible for maintaining public order.

Sewerage, flood protection, water, gas, electricity, highway maintenance, refuse collection, telephone, post, radio, TV broadcasting/detecting.

Emergency/rescue/specialised medical vehicle.

Circus/funfair vehicles.

Specialised breakdown vehicles.

Vehicles undergoing road tests for technical development, etc.

Non-commercial carriage of personal goods.

Milk collection from farms.

VEHICLE CATEGORIES cont

Category B (Exemptions from Community rules)
COMMUNITY DRIVERS' HOURS AND RECORDING EQUIPMENT
(EXEMPTIONS AND SUPPLEMENTARY PROVISIONS) REGULATIONS 1986

Passenger vehicle constructed and intended to carry not exceeding 17 persons including driver.

Public Authority Vehicles after 1.1.90 not in competition with professional road hauliers:
being an ambulance service or carrying staff; patients or medical supplies; social services vehicle for the aged or physically or mentally handicapped; coastguard or lighthouse vehicles; harbour vehicle within harbour limits; airport vehicle within airport limits; railway maintenance vehicle; or British Waterways maintenance vehicle.

being used by agricultural, horticultural, forestry or fishery undertaking (ie, carrying live fish or a catch of fish from where it was landed to place of processing), to carry goods within 50 km radius of its base.

Carrying animal waste or carcasses not intended for human consumption.

Carrying live animals between farm and market or between market and slaughterhouse.

Being used and specially fitted as a local market shop, door-to-door selling, mobile banking, worship, library or exhibitions.

Goods vehicle not over 7.5 tonnes carrying material or equipment for driver's use, within 50 km radius of base.

Operating exclusively on an island not over 2,300 sq km, not linked to Great Britian by bridge, ford or tunnel used by motor vehicles.

Goods vehicle not over 7.5 tonnes propelled by gas produced on the vehicle, or electricity.

Being used for driving instruction and not carrying goods for hire or reward.

Agricultural or forestry tractor after 1.1.90.

Used by RNLI for hauling lifeboats.

Vehicle manufactured before 1.1.47.

Steam propelled vehicle.

Vintage vehicle in rally etc.

Vehicle collecting sea coal and postal articles on national transport operations where max. weight of article does not exceed 3.5 tonnes or where vehicle is used by the Post Office to carry letters (exempt from recording equipment only).

VEHICLE CATEGORIES cont

Category C (Domestic Rules)

S 95 TRANSPORT ACT 1968
NONE OF THE BELOW WILL APPLY TO POLICE, FIRE BRIGADE, NAVY,
MILITARY OR AIR FORCE VEHICLES (S 102 TRANSPORT ACT 1968);
NOR TO TRAMCARS AND TROLLEY VEHICLES OPERATED UNDER
STATUTORY POWERS (S 102A TRANSPORT ACT 1968)

Vehicles and persons in the public service of the crown (S 102).

Public service vehicle (S 95).

Vehicle (not PSV) constructed or adapted to carry more than
12 passengers (S 95).

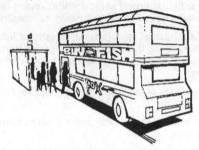

Goods vehicles, ie, heavy locomotive, light locomotive, motor
tractor, other motor vehicles so constructed that a trailer may by
partial superimposition be attached to the vehicle in such a manner
as to cause a substancial part of the weight of the trailer to be
borne by the vehicle, and any other goods vehicle constructed or
adapted to carry goods other than effects of passengers.

VEHICLE CATEGORIES cont

Category D (Modification of Driver's Hours)
DRIVERS' HOURS (GOODS VEHICLES) (MODIFICATIONS) ORDER 1986

Carrying on by him or his employer the profession of medical practitioner, nurse, midwife, dentist or veterinary surgeon.

Carrying out a service of inspection, cleaning, maintenance, repair, installation or fitting.

Commercial traveller only carrying goods for soliciting orders.

In course of employment by AA, RAC, or RSAC (Royal Scottish Automobile Club).

Carrying on by him or his employer the business of cinematography or radio or TV broadcasting.

Category E (Emergencies)
DRIVERS' HOURS (GOODS VEHICLES) (EXEMPTIONS) REGULATIONS 1986

Events which cause or are likely to cause such:
  a) danger to life or health of one or more individuals or animals,
  b) a serious interruption in the maintenance of public services for the supply of water, gas, electricity or drainage or of telecommunication or postal services, or
  c) a serious interruption in the use of roads, railways, ports or airports, as to necessitate the taking of immediate action to prevent the occurrence or continuance of such danger or interruption.

Events which are likely to cause such serious damage to property as to necessitate the taking of immediate action to prevent the occurrence of such damage.

DRIVER'S HOURS – COMMUNITY RULES

COUNCIL REGULATION (EEC) 3820/85

DAILY DRIVING: 9 hours
- May be extended twice in any one week to 10 hours.

WEEKLY REST: 45 hours
- Must be taken after no more than six daily driving periods.
- Periods may be reduced to minimum of 36 hours if taken where vehicle or driver normally based; or minimum of 24 hours if taken elsewhere. Such reductions must be compensated by an equivalent rest period taken en bloc before end of third week following, attached to another rest of at least 8 hours to be taken at the vehicle's parking place or driver's base, if requested.
- Weekly rest may be postponed until end of sixth day if total driving is no more than six daily periods.
- But on national or international passenger services other than regular services:

    may be postponed to the end of twelfth day if total driving is no more than 12 daily periods, or

    may be postponed until the week following and added on to that week's rest period.
- Weekly rest periods beginning in one week and continuing into the following week may be attached to either week.

FORTNIGHTLY DRIVING: 90 hours   ARTICLE 6

BREAK DURING DRIVING: 45 minutes   ARTICLE 7
- Must be taken after four and a half hours' driving unless beginning a rest period. May be replaced by 15-minute breaks during the driving period or immediately afterwards provided basic rule is complied with.
- For regular national passenger services in a 'relevant area' if it is not possible to take a break of at least 15 minutes, he may take 30 minutes immediately after a driving period of four hours maximum instead of the basic rule. The 'relevant areas' are the Boroughs of Camden, Kensington and Chelsea, Islington, and the cities of Westminster, Birmingham, Bristol, Leeds, Leicester, Nottingham and Oxford. During any driving break the driver may not carry out other work.
- Breaks may not be regarded as daily rest periods.
- During breaks the driver may not carry out other work. Waiting time and time travelling (not driving) in a vehicle, ferry or train is not regarded as 'other work'.

DRIVER'S HOURS – COMMUNITY RULES
cont COUNCIL REGULATION (EEC) 3820/85

DAILY REST: 11 consecutive hours
ARTICLE 8
- To be taken in each period of 24 hours.
- May be reduced to nine hours not more than three times per week provided an equivalent rest period in compensation is taken before the end of the following week but must be attached to another rest, of at least 8 hours at the vehicle's parking place or driver's base, if requested.
- If not reduced, the period may be taken on two or three separate occasions but one must be at least eight hours (the minimum period of rest is 1 hour) and total is increased to 12 hours.
- Eight hours are to be taken where there are two drivers, by each driver, during each period of 30 hours.
- May be taken in a stationary vehicle if fitted with a bunk.

INTERUPTION OF DAILY REST
ARTICLE 9
- If being transported by ferryboat or train rest period may be interrupted not more than once provided land rest period taken before or after that taken on board; period between the two portions of the rest period not to exceed 1 hour before embarkation or after disembarkation; driver must have access to bunk or couchette during both portions of the rest period; daily rest period is increased by 2 hours.

DEPARTURE FROM PROVISIONS
ARTICLE 12
- Provided road safety is not jeopardised, and to enable him to reach a suitable stopping place, the driver may depart from the above provisions to the extent necessary to ensure the safety of persons, of the vehicle or of its load. Such departures must be recorded on the record sheet or duty roster.

DRIVER'S HOURS – DOMESTIC RULES

SECTION 96 TRANSPORT ACT 1968

DAILY DRIVING: 10 hours

BREAKS: 30 minutes
Must be taken after five and a half hours' duty (or aggregate of five and a half hours if not continuous) unless taken during that period.

WORKING DAY: 11 hours
May be extended to up to 12.5 hours if during that day he is off duty for a period (or cumulation of periods) of not less than the amount by which the actual hours worked exceed 11 hours. And may be extended to 14 hours if:
a) all driving time is spent driving express or contract carriages; and
b) he is able to obtain not less than 4 hours rest.

DAILY REST: 11 hours
If all or greater part of the time is spent driving passenger vehicles, on one occasion during each working week may be reduced to nine and a half hours – does not apply in a week when each day's driving is not more than 4 hours.

WEEKLY DUTY: 60 hours
Does not apply in a week when each day's driving is not more than 4 hours.

WEEKLY REST: 24 hours
May fall wholly in that week or beginning in that week and ending in the next.
Does not apply in a week when each day's driving is not more than 4 hours.

Refer to selector to ascertain whether these rules are applicable.

DEFINITIONS

ARTICLE 1 COUNCIL REGULATION (EEC) 3820/85

PERMISSIBLE MAXIMUM WEIGHT

Means the maximum authorised operating weight of the vehicle fully laden.

DRIVER

Means any person who drives the vehicle even for a short period, or who is carried in the vehicle in order to be available for driving if necessary.

WEEK

Means the period between 00.00 hours on Monday and 24.00 hours on Sunday.

REGULAR PASSENGER SERVICES

Means national and international services which provide for the carriage of passengers at specified intervals along specified routes, passengers being taken up and set down at predetermined stopping points.

REST

Means any uninterrupted period of at least one hour during which the driver may freely dispose of his time.

CARRIAGE BY ROAD

Means any journey made on roads open to the public of a vehicle, whether laden or not, used for the carriage of passenger or goods.

RECORDS

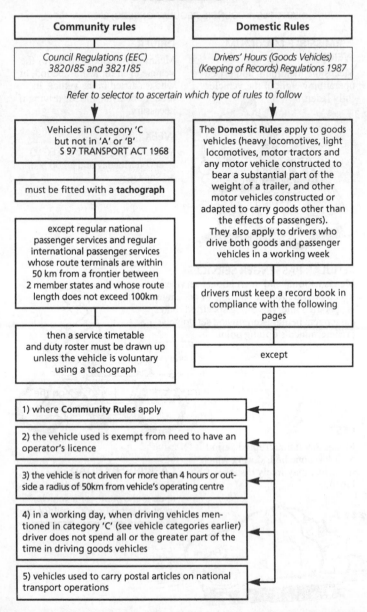

Community rules	Domestic Rules
Council Regulations (EEC) 3820/85 and 3821/85	*Drivers' Hours (Goods Vehicles) (Keeping of Records) Regulations 1987*

Refer to selector to ascertain which type of rules to follow

Vehicles in Category 'C but not in 'A' or 'B' S 97 TRANSPORT ACT 1968	The **Domestic Rules** apply to goods vehicles (heavy locomotives, light locomotives, motor tractors and any motor vehicle constructed to bear a substantial part of the weight of a trailer, and other motor vehicles constructed or adapted to carry goods other than the effects of passengers). They also apply to drivers who drive both goods and passenger vehicles in a working week
must be fitted with a **tachograph**	
except regular national passenger services and regular international passenger services whose route terminals are within 50 km from a frontier between 2 member states and whose route length does not exceed 100km	drivers must keep a record book in compliance with the following pages
then a service timetable and duty roster must be drawn up unless the vehicle is voluntary using a tachograph	except

1) where **Community Rules** apply

2) the vehicle used is exempt from need to have an operator's licence

3) the vehicle is not driven for more than 4 hours or outside a radius of 50km from vehicle's operating centre

4) in a working day, when driving vehicles mentioned in category 'C' (see vehicle categories earlier) driver does not spend all or the greater part of the time in driving goods vehicles

5) vehicles used to carry postal articles on national transport operations

RECORD BOOKS

DRIVERS' HOURS (GOODS VEHICLES) (KEEPING OF RECORDS)
REGULATIONS 1987

RECORD BOOKS

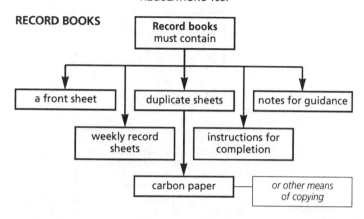

```
                    Record books
                    must contain

a front sheet      duplicate sheets      notes for guidance

         weekly record       instructions for
         sheets              completion

                carbon paper  ──  or other means
                                   of copying
```

ENTRIES

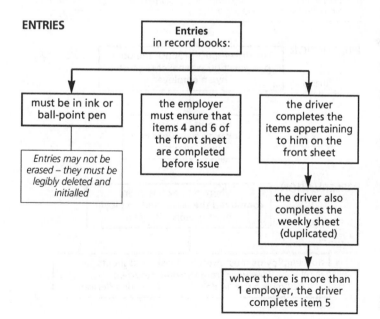

```
                    Entries
                    in record books:

must be in ink or    the employer         the driver
ball-point pen       must ensure that     completes the
                     items 4 and 6 of     items appertaining
                     the front sheet      to him on the
                     are completed        front sheet
                     before issue

Entries may not be                        the driver also
erased – they must be                     completes the
legibly deleted and                       weekly sheet
initialled                                (duplicated)

                                          where there is more than
                                          1 employer, the driver
                                          completes item 5
```

RECORD BOOKS cont

COMPLETED SHEETS

> At the end of a week the whole book is to be delivered to the employer within seven days of being completed

⬇

> the employer shall examine and sign the weekly sheet and duplicate, detach the duplicate and return the book to the driver before he is next on duty

> *If the book was full, the driver retains it for a further 14 days and then returns it to the employer*

> *A new book may not be started until the previous one is full*

PRODUCTION

> The driver must produce the book for inspection whenever requested by an employer

⬇

> he must have the book with him whenever he is on duty

PRESERVATION

> Where a book has been completed the driver and employer must preserve it intact

⬇

> employers must preserve books and sheets for one year from the date returned (following the 14 day drivers' retention period)

RECORD BOOKS continued

DRIVERS' HOURS (GOODS VEHICLES) KEEPING OF RECORDS)
REGULATIONS 1987

Model For Driver's Record Book
a. Front sheet

RECORD BOOK FOR DRIVERS IN ROAD TRANSPORT

1. Date book first used ....

2. Date book last used ....

3. Surname, first name(s), and address of holder of book ....
....
....

4. Name, address, telephone number and stamp (if any) of
employer/under-taking ....
....
....

5. Name, address, telephone number and stamp (if any) of any other
employer(s) ....
....
....

6. Operator's Licence No. (Nos) ....

---

b. Weekly sheet

WEEKLY SHEET							
1. DRIVER'S NAME			2. PERIOD COVERED BY SHEET WEEK COMMENCING (DATE).............................. TO WEEK ENDING (DATE)................................				
DAY ON WHICH DUTY	*REGISTRATION NO OF VEHICLE(S)*	*PLACE WHERE VEHICLE(S) BASED*	*TIME OF GOING ON DUTY*	*TIME OF GOING OFF DUTY*	*TIME SPENT DRIVING*	*TIME SPENT ON DUTY*	*SIGNA-TURE OF DRIVER*
MONDAY							
TUESDAY							
WEDNESDAY							
THURSDAY							
FRIDAY							
SATURDAY							
SUNDAY							
10. CERTIFICATION BY EMPLOYER			I HAVE EXAMINED THE ENTRIES IN THIS SHEET SIGNATURE...				

TACHOGRAPHS

COUNCIL REGULATION 3821/85

In EC countries the tachograph chart replaces the driver's log sheet.

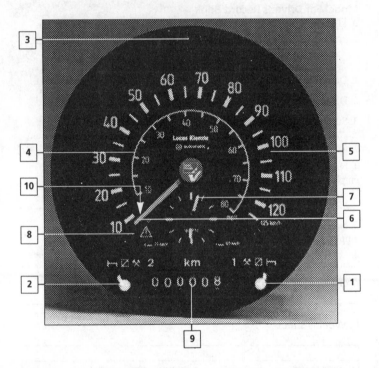

1. Driver work mode selector   **2.** Crew work mode selector   **3.** Lock
4. Miles/hour speed scale   **5.** Kilometres/hour Speed scale
6. Speedometer pointer   **7.** Clock   **8.** Clock operating Indicator
9. Odometer   **10.** RPM pointer

How the tachograph works

A tachograph is a speedometer and mileage counter fitted with a clock and recording mechanism. Instead of filling in a log sheet, the driver writes his name, the date and any other information onto a 'chart' and inserts it into a tachograph which then does the rest. The chart, in the form of a circular disc, is rotated by the clock mechanism and is marked by three sapphire-tipped styli which bear against it.

CHART ANALYSIS

1. Hours divisions. 2. Speed trace. 3. Driver mode: When the stylus is in the drive position and the vehicle is moving, the trace is broader than when the vehicle is stationary. 4. Distance trace: Each complete zig-zag represents 10 km. 5. Chart centre. 6. End of duty/driving. 7. Delay on route. 8. Delivery. 9. Work other than driving. 10. Rest period. 11. Start of duty/driving. 12. Name of driver. 13. Start place. 14. Finish place. 15. Start date. 16. Finish date. 17. Vehicle registration number. 18. Finish odometer reading. 19. Start odometer reading. 20. Total distance travelled (km).

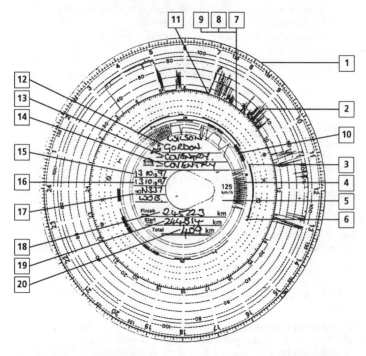

Distance Travelled

This is recorded by the innermost stylus. Every 10 km the stylus oscillates once, so that by counting the peaks, the journey length is measured.

Vehicle Movement

The middle stylus indicates when the vehicle is moving and hence records the hours at the wheel. By turning a knob, the driver can also record how the rest of his time has been apportioned between other work, eg loading and rest periods.

Speed

This is indicated by the outermost stylus and a jagged – as opposed to a smooth – trace indicates heavy use of the break and accelerator. A warning light goes on when a pre-selected speed is exceeded.

TACHOGRAPHS – FITTING/USE

COUNCIL REGULATION (EEC) 3821/85

Requirement

The requirement to install tachographs is brought about by Council Regulation (EEC) 3821/85 on recording equipment in road transport. *(ART 3).*
Refer to previous pages to ascertain which vehicles require tachographs to be fitted.

Type Approval is given by member states for tachographs and model record sheets, and an EC approval mark is issued. *(ARTS 5 & 6)*

Fitting

Tachographs may only be installed or repaired by fitters or workshops approved by the Secretary of State, and each has its special seal, a record of which is kept on a central registry. An installation plaque is then fitted which consists of the letter 'e' followed by the number designated to the member state. *(ART 12)*

Use

Both employers and drivers are responsible for ensuring the equipment works correctly. *(ART 13)*

The employer must issue sufficient suitable record sheets to drivers and the sheets must be kept by the employer for 1 year after their use. The sheets must be produced and handed over if requested by an authorised inspecting office. *(ART 14)*

Record sheets must be used at all times, starting as soon as the vehicle is taken over. Dirty or damaged sheets must not be used. If they become damaged they must be attached to the spare sheets after use. All times must be accurately recorded. *(ART 15)*

Crew members must also complete record sheets with their names, dates and places where the sheet begins and ends, registration number(s) of vehicle(s), odometer reading at the start and end of each journey and of both vehicles if he changes vehicles and the time of such change. *(ART 15(5))*

Where the driver is away from the vehicle and unable to operate the equipment, information relating to 'other periods of work', 'other periods of availability' (waiting time, time beside the driver or in a bunk whilst vehicle in motion) and break and daily rest periods, must be entered on the sheet either manually or automatically. *(ART 15 (2))*

TACHOGRAPHS – FITTING/USE cont

Tachographs and charts in use must be:

Calibrated	by DoT-approved calibration station
Re-calibrated /inspected	every six years or after repair and a simple check every two years
Sealed	by calibration centre's seal. The cables connecting the recording transmitter must be protected by a continuous plastic-coated stainless sheath with crimped ends.
Certified	that it is calibrated by affixing a plaque on or near the tachograph
Produced	by the driver for the current week and the last day of the previous week
Returned	to employer when completed within 21 days
Filed	by employer and kept for 12 months
Repaired	as soon as possible after becoming defective – once it has returned to base, not to be used until repaired. Drivers must mark on the record sheet or on a temporary sheet to be attached to the record sheet, all information not properly recorded by the equipment

Practical points

- Identify the record sheet in such a manner that it can be readily recognised in the future.
- Note odometer reading.
- Note details of calibration plaque.
- Note tyre sizes of tachograph drive axle.
- Check lead seals, note the numbers.
- Be sure, where charts are seized, that they are carefully preserved.
- Note time on tachograph clock, compare it with the true time and note any difference.
- Ensure that the chart has been inserted properly and the **chart** time is not 12 hours out.
- Check that the disc is of the correct type for the tachograph and the correct speed range.

TACHOGRAPH OFFENCES – DRIVER

Offence	Explanation
1. Not fitted	*Using a motor vehicle requiring a tachograph on a road when not fitted with a tachograph in accordance with the regulations, or which has been repaired otherwise than in accordance with 3821/85.*
CONTRARY TO ARTICLE 3, COUNCIL REGULATION (EEC) 3821/85 AND S 97(1)(B) TRANSPORT ACT 1968 AS AMENDED BY PASSENGER AND GOODS VEHICLES (RECORDING EQUIPMENT) REGULATIONS 1979 AND 1989.	
2. Dirty/damaged sheets	*Crew member using dirty or damaged record sheet.*
CONTRARY TO ART 15 (1) COUNCIL REGULATION (EEC) 3821/85 AND S 97 (1)(B) TRANSPORT ACT 1968 AS AMENDED BY PASSENGER AND GOODS VEHICLES (RECORDING EQUIP-MENT) REGULATIONS 1979.	
3. Dirty/damaged sheets	*Driver failing to attach dirty or damaged record sheet to duplicate Record Sheet.*
CONTRARY TO ARTICLE 15, COUNCIL REGULATIONS (EEC) 3821/85 AND S 97 (1)(B) TRANSPORT ACT 1968, AS AMENDED	
4. Not running	*Driver failing to ensure that Recording Equipment is running continuously from the time he took over the vehicle until relieved of responsibility.*
CONTRARY TO ARTICLE 15(2), COUNCIL REGULATION (EEC) 3821/85 AND S 97 (1)(B) TRANSPORT ACT 1968, AS AMENDED	
5. Time incorrect	*Driver failing to ensure that the time on the clock is correct for the country in which the vehicle is registered.*
CONTRARY TO ARTICLE 15(3), COUNCIL REGULATION (EEC) 3821/85 AND S 97(1)(B) TRANSPORT ACT 1968 AS AMENDED	
6. Improperly operated	*Driver failing to operate the switch mechanism to change to:* *– driving time* *– other periods of work* *– breaks from work and rest periods* *– other periods of availability* *– delete which is not applicable*
CONTRARY TO ARTICLE 15(3), COUNCIL REGULATION (EEC) 3821/85 AND S 97 (1)(B) TRANSPORT ACT 1968 AS AMENDED	

continued on next page

TACHOGRAPH OFFENCES – DRIVER
cont

Offence	Explanation
7. Entering information	Driver failing to enter information of any of the following details on the face of the record sheet: – surname and first name of driver – date and place sheet is first used also where it ends and date – registered number of vehicle and other vehicles used – odometer reading, start and end, and time of any change of vehicle.
CONTRARY TO ARTICLE 15 (5) REGULATION (EEC) 3821/85 AND S 97 (1) (B) TRANSPORT ACT 1968 AS AMENDED	
8. Production	Driver failing to produce record sheets of the current week and the last day of the previous week.
CONTRARY TO ARTICLE 15(7), COUNCIL REGULATION (EEC) 3821/85 AND S 97 (1)(B) TRANSPORT ACT 1968, AS AMENDED	
9. Written records	Crew member failing to keep a written record if tachograph is unserviceable or defective.
CONTRARY TO ARTICLE 16(2), COUNCIL REGULATION (EEC) 3821/85 AND S 97 (1)(B) TRANSPORT ACT 1968, AS AMENDED	
10. Written records	Driver failing to keep records.
CONTRARY TO ARTICLE 15(2), COUNCIL REGULATION (EEC) 3821/85 AND S. 97(1)(C) TRANSPORT ACT 1968, AS AMENDED	
11. Handing in	Driver failing to hand in previous record sheets after 21 days.
CONTRARY TO S 97A (1)(A), TRANSPORT ACT 1968, AS AMENDED	
12. Notification	Driver who was employed by two or more employers failing to notify each or all of the other employers detailed.
CONTRARY TO S 97A (1)(B), TRANSPORT ACT 1968, AS AMENDED	
13. Inspection	Driver failing to allow record sheets to be examined by Inspecting Officer.
CONTRARY TO S 99(4)(A), TRANSPORT ACT 1968 AS AMENDED	
14. Inspection	Driver failing to allow Inspecting Officer entry into vehicle for the purpose of examining record sheets.
CONTRARY TO S 99(4)(A), TRANSPORT ACT 1968, AS AMENDED	
15. Seals etc	Driver failing to ensure that equipment functions correctly and seals remain intact.
CONTRARY TO ARTICLE 13, COUNCIL REGULATION (EEC) 3821/85 AND S 97 (1) (B) TRANSPORT ACT 1968, AS AMENDED	

TACHOGRAPH OFFENCES – EMPLOYER

Offence	Explanation
1. Use etc	*Use, cause or permit any of offences 1 – 11 (see previous pages) committed by a driver.*
2. Supply	*Employer failing to issue sufficient number of record sheets (2 days' supply).*
CONTRARY TO ARTICLE 14 (1) COUNCIL REGULATION (EEC) 3821/85 AND S 97 (1)(B) TRANSPORT ACT 1968, AS AMENDED	
3. Retain	*Employer failing to retain record sheets (discs) for period of 12 months after use.*
CONTRARY TO ARTICLE 14(2), COUNCIL REGULATION (EEC) 3821/85 AND S 97(1)(B) TRANSPORT ACT 1968, AS AMENDED	
4. Inspection	*Employer failing to produce or hand over for inspection any records required to be kept.*
CONTRARY TO ARTICLE 14(2), REGULATION (EEC) 3851/85 AND S 97 (1)(B) TRANSPORT ACT 1968, AS AMENDED	
5. Not fitted	*Employer failing to fit tachograph in accordance with Regulations, or which has been repaired otherwise than in accordance with Art 16(1) of Council Regulation (EEC) 3821/85.*
CONTRARY TO S 97 (1)(A), TRANSPORT ACT 1968, AS AMENDED	
6. Inspection	*Employer failing to allow Inspecting Officer (including PC) to enter premises for the purpose of examining records, sheets, discs or vehicles.*
CONTRARY TO S 99(4), TRANSPORT ACT 1968, AS AMENDED	

Note: All above are summary offences with level 4 penalty and not endorsable, except that number 6 attracts a level 3 penalty.

TACHOGRAPH OFFENCES – GENERAL

SECTION 97AA TRANSPORT ACT 1968

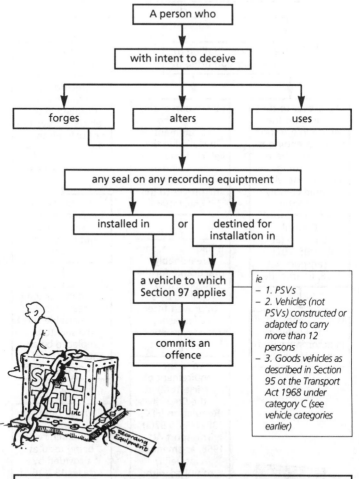

A person who

↓

with intent to deceive

↓

| forges | alters | uses |

↓

any seal on any recording equiptment

↓

| installed in | or | destined for installation in |

↓

a vehicle to which Section 97 applies

ie
- *1. PSVs*
- *2. Vehicles (not PSVs) constructed or adapted to carry more than 12 persons*
- *3. Goods vehicles as described in Section 95 ot the Transport Act 1968 under category C (see vehicle categories earlier)*

↓

commits an offence

↓

These are offences triable either way and the offender shall be liable on summary conviction to a fine not exceeding the statutory maximum (currently £5,000) or on conviction on indictment to imprisonment for a term not exceeding two years.

TACHOGRAPH DEFENCES

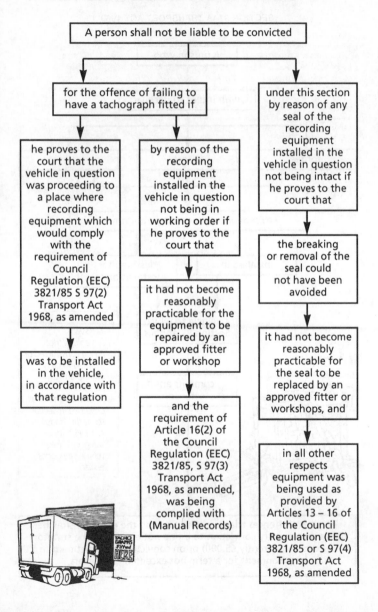

A person shall not be liable to be convicted

for the offence of failing to have a tachograph fitted if

he proves to the court that the vehicle in question was proceeding to a place where recording equipment which would comply with the requirement of Council Regulation (EEC) 3821/85 S 97(2) Transport Act 1968, as amended

was to be installed in the vehicle, in accordance with that regulation

by reason of the recording equipment installed in the vehicle in question not being in working order if he proves to the court that

it had not become reasonably practicable for the equipment to be repaired by an approved fitter or workshop

and the requirement of Article 16(2) of the Council Regulation (EEC) 3821/85, S 97(3) Transport Act 1968, as amended, was being complied with (Manual Records)

under this section by reason of any seal of the recording equipment installed in the vehicle in question not being intact if he proves to the court that

the breaking or removal of the seal could not have been avoided

it had not become reasonably practicable for the seal to be replaced by an approved fitter or workshops, and

in all other respects equipment was being used as provided by Articles 13 – 16 of the Council Regulation (EEC) 3821/85 or S 97(4) Transport Act 1968, as amended

TACHOGRAPH IRREGULARITIES

Problem	Cause
Speed stylus records below base line	Stylus bent to obtain lower speed recording. To obtain correct readings add the k/m below the line.
Breaks in distance trace	Driven with head open.
Interrupted recordings	Instrument door has been opened. Blank spaces appear because styli were not making contact.
Speed and/or RPM recordings stay at same level for unusually long time	Stylus has been blocked to prevent recordings of high road and/or engine speeds.
	To calculate the average road speed, multiply the mileage by 60 and divide the answer by the travelling time in minutes. The average will be higher than the maximum speed as indicated on the chart.
Overtracing	The chart has been turned back to conceal long breaks, or has not been replaced when completed.
Distance travelled does not correspond with odometer	Change of tyre size, two-speed adaptor or rear axle ratio, without necessary adjustment in the cable drive adaptor.
	An incorrect speed indication will also be shown.
All recordings vertical in same spot	Power supply to clock interrupted or intentionally blocked.

PART 5

MISCELLANEOUS

This section is intended as a 'catch-all' to cater for those aspects of traffic law which do not readily fall within other parts of the book. The major aspects include vehicle testing, drink driving, speed limits and the carriage of dangerous goods.

TESTING ON ROADS

SECTION 67 AND SCHED 2 ROAD TRAFFIC ACT 1988

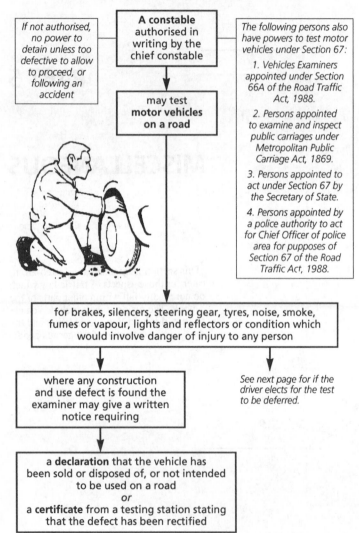

If not authorised, no power to detain unless too defective to allow to proceed, or following an accident

A constable authorised in writing by the chief constable

The following persons also have powers to test motor vehicles under Section 67:

1. Vehicles Examiners appointed under Section 66A of the Road Traffic Act, 1988.

2. Persons appointed to examine and inspect public carriages under Metropolitan Public Carriage Act, 1869.

3. Persons appointed to act under Section 67 by the Secretary of State.

4. Persons appointed by a police authority to act for Chief Officer of police area for pupposes of Section 67 of the Road Traffic Act, 1988.

may test motor vehicles on a road

for brakes, silencers, steering gear, tyres, noise, smoke, fumes or vapour, lights and reflectors or condition which would involve danger of injury to any person

where any construction and use defect is found the examiner may give a written notice requiring

See next page for if the driver elects for the test to be deferred.

a **declaration** that the vehicle has been sold or disposed of, or not intended to be used on a road
or
a **certificate** from a testing station stating that the defect has been rectified

Continued from previous page...

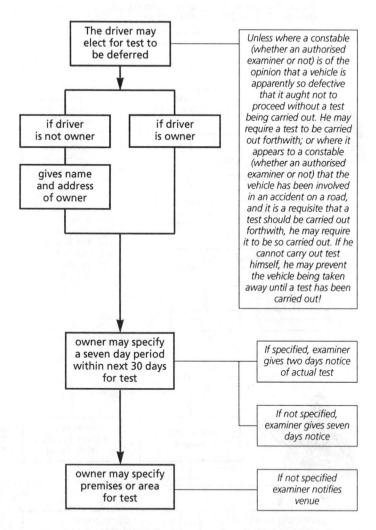

The driver may elect for test to be deferred

Unless where a constable (whether an authorised examiner or not) is of the opinion that a vehicle is apparently so defective that it aught not to proceed without a test being carried out. He may require a test to be carried out forthwith; or where it appears to a constable (whether an authorised examiner or not) that the vehicle has been involved in an accident on a road, and it is a requisite that a test should be carried out forthwith, he may require it to be so carried out. If he cannot carry out test himself, he may prevent the vehicle being taken away until a test has been carried out!

if driver is not owner

if driver is owner

gives name and address of owner

owner may specify a seven day period within next 30 days for test

If specified, examiner gives two days notice of actual test

If not specified, examiner gives seven days notice

owner may specify premises or area for test

If not specified examiner notifies venue

It is an offence to obstruct an authorised constable, (or authorised examiners) or to fail to comply with a lawful requirement.

TESTING ON PREMISES

REG 74 ROAD VEHICLES (CONSTRUCTION AND USE) REGULATIONS 1986
REG 28 ROAD VEHICLES LIGHTING REGULATIONS 1989

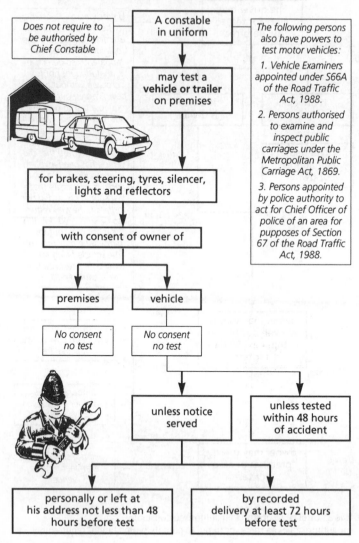

Does not require to be authorised by Chief Constable

A constable in uniform

The following persons also have powers to test motor vehicles:

1. Vehicle Examiners appointed under S66A of the Road Traffic Act, 1988.

may test a **vehicle or trailer** on premises

2. Persons authorised to examine and inspect public carriages under the Metropolitan Public Carriage Act, 1869.

3. Persons appointed by police authority to act for Chief Officer of police of an area for pupposes of Section 67 of the Road Traffic Act, 1988.

for brakes, steering, tyres, silencer, lights and reflectors

with consent of owner of

premises

vehicle

No consent no test

No consent no test

unless notice served

unless tested within 48 hours of accident

personally or left at his address not less than 48 hours before test

by recorded delivery at least 72 hours before test

REMOVAL OF VEHICLES

REGS 3 AND 4 REMOVAL AND DISPOSAL OF VEHICLES REGULATIONS 1986
SECTION 91 ROAD TRAFFIC OFFENDERS ACT 1988

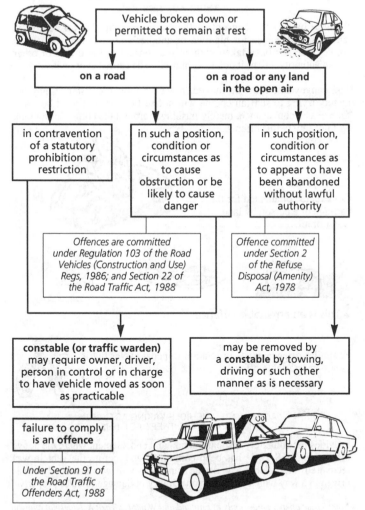

Vehicle broken down or
permitted to remain at rest

on a road

**on a road or any land
in the open air**

in contravention
of a statutory
prohibition or
restriction

in such a position,
condition or
circumstances as
to cause
obstruction or be
likely to cause
danger

in such position,
condition or
circumstances as
to appear to have
been abandoned
without lawful
authority

*Offences are committed
under Regulation 103 of the Road
Vehicles (Construction and Use)
Regs, 1986; and Section 22 of
the Road Traffic Act, 1988*

*Offence committed
under Section 2
of the Refuse
Disposal (Amenity)
Act, 1978*

constable (or traffic warden)
may require owner, driver,
person in control or in charge
to have vehicle moved as soon
as practicable

may be removed by
a **constable** by towing,
driving or such other
manner as is necessary

failure to comply
is an **offence**

*Under Section 91 of
the Road Traffic
Offenders Act, 1988*

*Note: Reference to traffic wardens having power under reg 3 (above) to require
vehicle to be removed only applies in England and Wales.*

TAKING A CONVEYANCE WITHOUT AUTHORITY

THEFT ACT 1968

Without having the consent of the owner or other lawful authority, taking a conveyance for his own or another's use. Or knowing that a conveyance has been taken without the consent of the owner or other lawful authority, drives it or allows himself to be carried in or on it.

The conveyance must be moved, however short the distance may be, merely trying to start an engine will not suffice. Also, it must be taken for use as a conveyance, merely pushing it around the corner for a prank will not satisfy this offence.

S 12(1)

Conveyance

Constructed or adapted for the carriage of a person by land, water or air.

● This is an arrestable offence

A similar offence exists in relation to pedal cycles but it is not an arrestable offence.

S 12(5)

AGGRAVATED VEHICLE-TAKING ACT 1992
adds S 12A TO THE THEFT ACT 1968.

Provides for obligatory disqualification and endorsement where the above offence under S 12(1) has been committed and, before the vehicle was recovered, the vehicle was driven dangerously or was damaged or was driven in a way which led to personal injury or damage to other property.

Note: These offences only apply in England and Wales (as Theft Act does not apply to Scotland) – Scots officers should consult Section 178 of the Road Traffic Act, 1988; Re: Taking of Motor Vehicles without Consent etc.

VEHICLE INTERFERENCE

SECTION 9 CRIMINAL ATTEMPTS ACT 1981

A person is guilty of this offence if he interferes with

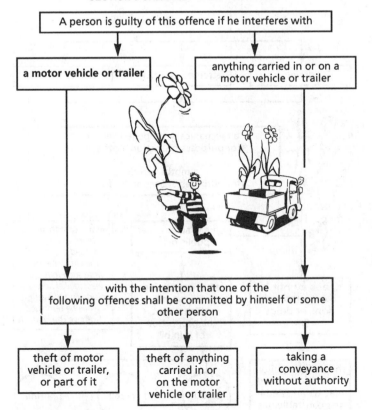

a motor vehicle or trailer

anything carried in or on a
motor vehicle or trailer

with the intention that one of the
following offences shall be committed by himself or some
other person

theft of motor
vehicle or trailer,
or part of it

theft of anything
carried in or
on the motor
vehicle or trailer

taking a
conveyance
without authority

**Any arrest must be in accordance with the
Police and Criminal Evidence Act 1984**

Note:
1. The above legislation is only applicable to England and Wales.
*2. A person may still be guilty of an offence under S 25 of the Road Traffic Act 1988,
if, while a motor vehicle is on a road or local authority parking place, he gets onto
the vehicle or tampers with the brakes or other parts of its mechanism.*

DRINK/DRIVING

SECTIONS 4 AND 5 ROAD TRAFFIC ACT 1988

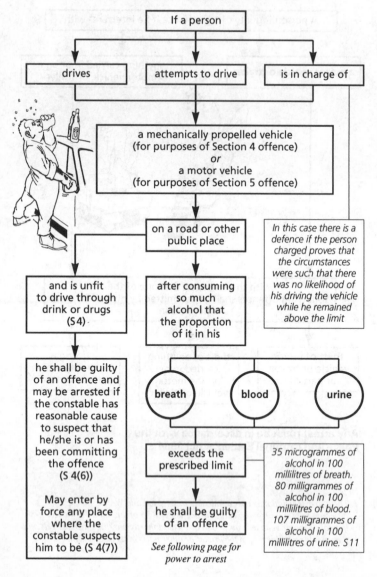

If a person

drives — attempts to drive — is in charge of

a mechanically propelled vehicle
(for purposes of Section 4 offence)
or
a motor vehicle
(for purposes of Section 5 offence)

on a road or other public place

In this case there is a defence if the person charged proves that the circumstances were such that there was no likelihood of his driving the vehicle while he remained above the limit

and is unfit to drive through drink or drugs (S 4)

after consuming so much alcohol that the proportion of it in his

breath — blood — urine

he shall be guilty of an offence and may be arrested if the constable has reasonable cause to suspect that he/she is or has been committing the offence (S 4(6))

May enter by force any place where the constable suspects him to be (S 4(7))

exceeds the prescribed limit

he shall be guilty of an offence

*35 microgrammes of alcohol in 100 millilitres of breath.
80 milligrammes of alcohol in 100 millilitres of blood.
107 milligrammes of alcohol in 100 millilitres of urine. S 11*

See following page for power to arrest

BREATH TESTS

SECTION 6 ROAD TRAFFIC ACT 1988

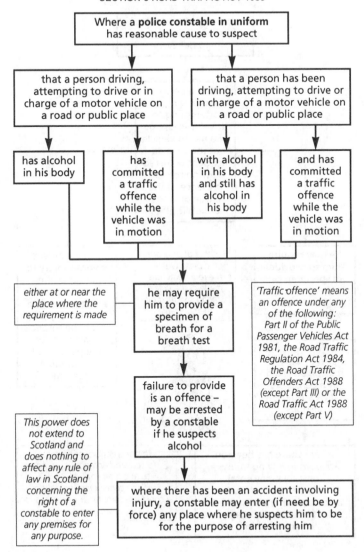

Where a **police constable in uniform** has reasonable cause to suspect

that a person driving, attempting to drive or in charge of a motor vehicle on a road or public place

that a person has been driving, attempting to drive or in charge of a motor vehicle on a road or public place

has alcohol in his body

has committed a traffic offence while the vehicle was in motion

with alcohol in his body and still has alcohol in his body

and has committed a traffic offence while the vehicle was in motion

either at or near the place where the requirement is made

he may require him to provide a specimen of breath for a breath test

'Traffic offence' means an offence under any of the following: Part II of the Public Passenger Vehicles Act 1981, the Road Traffic Regulation Act 1984, the Road Traffic Offenders Act 1988 (except Part III) or the Road Traffic Act 1988 (except Part V)

failure to provide is an offence – may be arrested by a constable if he suspects alcohol

This power does not extend to Scotland and does nothing to affect any rule of law in Scotland concerning the right of a constable to enter any premises for any purpose.

where there has been an accident involving injury, a constable may enter (if need be by force) any place where he suspects him to be for the purpose of arresting him

BREATH TESTS continued

SECTION 6 ROAD TRAFFIC ACT 1988

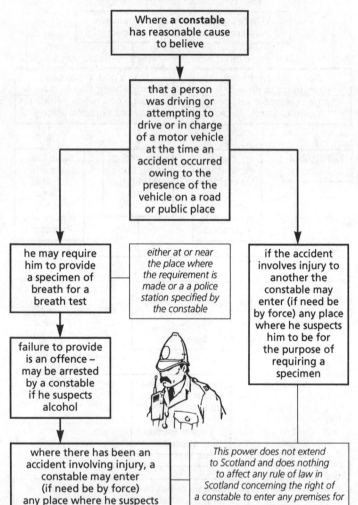

Where **a constable** has reasonable cause to believe

that a person was driving or attempting to drive or in charge of a motor vehicle at the time an accident occurred owing to the presence of the vehicle on a road or public place

he may require him to provide a specimen of breath for a breath test

either at or near the place where the requirement is made or a a police station specified by the constable

if the accident involves injury to another the constable may enter (if need be by force) any place where he suspects him to be for the purpose of requiring a specimen

failure to provide is an offence – may be arrested by a constable if he suspects alcohol

where there has been an accident involving injury, a constable may enter (if need be by force) any place where he suspects him to be for the purpose of arresting him

This power does not extend to Scotland and does nothing to affect any rule of law in Scotland concerning the right of a constable to enter any premises for any purpose.

SPECIMENS – VENUE

SECTION 7 ROAD TRAFFIC ACT 1988

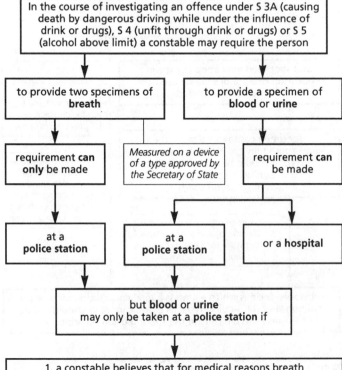

In the course of investigating an offence under S 3A (causing death by dangerous driving while under the influence of drink or drugs), S 4 (unfit through drink or drugs) or S 5 (alcohol above limit) a constable may require the person

to provide two specimens of **breath**

to provide a specimen of **blood** or **urine**

requirement **can only** be made

Measured on a device of a type approved by the Secretary of State

requirement **can** be made

at a **police station**

at a **police station**

or a **hospital**

but **blood** or **urine** may only be taken at a **police station** if

1. a constable believes that for medical reasons breath cannot or should not be required.
2. a reliable device is not available at the police station or it is not practicable to use such a device there.
3. offence under S 3A or 4 is involved and medical practitioner advised that the condition of the person might be due to some drug.

A request may then be made even where the person has already provided or been required to provide two specimens of breath.

Note: All motorists judged by the Intoximeter to be over the limit, and those who fail to give a sample of breath, have the option of giving a blood test.

SPECIMENS – PROCEDURE

SECTIONS 8 AND 9 ROAD TRAFFIC ACT 1988

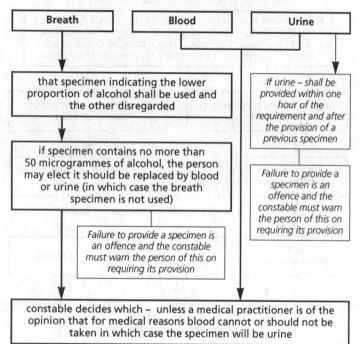

HOSPITALS

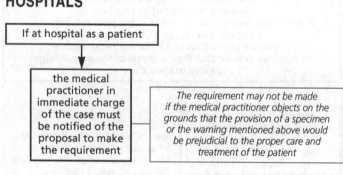

SPEED LIMITS

ROAD TRAFFIC REGULATION ACT 1984

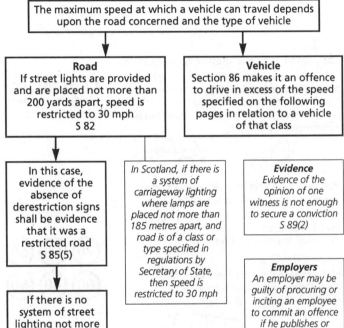

The maximum speed at which a vehicle can travel depends upon the road concerned and the type of vehicle

Road
If street lights are provided and are placed not more than 200 yards apart, speed is restricted to 30 mph
S 82

Vehicle
Section 86 makes it an offence to drive in excess of the speed specified on the following pages in relation to a vehicle of that class

In this case, evidence of the absence of derestriction signs shall be evidence that it was a restricted road
S 85(5)

In Scotland, if there is a system of carriageway lighting where lamps are placed not more than 185 metres apart, and road is of a class or type specified in regulations by Secretary of State, then speed is restricted to 30 mph

Evidence
*Evidence of the opinion of one witness is not enough to secure a conviction
S 89(2)*

If there is no system of street lighting not more than 200 yards (185 metres in Scotland) apart then there must be traffic signs

Employers
An employer may be guilty of procuring or inciting an employee to commit an offence if he publishes or issues a time-table or schedule or gives directions to complete a journey within such a time as cannot be achieved without exceeding the speed limit. S 89(4)

SPEED LIMITS continued

SECTION 86 AND SCHED 6 ROAD TRAFFIC REGULATION ACT 1984

Cars, small vans and dual-purpose vehicles

This limit was set by the 70 mph, 60 mph and 50 mph (Temporary Speed Limit) Order 1977, which was continued indefinitely by SI 1978 No 1548. The limit refers to all vehicles unless a lesser one applies.

Passenger vehicle, motor caravan or dual purpose vehicle without trailer

uw over 3.05 tonnes or adapted to carry more than 8 passengers.
a) Overall length n/e 12 metres

b) Overall length over 12 metres
Note: Coaches which could exceed the motorway limit must be fitted with a governor.

Invalid carriage

Passenger vehicle, motor caravan, car-derived van or dual purpose vehicle drawing one trailer

As above, drawing more than one trailer

SPEED LIMITS continued

SECTION 86 AND SCHED 6 ROAD TRAFFIC REGULATION ACT 1984

Goods vehicle

With max laden weight n/e 7.5 tonnes but which is not an articulated vehicle, or is not drawing a trailer, or is not a car-derived van.

(A 'car-derived van' is a goods vehicle derivative of a passenger vehicle and which has a maximum laden weight not over 200 kg.)

Drawing 1 trailer (other than a car-derived van) – aggregate max. laden weight of both n/e 7.5 tonnes.

Goods vehicle other than a car-derived van drawing more than 1 trailer.

Goods vehicle max. laden weight over 7.5 tonnes not drawing trailer

Goods vehicle drawing 1 trailer with aggregate max. laden weight of vehicle and trailer over 7.5 tonnes.

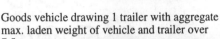

Articulated goods vehicle

Max laden weight n/e 7.5 tonnes.

Max laden weight over 7.5 tonnes

SPEED LIMITS continued

SECTION 86 AND SCHED 6 ROAD TRAFFIC REGULATION ACT 1984

Special types vehicles
Cat I

(60) (50) (40)

Cat II

(40) (35) (30)

Cat III

(30) (25) (20)

Motor tractor
Light or heavy locomotive with required springs
& wings (other than industrial tractor).

(40) (30) (30)

As above drawing 1 trailer also complying with
springs and wings.

(40) (30) (30)

Vehicle and/or trailer as above not complying
with springs and wings.

(20) (20) (20)

Vehicle (and trailer if drawn) where at least one
wheel has a resilient tyre and all other (if any)
have pneumatic tyres.

(20) (20) (20)

Vehicle (or trailer if drawn) where any wheel has
not either a pneumatic or resilient tyre *(does not
apply if track-laying)*.

(5) (5) (5)

Works truck

(18) (18) (18)

Industrial tractor

(N/A) (18) (18)

Agricultural motor vehicle

(40) (40) (40)

Vehicle displaying 'Low Platform Trailer'
plate (LL). *REG 100A RV (CON & USE) REGS 1986*

(40) (40) (40)

Vehicle displaying 'Restricted Speed Vehicle'
plate (50). *REG 100A RV (CON & USE) REGS 1986*

(50) (50) (50)

SPEED LIMITERS

REGS 36A, 36B AND 70A ROAD VEHICLES (CONSTRUCTION AND USE)
REGULATIONS 1986

The following vehicles must be fitted with a device designed to limit the maximum speed by controlling its engine power

Coaches

First used on or after 1.4.74 and before 1.1.88 having a **maximum speed exceeding 70 mph**

or first used on or after 1.1.88, having max gross weight over 7.5 tonnes and **maximum speed exceeding 65 mph**

Goods Vehicles

Having gross weight over 7,500kg but not over 12,000 kg, first used on or after 1.8.92 and **speed exceeding 60 mph**, must have a speed limiter fitted and calibrated to not exceed 60 mph.

If it has a gross weight over 12,000 kg first used on or after 1.1.88 and **speed exceeding 56 mph**, the limiter must be calibrated to not exceed 85 kmh and the stabilised speed of the vehicle must not exceed 90 kmh.

The limiter must be calibrated to a set speed **not exceeding 70 mph or 65 mph** as appropriate and **sealed**

Exemptions relate to a vehicle being taken for a speed limiter to be installed, calibrated, repaired or replaced, or completion of a journey after it has ceased to function

Exemptions relate, in addition to those on the left, to naval, military or air force vehicles; fire, ambulance or police vehicle; or only passing between private premises for not more than 6 miles per week

Note:
1. *The limiter must be maintained in good and efficient working order.*
2. *A plate must be displayed in the driving compartment in a conspicuous position clearly and indelibly marked with the speed at which it has been set.*
3. *The limiter must be sealed to prevent improper interference.*

TRANSPORT OF DANGEROUS GOODS

CARRIAGE OF DANGEROUS GOODS BY ROAD REGULATIONS 1996

Exemptions

Schedule 2 provides a number of exemptions from the regulations. The main ones are listed below but reference should be made to the schedule to ascertain specific technical details.

The regulations do not apply to:
1. A motor vehicle registered outside the U.K. where carriage is restricted to within G.B. and conforms to the provisions of the European Agreement concerning the International Carriage of Dangerous Goods by Road (ADR);
2. An international transport operation conforming with the provisions of ADR;
3. An international transport operation subject to a bilateral or multilateral agreement and the vehicle is owned by, or is under the control of, the armed forces of a country which is a contracting party to the ADR;
4. Certain dangerous goods being carried in an agricultural or forestry tractor, mobile machinery, a vehicle with fewer than 4 wheels, a vehicle with a design speed of 25 mph or less, or a vehicle owned by or under the control of the armed forces;
5. Explosives;
6. Flammable liquid carried in a tank or prover pipe used for the calibration of metering equipment or measurement of petroleum fuel deliveries;
7. Goods used solely in connection with the operation with the vehicle, container or tank;
8. Live animals;
9. Radioactive material;
10. A vehicle not being used for, or in connection with, work;
11. A vehicle used for the internal transfer of goods in private premises;
12. A road construction vehicle.

Definitions

Meaning of 'operator':
1. Of a container or vehicle:
    i)   the person having a place of business in G.B. and at the time has the management of it; or
    ii) if no person satisfies the above, the driver of the vehicle.
2. Of a tank other than the carrying tank of a road tanker
    i)   The person having a place of business in G.B. and who owns the tank;
    ii) If no person satisfies (i), the person having a place of business in G.B. and who acts as agent for the owner;
    iii) If no person satisfies (i) or (ii), the person who, having a place of business in G.B. has management of the tank at that time; or
    iv) if no person satisfies (i), (ii) or (iii), the driver of the vehicle.

Meaning of dangerous goods:
Any explosive, radioactive material, goods listed in a document approved by the Health and Safety Commission, and any other goods which have one or more dangerous properties as listed in Sched 1 to the 1994 Regs.

CARRIAGE OF DANGEROUS GOODS – DUTIES OF THE OPERATOR

Suitability of Vehicles, etc.

Ensure that the requirements relating to the construction and design of vehicles and tanks, and the filling, examination, testing and certification of tanks are complied with.   *REG 6*

Ensure that the container, tank or vehicle is suitable for the carriage of the goods and has been adequately maintained.   *REG 10*

Ensure that the vehicle has no more than one trailer or semi-trailer; is suitably sheeted (or enclosed) if the packages are sensitive to moisture; and that the vehicle or container complies with specific requirements having regard to the type of goods carried.   *REG 10 AND SCHED 7*

Shall not cause or permit the carriage of any dangerous goods in a tank unless a certificate has been issued stating that; the tank has been examined and tested, conforms to an approved design, and is suitable for the intended purpose.   *REG 11*

Consignor's Declaration

Shall not permit the carriage of dangerous goods unless he has obtained a declaration from the consignor stating that the goods are in a fit state to be carried.   *REG 12*

Transport Documentation

Ensure that the driver is in possession of the Transport Documentation, comprising:

a) Information relating to the goods, e.g. designation, classification code, UN number, mass and number of any packages, mass of any container or tank, details of the consignor, and the consignor's declaration;

b) Details of the total mass or volume carried;

c) Emergency action code, where appropriate;

d) Prescribed temperature, where appropriate;

e) Emergency information regarding measures to be taken in the event of an accident.   *REG 14*

Must keep a copy of the information contained in the Transport Documentation (other than emergency information) for 3 months after completion of the journey.   *REG 16*

CARRIAGE OF DANGEROUS GOODS – DUTIES OF THE OPERATOR continued

Display of Information

Ensure that the required information (orange-coloured panels, telephone
number and danger signs) is displayed.   *REG 17*

Shall not cause or permit the display of information if dangerous goods are
not being carried, or which would be likely to confuse the emergency
services.   *REG 17*

Ensure that any panel or sign containing information is kept clean and free
from obstruction.   *REG 17*

Ensure that any panel or sign which does not relate to the goods being
carried is covered or removed.   *REG 17*

Health and Safety

Ensure the manner of loading, stowage and unloading does not create or
increase the risk to health and safety of any person.   *REG 19*

Cleaning

Ensure that vehicles, tanks and containers are cleaned after use.   *REG 19*

Equipment

Ensure that the vehicle is equipped so that the driver can comply with the
instructions contained in the emergency information, and that, if toxic gases
are carried, the crew are supplied with suitable respiratory protective
equipment.   *REG 21*

Ensure that the vehicle is equipped with suitable fire extinguishers.   *REG 23*

Parking

Ensure that when the vehicle is parked it is supervised by a person over
18 years of age or a member of the armed forces, or parked in an isolated
position, having been properly secured.   *REG 24*

CARRIAGE OF DANGEROUS GOODS – DUTIES OF THE DRIVER

Carriage of Passengers

Shall not carry any person in the vehicle other than a crew member.   *REG 12*

Opening of Packages

Shall not open any package unless authorised by the operator.   *REG 12*

Carrying Food

If carrying infectious substances or toxic goods (or if it has done so and has not yet been cleaned) shall not carry food in the vehicle unless it is effectively separated or adequately protected from the risk of contamination.   *REG 12*

Transport Documentation

Ensure that the Transport Documentation (see list under "Duties of Operator") is kept readily on the vehicle and produced on request to a police constable or goods vehicle examiner.   *REG 15*

Where a trailer is detached from the motor vehicle for parking, shall give the Transport Documentation (or copy) to the occupier of the premises and attach a copy to the trailer in a readily visible position.   *REG 15*

Any documentation relating solely to goods which are not being carried must be either removed from the vehicle or placed in a securely closed container clearly marked to show that it does not relate to goods being carried.   *REG 15*

Display of Information

Must not cause or permit any information (orange coloured panels, telephone number and danger sign) to be displayed if dangerous goods are not being carried or if it would be likely to excuse the emergency services.
REG 17

Ensure that any panel or sign is kept clean and free from obstruction. *REG 17*

Any panel or sign displayed which does not relate to the goods being carried must be covered or removed.   *REG 17*

Health and Safety

Ensure the manner of loading, stowage or unloading is not liable to create or increase the risk to health and safety of any person.   *REG 19*

CARRIAGE OF DANGEROUS GOODS – DUTIES OF THE DRIVER continued

Cleaning

Ensure that vehicles, containers and tanks are cleaned after use.   *REG 19*

Use of Tanks

Where B tank is used, it must not be overfilled, and all openings and valves must be securely closed before commencement and during the journey.

REG 19

Emergencies

In the event of an accident or emergency must comply with any instructions laid down in the emergency information and if the situation cannot be brought under immediate control shall notify the emergency services by the quickest possible means.   *REG 22*

Parking

Ensure that when the vehicle is parked, it is supervised by a person over the age of 18 years or a member of the armed forces, or is parked in an isolated position, having been properly secured. When parked, the parking brake must be applied.   *REG 24*

CARRIAGE OF DANGEROUS GOODS – Display of Orange-Coloured Panels

REG 17 & SCHED 10

TYPE OF VEHICLE	INFORMATION REQUIRED	REMARKS
Any vehicle carrying dangerous goods (expect a trailer not attached to a vehicle)	Orange-coloured panel conforming to fig.1	Displayed at the front of vehicle
a vehicle carrying dangerous goods in packages	Orange-coloured panel conforming to fig.1	Displayed at the rear of the vehicle
A vehicle carrying only one type of dangerous goods in a tank	Orange-coloured panel conforming to fig. 2 bearing the appropriate UN number and emergency action code	Displayed at the rear of the vehicle and on both sides of the tank, the frame of the tank, or the vehicle, provided it is immediately below the tank.
A vehicle carrying a multi-load in tanks	Orange-coloured panel conforming to fig.3 bearing the appropriate emergency action code.	Displayed at rear of the vehicle
	Orange-coloured panel conforming to fig. 2 bearing appropriate UN number and emergency action code.	Displayed on both sides of each tank or, where there is more than one compartment, each compartment.
	If deisel, gas oil, heating oil, light petrol, motor spirit, gasoline or kerosene are being carried, the vehicle will be treated as if it was carrying only one type of goods. The UN number and emergency action code will be those for the most hazardous of the goods being carried.	At least one on each side must conform to fig. 2 the remainder conform to fig. 4 bearing the appropriate UN number. They may be displayed on both sides of the frame of each tank or on both sides of the vehicle provided they are immediately below the tank or compartment
A vehicle carrying only one type of goods in bulk in the vehicle or a container.	As for a vehicle carrying only one type of goods in a tank.	
A vehicle carrying a multi-load in bulk in the vehicle or a container	As for a vehicle carrying a multi load in tanks.	

Display of Orange-Coloured Panels continued...

All panels must be rigid, vertical and in the form of a plate. But if a tank container or bulk container the panels may be replaced by orange-coloured self-adhesive sheets or orange-coloured paint provided the material used is weather resistant and durable.

Figure 1:
Orange-coloured
panel

Height not less than
300mm

Base 400mm

All black borders
15mm or less

Figure 2:
Orange-coloured
panel displaying
the emergency
action code and
the UN number

*The emergency action
code shall be inscribed in
the upper half; and the
UN number shall be
inscribed in the lower half*

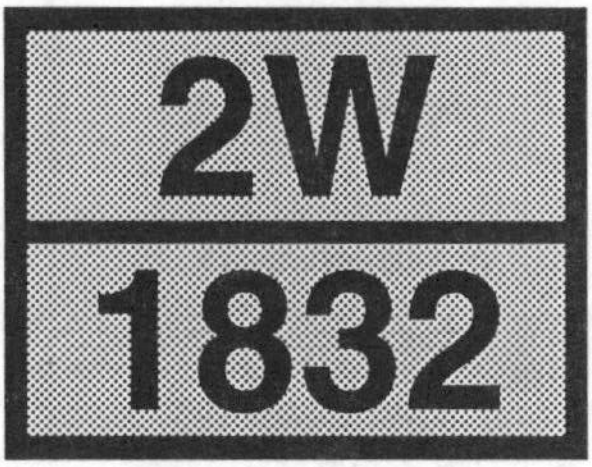

Height not less than
300mm

Base 400mm

All black borders
15mm or less

Horizontal black
line at mid height
of 15mm stroke
width

Figure 3:
Orange-coloured
panel displaying
the emergency
action code

*The emergency action
code shall be inscribed
in the upper half*

Height not less than
300mm

Base 400mm

All black borders
15mm or less

Horizontal black
line at mid height
of 15mm stroke
width

Figure 4:
Orange-coloured
panel displaying
UN number

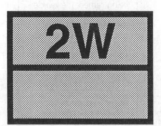

Height not less than
150mm

Base 400mm

All black borders
15mm or less

CARRIAGE OF DANGEROUS GOODS

REG 17 & SCHED 10

Display of Telephone Number

Where dangerous goods are being carried in a tank (or tanks) the telephone number shall be displayed:

a)   at the rear of the vehicle;
b)   on both sides of:
    i)   the tank (or each tank in the case of a multi-load),
    ii)   the frame of the tank(s), or
    iii) the vehicle; and
c)   in the immediate vicinity of the orange coloured panels.

The telephone number shall be black, not less than 30mm high, and on an orange background.

However, the telephone number may be substituted by the words:
    "CONSULT LOCAL DEPOT" or "CONTACT LOCAL DEPOT"
provided:

a)   the name of the operator is clearly marked on the tank or vehicle;
b)   the chief fire officer of every area through which the goods will pass has been notified in writing of the address and telephone number of that local depot; and
c)   each fire officer has agreed in writing to the arrangements.

Display of Danger Signs

Where a vehicle is carrying dangerous goods a danger sign appropriate to those goods (see following page) must be displayed:

a)   if the goods are carried in packages in a container, on at least one side of the container;
b)   if in a tank container or in bulk in a container, on each side of the container;
c)   if in a tank other than a tank container, or if in bulk other than in a container, on each side and at the rear of the vehicle.

Display of Hazard Warning Panels

Instead of individually displaying the orange coloured panels, telephone number and danger signs, the information may be displayed on a hazard warning panel as per the below example.

The emergency action code shall be inscribed in the upper half and the UN number in the lower half of the orange coloured panel and the telephone number (or text as the case may be) beneath the UN number

Width 400mm

Height not less than 300mm

Horizontal black line at mid height of 15mm stroke width

Height not less than 400mm

Al black borders 15mm or less

Width not less than 700mm

DANGEROUS SUBSTANCE SIGNS

CLASSIFICATION	HAZARD WARNING SIGN	CLASSIFICATION	HAZARD WARNING SIGN
Non-flammable compressed gas	COMPRESSED GAS (Green background)	Toxic gas	TOXIC GAS (White background)
Flammable solid	(Red stripes on white)	Flammable gas	FLAMMABLE GAS (Red background)
Spontaneously combustible substance	(White b/g upper) SPONTANEOUSLY COMBUSTIBLE (Red b/g lower)	Flammable liquid	FLAMMABLE LIQUID (Red background)
Substance which in contact with water emits flammable gas	DANGEROUS WHEN WET (Blue background)	Toxic substance	TOXIC (White background)
Oxidising substance	OXIDIZING AGENT (Yellow background)	Harmful substance	(White background)
Organic peroxide	(Yellow background) ORGANIC PEROXIDE	Corrosive substance	CORROSIVE (Black and white)
Multi loads	(White background)	Other dangerous substance	(Black and white)

TRANSPORT OF RADIOACTIVE SUBSTANCES

RADIOACTIVE MATERIAL (ROAD TRANSPORT) (GREAT BRITAIN)
REGULATIONS 1996

The regulations do not apply to:
a) Implantations in the body;
b) International transport operations complying with the European Agreement concerning the International Carriage of Dangerous Goods by Road (ADR);
c) The transport of an Instrument of War on behalf of a U.K. Government Department or visiting forces;
d) Luminous devices for persons or vehicles;
e) Not more than 500 domestic smoke detectors; or
f) Not more than 5 gaseous tritium light devices.   *REG 3*

General Prohibitions

Transporting material is prohibited if:
a) in a Public Service Vehicle;
b) in a vehicle which is carrying explosives;
c) in a package which is damaged, unless the consignor has issued a declaration (which has to be carried on the vehicle) of the damage;
d) the label of any package does not correspond with its contents;
e) the carrier is not the consignor of that material, or does not hold the transport documents for the material (does not apply to material arriving from Northern Ireland and which meets the requirements of N.I. regulations);
f) the material has not been suitably packaged (the schedules to the regulations lay down specific requirements) or, if not required to be packaged does not comply with laid down requirements;
g) the material is liquid, unless in a tank the opening of which is above the level of the liquid, and the pipe connections of the shell walls are below the level of the liquid;
h) when reasonable care has not been exercised by the consignor and carrier to ensure that there will be no injury to health or damage to property or the environment.
i) goods other than radioactive material is being transported in a tank which has at any time contained radioactive material.   *REGS 5 - 9*

Tampering with, and Security of Packages and Labels

1) No person shall wilfully damage, or open without reasonable cause, any package in the course of transport.
2) No person other than the carrier shall remove material from a vehicle whilst in the course of transport, or alter the position of any package in the vehicle except on instructions from the carrier, consignor or consignee, or for reasonable cause.
3) The carrier shall exercise all reasonable care to ensure that the package is secured against unlawful removal and is securely stowed during transport.
4) No person shall remove, without reasonable cause from a package in the course of transport, any label or warning sign or mark required by these regulations, or wilfully deface such.
5) No person shall remove, without reasonable cause any label, notice, placard or plate required to be carried by the vehicle, or wilfully deface such.

RADIOACTIVE SUBSTANCES continued

Duties of the Driver

a) must exercise reasonable care to ensure that none of the material is lost, escapes or is unlawfully removed from the vehicle;

b) must not without reasonable cause leave the vehicle unattended in a public place;

c) shall not park the vehicle anywhere for more than I hour unless there is a clear space of at least 2 metres at both sides and at both ends of the vehicle. (This requirement does not apply if the material is contained in excepted packages, industrial packages, or Type A packages bearing category 1-WHITE labels);

d) must keep on the vehicle until the material has been delivered the documents required to be carried; and

e) shall immediately notify the police and the consignor if:

   i) material has been lost, escapes or has been unlawfully removed from the vehicle; or

   ii) any package has been opened or otherwise damaged; or

   iii) the vehicle has overturned, suffered serious damage, or has been involved in a fire.

Transport Documents

The consignor must give to the carrier or driver the following documents:

a) a **transport document** containing the name, address and telephone number of the consignor; the name and address of the consignee; the shipping name of the material; the U.N. Class Number '7'; the words 'RADIOACTIVE MATERIAL'; the U.N. material number; for low specific activity material, the notation 'LSA-I, II or III' as appropriate; for surface contaminated object, the notation 'SCO-I or II' as appropriate; the name or symbol of each radionuclide; a description of the physical and chemical form of the material; the maximum activity of the radioactive contents; the category of the package, i.e., 'I-WHITE, II-YELLOW or III-YELLOW' according to the radiation level, the lower number indicating a lower level; other technical information; and a declaration by the consignor as to the accuracy of the information given;

b) a **statement** for the carrier:

   i) specifying any action to be taken by the carrier;

   ii) explaining operational instructions for loading, stowage, handling etc.;

   iii) laying down restrictions on the mode of transport or conveyance, and routing instructions; and

   iv) specifying the appropriate emergency arrangements.

Production of Documents

The consignor must keep a copy of the transport document or a copy of the number and type of packages transported for 2 years. A Police Constable, examiner or inspector may require the carrier or driver to produce any documents required to be carried.

Marking Labelling and Placarding

The consignor must:

a) ensure that each package is suitably marked with its gross mass, type of package design, identification mark of package design, and unique serial number; and

RADIOACTIVE SUBSTANCES continued

b) ensure that each package, overpack, tank and freight container bears the appropriate labels (see later) containing information as to contents, maximum radioactivity of contents, transport index (radiation exposure control), and (except tank containers and overpacks) the assigned U.N. number.

The carrier must:
a) ensure that the appropriate placards are displayed (see later); and
b) in addition, ensure that an appropriate 'ADR' plate is displayed, or that a notice in the following form is displayed:

This vehicle is carrying

RADIOACTIVE
MATERIAL

In case of accident get in touch at once with

THE POLICE

and

(particulars of owner/operator of vehicle)

The notice must conform with the following:
a) Not less than 12 cm square. Lettering to be black, bold and legible (embossed or stamped). The word 'RADIOACTIVE' to be not less than 12 mm high and all other capital letters to be not less than 5 mm high;
b) Fireproof;
c) Securely posted in the cab, visible to the driver but not obstructing his view, and only displayed when the vehicle is transporting such material;
d) Contain the name, address and telephone number of the owner (if hired, 'owner' means person in possession) or operator of the vehicle.

Restrictions on Travel in Vehicles

No person shall travel in a vehicle which is transporting radioactive material unless:
a) he is the carrier or has the permission of the carrier;
b) he travels in a personnel compartment; and
c) the material is transported in a goods compartment.

No person except the driver and his assistant(s) may travel in a vehicle transporting a package, overpack, tank or freight container bearing category 'II – YELLOW' or 'III – YELLOW' labels.

Type of vehicle/load	Type of placard	Fitting Requirements
Large freight containers carrying packages other than excepted packages, and tanks	Fig. 5 (4 placards) Alternatively, enlarged Fig. 2, 3 or 4 with min. dimensions as for Fig. 5.	Vertically to each side wall and each end wall.
Unpacked LSA-1 or SCO-1 or packaged commodity with a single U.N number	Either U.N number to be displayed in lower half of Fig 5, or Fig. 6.	Letters to be black and not less than 65 mm high. If Fig. 6 is used, it is to be fitted adjacent to the main placard on all 4 sides of the container or tank.
Vehicle labelled with Fig. 2, 3 or 4	Fig. 5	On each of the 2 external walls and the external rear wall. If no sides, fitted directly to the cargo-carrying unit.
All vehicles transporting radioactive material	Either an "ADR" plate or or a "RADIOACTIVE" notice as previously described. This is in addition to any other placard required.	Inside cab
Type B(U) or B(M) packages so labelled	Fig. 1 trefoil	On the outside of the outermost receptacle. Must be resistant to fire and water.

Figure 1:
Basic trefoil symbol with proportions based on a central circle of radius X. The minimum allowable size of X shall be 4mm.

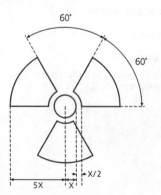

Figure 2:
Category I – WHITE label. The background colour of the label shall be white, the colour of the trefoil and the printing shall be black, and the colour of the category bar shall be red.

Figure 3:
Category II – YELLOW label. The background colour of the upper half of the label shall be yellow and the lower half white, the colour of the trefoil and the printing shall be black, and the colour of the category bars shall be red.

Figure 4:
Category III – YELLOW label. The background colour of the upper half of the label shall be yellow and the lower half white, the colour of the trefoil and the printing shall be black, and the colour of the category bars shall be red.

Figure 5:
Placard. Minimum dimensions are given: when larger dimensions are used the relative proportions must be maintained. The figure '7' shall not be less than 25mm high. The background colour of the upper half of the placard shall be yellow and the lower half white, the colour of the trefoil and the printing shall be black. The use of the word 'RADIOACTIVE' in the bottom half is optional to allow the alternative use of this placard to display the appropriate United Nations Number for the consignment.

Figure 6:
Placard for separate display of the United Nations Number. The background colour of the placard shall be orange and the border and United Nations Number shall be black. The symbol '••••' denotes the space in which the appropriate United Nations Number for radioactive material, as specified in Appendix I, shall be displayed.

THE EMERGENCY ACTION CODE (HAZCHEM CODE)

Hazchem card

| front | back |

Hazchem scale

FOR FIRE OR SPILLAGE

| Hazchem | Issue No 2 |
| UN No | |

1	**JETS**
2	**JETS**
3	**FOAM**
4	**DRY AGENT**

P	V	FULL	
R			
S	V	BA	DILUTE
S		BA for FIRE only	
T		BA	
T		BA for FIRE only	
W	V	FULL	
X			
Y	V	BA	CONTAIN
Y		BA for FIRE only	
Z		BA	
Z		BA for FIRE only	
E		CONSIDER EVACUATION	

Notes for Guidance

FOG
In the absence of fog equipment a fine spray may be used.

DRY AGENT
Water **must not** be allowed to come into contact with the substance at risk.

V
Can be violently or even explosively reactive.

FULL
Full body protective clothing with BA.

BA
Breathing apparatus plus protective gloves.

DILUTE
May be washed to drain with large quantities of water.

CONTAIN
Prevent, by any means available, spillage from entering drains or water course.

I.C.I. EMERGENCY TEL. -
I.C.I. C + P RUNCORN   01928 572000
I.C.I. C + P AVONMOUTH   01272 923601
I.C.I. C + P ESTON GRANGE 01642 452461

For you own protection the following points are worthy of note:

- 'V' is intended to warn against unexpected or possibly hazardous events which could occur due to the ignition of flammable gas, rapid acceleration of combustion due to the involvement of an oxidiser, or the reaction with water, which is itself violent – generating large quantities of steam or flammable gases which may subsequently ignite.

- 'FULL' indicates that the material presents hazards to the skin, eyes and respiratory system. Certain chemicals have the capability of inflicting severe poisoning which could prove fatal when splashed on the skin. If in doubt about a material, seek further advice before approaching too close.

- 'BA' it is probable that the substance will affect the respiratory system and/or eyes. Again – operations room have up-to-date information on most chemicals.

Below is an example of a Tremcard. Such information is readily available in most operations rooms, and advice can be relayed to the officer at the scene of an incident within seconds.

TRANSPORT EMERGENCY CARD (Road)

Cargo   **SODIUM CYANIDE (Solution)**

Usually colourless or yellow solution with perceptible odour.

Nature of Hazard   Severe poisoning perhaps fatal when splashed on skin or swallowed

Contact with an acid may cause toxic fumes: hydrogen cyanide Heating will cause pressure rise with risk of bursting

Protective Devices   Suitable respiratory protective device
Goggles giving complete protection to eyes

Plastic or rubber gloves and boots
Special first aid equipment

EMERGENCY ACTION Notify police and fire brigade immediately

Eyewash bottle with clean water

- Stop the engine
- Mark roads and warn other road users
- Keep public away from danger area
- Keep upwind

- Contain leaking liquid with sand or earth; consult an expert
- Prevent liquid entering sewers, vapour may create toxic atmosphere
- If substance has entered a water course or sewer or contaminated soil or vegetation advise police.

Fire
- Keep containers cool by spraying with water if exposed to fire

First aid
- Special treatment is required. Emergency kit in vehicle's first aid box
- If the substance has got into the eyes, immediately wash out with plenty of water for at least 15 minutes.
- Remove contaminated clothing immediately and wash affected skin with plenty of water
- Seek medical treatment when anyone has symptoms apparently due to swallowing, inhalation or contact with skin or eyes.
- Even if there are no symptoms send to doctor and show him this card.

Additional information provided by manufacturer or sender.

ANIMALS IN TRANSIT

TRANSIT OF ANIMALS (ROAD AND RAIL) ORDER 1975

Is the vehicle carrying:

- cattle?
- horses?
- sheep?
- swine?
- goats?

IF 'YES'

(The following applies for • cattle • horses • sheep • swine • goats)

Loading and unloading
See section A

Carriage
see section B

Construction of vehicles
see section C

Carriage in receptacle
• must not be placed on top of one another *and*
• must be soundly constructed, suitable for the species, labelled, 'upright' indicated, secured to prevent displacement , readily accessible

Feeding and watering
Must be fed and watered at maximum of 12-hour intervals unless whole journey can be completed in 15 hours

IF 'NO'

(The following applies to all other mammals and four-footed beasts • all fish • reptiles • crustaceans • any cold-blooded creatures • poultry and birds of any species)

- Loading and unloading
- carriage
- construction of vehicles

Must not be done in a manner which is likely to cause suffering or injury, eg, by inadequate construction, insecure fittings, contact with obstructions, exposure to weather, inadequate fresh air, overcrowding, or any other cause

Carriage in receptacle
must be soundly constructed, suitable for the species, labelled, 'upright' indicated, secured to prevent displacement , readily accessible

Feeding and watering
Must be adequately fed and watered at suitable intervals

ANIMALS IN TRANSIT
SECTION A – LOADING AND UNLOADING

Unless floor of vehicle is not over 31 cms from the ground, loading and unloading must be by means of

- ramp (either carried on the vehicle or not)
- loading bank
- mechanical lifting gear
- manual lifting or carrying.

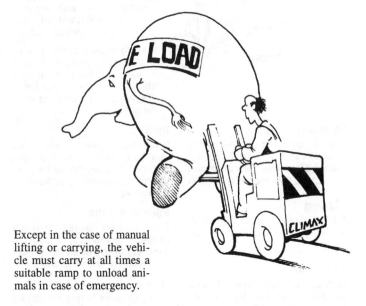

Except in the case of manual lifting or carrying, the vehicle must carry at all times a suitable ramp to unload animals in case of emergency.

To prevent animals falling or injuring limbs, ramps must be fitted with suitable constructed guards not less than 1.3 metres above the ramp. (Does not apply to horse boxes if horse is led from the vehicle

SECTION B – CARRIAGE

Space

The space available, whether divided by partition or not, must not exceed

- sheep   3.1 metres
- swine   3.1 metres
- goats   3.1 metres
- horses   3.7 metres
- calves   2.5 metres
- cattle   such length which will not allow throwing about

Having regard to the size of the animals being carried, if space is not filled to capacity then, to prevent animals being thrown about, partitions must be provided

Partitions

The vehicle must be divided by partitions so that space is not less than 1.27 metres for cattle and horses, and 0.76 metres for others

Lighting

Artificial lighting must be provided to facilitate tending to the animals

Headroom

Each animal must have sufficient headroom, and in the case of horses there must be a minimum of 1.98 metres between floor and roof

Overcrowding

There must be no overcrowding which causes unnecessary suffering or injury

Roof

If more than two floors, sheep may be carried on the top floor without a covering so long as injury or unnecessary suffering is not caused

Injury/suffering

Must not be caused through exposure to weather, inadequate fresh air, falling or escaping from the vehicle or any other cause

Horses

If two or more horses are carried in a undivided vehicle, the hind feet of each animal must be unshod

Each horse must be tied and supported against the motion of the vehicle

Floor

If the floor is not made of an anti-slip material – sand or some other substance must be provided to give foothold

ANIMALS IN TRANSIT
SECTION C – CONSTRUCTION OF VEHICLES

Construction
Must be substantial and capable of withstanding the weight of the animal being thrown against it

Inspection
Apertures must be provided (or doors) together with suitable footholds to facilitate inspection at each floor level from outside the vehicle

Wheel arches
Any wheel arch protruding inside must be covered with permanent shields to prevent injury or suffering

Tying points
Where animals are required to be secured, the vehicle must be equipped with suitable tying points.

Lifting gear
Where there is more than one floor, internal ramps or lifting gear must be carried at all times

Floors
Floors and ramps to be anti-slip or fitted with suitable foot battens.

Partition fittings
To be provided not more than one metre apart along entire length of the body. Does not apply to horse-boxes designed to carry horses facing the front or rear of the vehicle.

Projections
Must be free from sharp edges or projections likely to cause injury or suffering

Electrical fittings
All electrical fittings must be protected to prevent contact with animals.

Ramp barriers
Must be provided with barriers or straps to prevent animals falling from the vehicle when the ramp is lowered

REPORTING OF ACCIDENTS
SECTION 170 ROAD TRAFFIC ACT 1988

IF, OWING TO THE PRESENCE OF A

mechanically propelled vehicle

ON A **road**

AN **accident** OCCURS

WHICH CAUSES

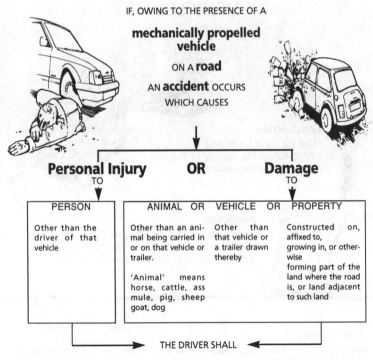

Personal Injury TO	**OR**	**Damage** TO

PERSON	ANIMAL OR	VEHICLE OR	PROPERTY
Other than the driver of that vehicle	Other than an animal being carried in or on that vehicle or trailer. 'Animal' means horse, cattle, ass mule, pig, sheep goat, dog	Other than that vehicle or a trailer drawn thereby	Constructed on, affixed to, growing in, or otherwise forming part of the land where the road is, or land adjacent to such land

THE DRIVER SHALL

STOP

AND IF REQUESTED TO DO SO GIVE HIS NAME AND ADDRESS AND THE
NAME AND ADDRESS OF THE OWNER OF THE VEHICLE AND PARTICULARS OF THE
VEHICLE TO ANY PERSON HAVING GROUNDS FOR REQUIRING   S 170(2)

IF HE DOESN'T GIVE HIS NAME AND ADDRESS HE MUST
AS SOON AS PRACTICABLE AND IN ANY CASE WITHIN 24 HOURS

report to the police   S 170(3) AND (6)

IF THE ACCIDENT INVOLVES PERSONAL INJURY HE MUST ALSO

PRODUCE INSURANCE
AT THE TIME OF THE ACCIDENT OR, IF HE FAILS TO DO SO,
TO THE POLICE AS SOON AS REASONABLY PRACTICABLE AND, IN ANY CASE,
WITHIN 24 HOURS (But he will not be guilty of the offence of failing to produce
the insurance if he does so within 7 days).   S 170(5) AND (6)

POWERS OF ARREST WITHOUT WARRANT

SECTION 24 POLICE AND CRIMINAL EVIDENCE ACT 1984

ANY PERSON MAY ARREST

Anyone who is in the act of committing an arrestable offence	Where an arrestable offence has been committed: ● anyone who is guilty of the offence ● anyone whom he/she has reasonable grounds for suspecting to be guilty of it	anyone whom he/she has reasonable grounds for suspecting to be committing an arrestable offence

A constable may arrest

where he has reasonable grounds for suspecting an arrest offence has been committed – anyone who he has reasonable grounds for suspecting to be guilty of the offence	Anyone who is about to commit an arrestable offence or whom he has reasonable grounds for suspecting to be about to commit an arrestable offence*

Note:
* Arrestable offence (see following page).
Note: Not applicable to Scotland.

ARRESTABLE OFFENCE

Arrestable offence means:

- Offences for which the sentence is fixed by law.

- Offences for which a person of 21 years of age or over (not previously convicted) may be sentenced to imprisonment for a term of five years or more.

- Committing: conspiring to commit; attempting to commit; or inciting; aiding, abetting, counselling or procuring any of the following offences:

- offences for which a person may be arrested under the Customs and Excise Acts, as defined in S 1(1) of the Customs and Excise Management Act 1979;

- offences under the Official Secrets Act – that are not arrestable offences by virtue of the term of imprisonment for which a person may be sentences in respect of them;

- offences under Ss 14 (indecent assault on a woman), 22 (causing prostitution of women, or 23 (procuration of girl under 21) of the Sexual Offences Act 1956;

- Offences under S 12(1) (taking motor vehicle or other conveyance without authority etc)

or S 25(1) (going equipped for stealing etc) of the Theft Act 1968; and

- offences under S 1 of the Public Bodies Corrupt Practices Act 1889 (corruption in office) or S 1 of the prevention of Corruption Act 1906 (corrupt transactions with agents)

- offences under the Football (Offences) Act 1991

- offences of publishing obscene matter (Obscene Publications Act 1959, S 2) or indecent photographs of children (Protection of Children Act 1978, S 1) or publishing etc material likely to cause racial hatred (Public Order Act 1986, S 19).

Note: Not applicable to Scotland.

POWERS OF ARREST WITHOUT WARRANT

SECTIONS 24 AND 25 POLICE AND CRIMINAL EVIDENCE ACT 1984

Note – not applicable for an arrestable offence

> Where **a constable** has reasonable grounds to suspect

> that any offence which is not an arrestable offence has been or is being committed or attempted

> he may arrest the relevant person *

> if it appears to him that service of a summons is impracticable or inappropriate

> because any of the general arrest conditions ** is satisfied

Notes

The relevant person *

Any person whom the constable has reasonable grounds to suspect of having committed, or having attempted to commit, or of being in the course of committing or attempting to commit the offence.

General arrest conditions **

See opposite.

Not applicable to Scotland.

GENERAL ARREST CONDITIONS

SECTION 25 POLICE AND CRIMINAL EVIDENCE ACT 1984

Identify

> That the name of the relevant person is unknown to, and cannot be readily ascertained by, the constable; or
>
> That the constable has reasonable grounds for doubting whether a name furnished by the relevant person as his name, is his real name

Address for service

> That the relevant person has failed to furnish a satisfactory address for service; or
>
> that the constable has reasonable grounds for doubting whether an address furnished by the relevant person is a satisfactory address for service

> 'Satisfactory for service' means that the relevant person will be at that address sufficiently long to serve a summons; or that some other specified person will accept service for him.

Preventative measures

> That the constable has reasonable grounds for believing that arrest is necessary to prevent the relevant person:
> - causing physical injury to himself or any other person;
> - suffering physical injury;
> - causing loss of, or damage to, property;
> - committing an offence against public decency where members of the public could not be expected to avoid him;
> - causing an unlawful obstruction on the highway.

Protection

> That the constable has reasonable grounds for believing that arrest is necessary to protect a child or other vulnerable person from the relevant person.

Not applicable to Scotland.

MODE OF ARREST

SECTIONS 28 AND 30 POLICE AND CRIMINAL EVIDENCE ACT 1984

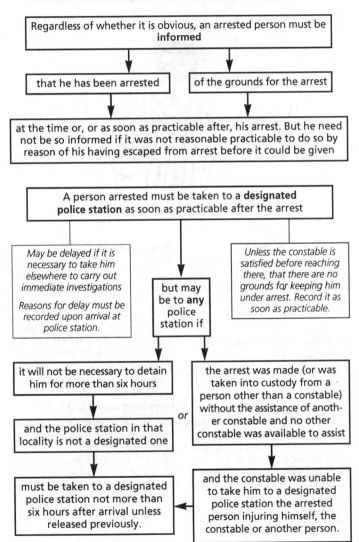

Regardless of whether it is obvious, an arrested person must be **informed**

that he has been arrested

of the grounds for the arrest

at the time or, or as soon as practicable after, his arrest. But he need not be so informed if it was not reasonable practicable to do so by reason of his having escaped from arrest before it could be given

A person arrested must be taken to a **designated police station** as soon as practicable after the arrest

May be delayed if it is necessary to take him elsewhere to carry out immediate investigations

Reasons for delay must be recorded upon arrival at police station.

but may be to **any** police station if

Unless the constable is satisfied before reaching there, that there are no grounds for keeping him under arrest. Record it as soon as practicable.

it will not be necessary to detain him for more than six hours

and the police station in that locality is not a designated one

or

the arrest was made (or was taken into custody from a person other than a constable) without the assistance of another constable and no other constable was available to assist

must be taken to a designated police station not more than six hours after arrival unless released previously.

and the constable was unable to take him to a designated police station the arrested person injuring himself, the constable or another person.

Not applicable to Scotland.

ROAD CHECKS

SECTION 4 POLICE AND CRIMINAL EVIDENCE ACT 1984

Under certain circumstances, a police constable needs authority to carry out a road check

What is a road check?

The exercise in a locality of the power conferred by S 163 of the Road Traffic Act 1988, to stop either all vehicles or vehicles selected by any criterion

What type of check needs to be authorised?

Where it is necessary to ascertain whether a vehicle is carrying:
- a person who has committed a serious arrestable offence (other than a traffic or excise offence) and may be in the locality
- a person who is a witness to a serious arrestable offence
- a person who intends to commit a serious arrestable offence and may be in the locality
- a person who is unlawfully at large any may be in the locality

Who can authorise it?

Normally a Superintendent must authorise it in writing. But may be authorised by an officer below that rank as a matter of urgency, in which case, as soon as practicable, he must make a written record of the time he gives it and cause a Superintendent to be informed

The locality at which the check is to be carried out must be specified

How long may it last?

The Superintendent or above (not below) must specify a period, not exceeding seven days, during which it may take place (may be renewed in writing). He may direct whether it shall be continuous or conducted at specified times

Not applicable to Scotland.

STOP AND SEARCH

Serious Violence

Where a Superintendent or above (or inspector if incident is imminent) reasonably believes that incidents involving serious violence may take place in his area and it is expedient to prevent their occurrence he may authorise (in writing) stopping and searching of persons and vehicles in that locality for a period not exceeding 24 hours for offensive weapons or dangerous instruments. Constable in uniform may stop any person or vehicle and make any search he thinks fit whether or not he has any grounds for suspecting that weapons or articles of that kind are present.

S 60 CRIMINAL JUSTICE AND PUBLIC ORDER ACT 1994

Prevention of Terrorism

Where it appears to an officer of the rank of Commander/Assistant Chief Constable that it is expedient in order to prevent acts of terrorism (connected with Northern Ireland or of any description but not connected solely with the affairs of the UK) he may authorise the stopping and searching of person or vehicles (including ships and aircraft) for up to 28 days in a specified locality. In the exercise of these powers a constable may stop any vehicle or person and make any search he thinks fit whether or not he has any grounds for suspecting that articles of terrorism are being carried.

S 81 CRIMINAL JUSTICE AND PUBLIC ORDER ACT 1994

Raves – stopping persons from attending

If a constable in uniform reasonable believes that a person is on his way to a gathering to which S 63, Criminal Justice and Public Order Act 1994 applies, and in respect of which a direction is in force, he may stop that person and direct him not to proceed in the direction of that gathering. This power may be exercised within five miles of the boundary of the site of the gathering. Failure to comply is an offence and a constable in uniform who reasonably suspects that person is committing the offence may arrest him without warrant

S 65 CRIMINAL JUSTICE AND PUBLIC ORDER ACT 1994

TAXI TOUTS

SECTION 167 CRIMINAL JUSTICE AND PUBLIC ORDER ACT 1994

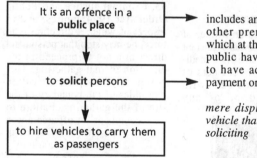

It is an offence in a **public place** → includes any highway and any other premises or place to which at the material time the public have or are permitted to have access, whether on payment or otherwise

to **solicit** persons →

mere display of a sign on a vehicle that it is for hire is not soliciting

to **hire** vehicles to carry them as passengers

Does not include soliciting persons to hire licensed taxis or public service vehicles on behalf of a holder of a PSV operator's licence with his authority.

● **This is an arrestable offence**

Not applicable to Scotland.

BUILDERS' SKIPS

HIGHWAYS ACT 1980

Offences   *S 139*

- Depositing a skip without the written permission of the highway authority
- Failing to comply with any conditions contained in the authorisation
- Not having skip properly lighted at night
- Not having it removed as soon as reasonable practicable after it has been filled
- Not having name and address or telephone number of owner clearly and indelibly marked on the skip.

'Skip'

A container designed to be carried on a vehicle and deposited on a road for the collection and removal of rubble etc.

Markers

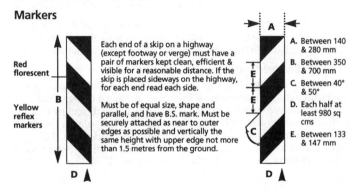

Each end of a skip on a highway (except footway or verge) must have a pair of markers kept clean, efficient & visible for a reasonable distance. If the skip is placed sideways on the highway, for each end read each side.

Red florescent

Yellow reflex markers

Must be of equal size, shape and parallel, and have B.S. mark. Must be securely attached as near to outer edges as possible and vertically the same height with upper edge not more than 1.5 metres from the ground.

A. Between 140 & 280 mm
B. Between 350 & 700 mm
C. Between 40° & 50°
D. Each half at least 980 sq cms
E. Between 133 & 147 mm

BUILDERS' SKIPS (MARKINGS) REGULATIONS 1984

Proceedings

may be taken against the owner * and/or any person whose act resulted in the offence

* If hired for more than a month or subject of an HP agreement, hirer becomes the owner. An owner hiring out his skip mist ensure hirers are aware of their duties.

Defence

That the offence was a result of an act or default of another and reasonable precautions had been taken to avoid any contravention

Police powers

A constable in uniform may require the owner to remove or re-position the skip as soon as possible. The constable has power to remove or re-position it himself and any expenses incurred may be recovered from the owners.   *S 140(2)*

Not applicable to Scotland – See Scots provisions re Builder's Skips in Roads (Scotland) Act, 1984.

NOTICE OF INTENDED PROSECUTION

SECTIONS 1 AND 2 ROAD TRAFFIC OFFENDERS ACT 1988

In relation to certain offences, a person will not be convicted *unless:*

At the time of the offence he was warned that the question of prosecuting him would be considered	within 14 days of the offence a summons was served on him	within 14 days of the offence a notice of intended prosecution was sent to the driver or rider (or in the case of motor vehicles, the registered keeper)

By delivering it to him; by addressing it to him and leaving it at his last known address; or by sending it by registered post, recorded delivery service or first class post addressed to him at his last known address

But the above requirement will not apply if, at the time of the offence or immediately thereafter, an accident occurs owing to the presence on a road of a vehicle in respect of which the offence was committed

Offences involved include *(SCHED 1)*

● Dangerous driving ● Careless and inconsiderate driving ● Leaving a vehicle in a dangerous position ● Dangerous cycling ● Careless and inconsiderate cycling ● Failing to comply with traffic directions ● Failing to comply with traffic signs (see below) ● Exceeding a speed limit or restriction under S14 and S16 (temporary restrictions), S17 (Special Roads), S88 (temporary minimum speed limits) or S89 (speeding generally) of The Road Traffic Regulation Act 1984.

Signs

The offence concerns only the following signs which are contained in Reg 10 of The Traffic Signs Regulations And General Directions 1994. Contravention of others should be dealt with under the relevant order

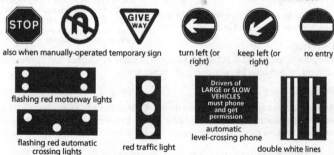

STOP — also when manually-operated temporary sign

GIVE WAY

turn left (or right)

keep left (or right)

no entry

flashing red motorway lights

flashing red automatic crossing lights

red traffic light

Drivers of LARGE or SLOW VEHICLES must phone and get permission — automatic level-crossing phone

double white lines

Also: ● weak bridge weight limit contravention ● height limit contravention ● route for use by buses, tram cars, pedal cycles only

CRASH HELMETS

If a person driving or riding
on a motor cycle uses eye
protectors. they must be of
a type prescribed (conforming to the relevant British
Standard and so marked.)

Protective Headgear

Every person driving or riding on a motor bicycle
(otherwise than as a passenger in a sidecar) on a road.

● must wear protective headgear.

● must be securely fasted to the head of the wearer by means
of straps or other fastening provided for that purpose.

● must bear a mark indication compliance with the British
Standard.

● or be of a type which , by virtue of its shape, material
and construction could reasonable be expected to afford
protection similar to, or greater than, a helmet which
conforms to the British Standard.

BS 6658/1985

A person who drives or rides a motorcycle in
contravention of the foregoing commits an offence. Note
that provided the person committing the offence is 16
years or over no other person can be charged with aiding
and abetting or causing or permitting the offence.
S16(4) RTA 1988

The regulations do not apply to

● mowing machine

● vehicle being propelled by a person on foot

● follower of Sikh religion while wearing a turban
ROAD TRAFFIC ACT 1988, S 16

'Motor bicycle'

means a two-wheeled motor cycle with or without a sidecar. If the distance between the wheels is less than 460mm they shall be regarded as
one wheel
*MOTOR CYCLES (PROTECTIVE HELMETS) REGULATIONS 1980
S 16, ROAD TRAFFIC ACT 1988*

MOTORWAYS

MOTORWAYS TRAFFIC (ENGLAND AND WALES) REGULATIONS
1982, AS AMENDED and MOTORWAYS TRAFFIC (SCOTLAND)
REGULATIONS 1995 WERE MADE UNDER THE PROVISIONS OF SECTION
17 ROAD TRAFFIC REGULATION ACT 1984
The following details apply under respective regulations to both sides of the
border. The numbers of the scots regulations are shown in brackets.

Driving

Must not drive on any part of the
motorway other than the carriageway.
REG 5 (REG 4)
Must drive with the central reservation
on the right or offside unless
directed otherwise.   *REG 6 (REG 5)*

Stopping

Must not stop or remain at rest on a
carriageway or verge unless broken
down (includes mechanical defect,
lack of fuel, water or oil), involved in
an accident, illness, emergency, to
recover or remove an object on the
motorway, or to give help to a person
in such circumstances.

If stoppage is necessary on the carriageway the vehicle must be moved
onto the verge as soon as practicable.
If stopped on the verge, must not cause
obstruction or danger to vehicles on
the carriageway, and shall not remain
at rest longer than is necessary in the
circumstances.   *REG 7 (REG 6)*

Reversing

A vehicle shall not be reversed unless
it is necessary to enable it to move
forward or to be connected to another
vehicle.   *REG 8 (REG 7)*

L Drivers

Persons who have not passed a test to
drive must not use the motorway.
(Does not apply to large goods
vehicles or passenger-carrying vehicle
(over 16 passengers, or over 8 and for
hire or reward)).   *REG 11 (REG 10)*

Lanes (three-lane motorways)

The following vehicles may not use
the right hand lane of a 3 lane (or
more) carriageway: Goods vehicle
max laden weight over 7.5 tonnes;
passenger vehicle constructed or
adapted to carry more than 8 seated
passengers in addition to the driver,
with maximum laden weight over 7.5
tonnes; motor vehicle drawing a trailer;
motor tractor, light locomotive or heavy
locomotive; except when necessary to
pass an exceptionally wide load.
REG 12 (REG 11)

Pedestrians

Prohibited from using any part of the
motorway except when necessary to
do so as a result of accident, emergency or vehicle at rest on motorway
as a result of circumstances specified
in Regulation 7 (above), or with permission of constable to investigate
accident, or he is performing his duty
as constable, member of fire brigade,
or ambulance service, or where necessary to carry out maintenance, repairs
cleaning, etc, of motorway or struc-
tures on, under, over motorway, or to
remove vehicles from motorway, or
carry out serveys, inspections, etc,
under authority of Secretary of State.
*REG 15 (REG 13 – note REG 7 (above)
for Scots is REG 6)*

Animals

Not to be allowed to leave the vehicle,
but if this is necessary, must not be
allowed on the carriageway and must
be on a lead or dept under proper control
REG 14 (REG 12)

 **EYESIGHT**

If a driver's eyesight is such (whether through a defect which cannot be corrected or which is not for the time being corrected) that he cannot comply with the following requirements, he commits an offence:
He must be able to read a car's number plate in good daylight
at a distance of
20.5 metres
(with the aid of glasses or contact lenses if worn)
and comprising letters and figures 79.4 mm high
The above requirement does not apply to the driving of vehicles in group 'K' (mowing machine or pedestrian controlled vehicle).

A constable who suspects that a driver may be guilty of this offence may require him to submit to a test using no other means of correction than he used at the time of driving. It is an offence to refuse to submit to the test.

S. 96 ROAD TRAFFIC ACT 1988
MOTOR VEHICLE (DRIVING LICENCES) REGULATIONS 1987, SCHED 4

PHYSICAL HEALTH

- An applicant for a driving licence must declare whether or not he/she is suffering from or has suffered from a relevant or prospective disablilty – making a false declaration is an offence.

- A licence holder who becomes aware that his is suffering from a relevant or prospective disablilty (which will last for longer than three months) must inform the Secretary of State who may then serve notice on the licence holder, revoking the licence.

- The following disabilities are prescribed by Reg 24:
    - epilepsy
    - severe mental handicap
    - liability to sudden attacks of giddiness or fainting
    - the implant of a heart regulator or pacemaker to prevent such attacks

SS 91-93, ROAD TRAFFIC ACT 1988
REG 24, MOTOR VEHICLES (DRIVING LICENCES) REGULATIONS 1987

STOPPING DISTANCES

Highway Code

Speed (MPH)	20	30	40	50	60	70
Distance (feet)	40	75	120	175	240	315

DRIVING INSTRUCTION

SECTIONS 123, 135 AND 137 ROAD TRAFFIC ACT 1988
MOTOR CARS (DRIVING INSTRUCTION) REGULATIONS 1989

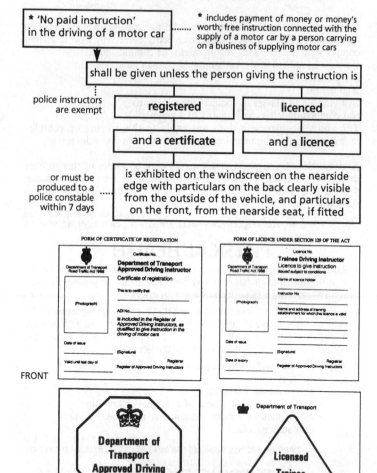

It is also an offence for an unregistered person to use a title, wear a badge, or use any description implying that he is registered. The badge referred to is similar to that displayed on the back of the certificate (see above).

MISCELLANEOUS DRIVING OFFENCES
DEFINITIONS AND MAXIMUM PENALTIES
ROAD TRAFFIC ACT 1988, ROAD TRAFFIC OFFENDERS ACT 1988

Definition of 'dangerously'   RTA S 2A

A person drives dangerously if
- the way he drives falls far below what would be expected of a competent driver, and
- it would be obvious to a competent and careful driver that driving in that way would be dangerous.
- it is obvious to competent and careful driver that driving the vehicle in its current state would be dangerous.

'Public place'

MOTOR VEHICLES (OFF ROAD EVENTS) REGULATIONS 1992, SI 1992 NO 1370

It must be proved that:

(a) the public at large have access to the place, and not just a special class of the public; and

(b) the access is express or implied by the owner. (D.P.P. v Vivier 1991)
Not an offence against Ss 1, 2 or 3, Road Traffic Act if at an authorised motoring event

Causing death by dangerous driving   (RTA S 1)

A person who causes the death of another person by driving a mechanically propelled vehicle dangerously on a road or other public place is guilty of an offence.
10 years' prison sentence and/or unlimited fine – obligatory 2 years' disqualification and re-test – obligatory 3-11 points

Dangerous driving   (RTA S 2)

A person who drives a mechanically propelled vehicle dangerously on a road or other public place is guilty of an offence.
6 months' prison sentence and or statutory max fine – obligatory 12 months' disqualification and re-test – obligatory 3-11 points

Careless or inconsiderate driving   (RTA S 3)

A person who drives a mechanically propelled vehicle on a road or other public place without due care and attention or without reasonable consideration for other persons using the road is guilty of an offence.
Level 4 fine – discretionary disqualification – obligatory 3-9 points

Causing death by careless driving having consumed alcohol (RTA S 3A)

A person who causes the death of another person by driving a mechanically propelled vehicle on a road or other public place without due care and attention, or without reasonable consideration for other persons using the road or other public place and

- he is at the time of driving, unfit through drink or drugs, or
- has consumed so much alcohol that the proportion in his breath, blood or urine at that time, exceeds the prescribed limit, or
- he is, within 18 hours after that time, required to provide a specimen in pursuance of S 7 of this Act, but without reasonable excuse fails to provide it, is guilty of an offence.

10 years' prison sentence and or fine – obligatory 2 years' disqualification and re-test – obligatory 3-11 points

Dangerous or careless cycling (RTA SS 28 AND 29)

A person who rides a cycle on a road dangerously, without due care and attention or without reasonable consideration for other persons using the road is guilty of an offence.

Fine level 4 – fine level 3 for careless or inconsiderate cycling

Causing danger to road users (RTA S 22A)

A person who, intentionally and without lawful authority or reasonable cause,

- causes anything to be on or over a road, or
- interferes with a motor vehicle, trailer or cycle, or
- interferes directly or indirectly with traffic equipment, (traffic signs, barriers, etc)

in such circumstances that it would be obvious to a reasonable person that to do so would be dangerous, is guilty of an offence.

7 years' imprisonment and unlimited fine – on summary trial, 6 months' imprisonment and statutory maximum fine

Driving with excess alcohol RTA S 5(1)(A)

6 months and/or fine level 5 – obligatory disqualification 1 year min – obligatory 3-11 points

In charge with excess alcohol RTA S 5(1)(B)

4 months and/or fine level 4 – discretionary disqualification – obligatory 10 points

Failing to provide specimen of breath RTA S 6

Fine level 3 – forfeiture of vehicle – obligatory disqualification – obligatory 4 points

Failing to provide specimen for laboratory analysis RTA S 7

6 months or level 5 or both – obligatory disqualification 3-11 points (where driving or attempting to drive) – otherwise 3 months or level 4 – discretionary disqualification – 10 points

Construction and use RTA S 41A

Breach of requirements re brakes steering or tyres

Level 5 – discretionary disqualification – obligatory 3 points

MISCELLANEOUS DRIVING OFFENCES
DEFINITIONS AND MAXIMUM PENALTIES
ROAD TRAFFIC REGULATION ACT 1984

Pedestrian crossing contravening regulations
RTRA S 25 'ZEBRA' PEDESTRIAN CROSSING REGULATIONS 1971 REG 8

Failing to accord precedence to a foot passenger within the limits of the crossing

Level 3 fine – obligatory 3 points

Speeding
RTRA S 89(1)

Fine level 3 – discretionary disqualification – obligatory 3-6 points or 3 points (fixed penalty)

Racing and speed trials on public highway (in Scotland public road)
RTA S 12

Fine level 4 – obligatory disqualification – obligatory endorsement – 3-11 points

No insurance
RTA S 143

Fine level 5 – discretionary disqualification – obligatory 6-8 points

Driving while disqualified
RTA S 103

6 months and/or level 5 discretionary disqualification – obligatory 6 points

Leaving vehicle in dangerous position
RTA S 22

Level 3 fine – discretionary disqualification – obligatory 3 points

PARKING

SECTION 99 ROAD TRAFFIC REGULATION ACT 1984 AND
REMOVAL AND DISPOSAL OF VEHICLES REGULATIONS 1986

- within 10m of junction
- parking unlit at night – *see section 3*
- obstruction of road – *see earlier in this section*

Removal of vehicles illegally, obstructively or dangerously parked or abandoned or broken down

Regulations may be made (see below) to permit the removal of vehicles at rest on a road in contravention of any statutory prohibition or restriction or in such a position or in such condition or in such circumstances as to cause obstruction to persons using the road or as to cause danger to such persons. Reg 4 of the Regulations empowers a constable to remove a vehicle which he could require to be removed or which has been abandoned on a road or on land in the open air.

Emergency removal   ROAD TRAFFIC REGULATION ACT 1984, S 49(4), (4A).

A vehicle left in an authorised parking place may be removed in an emergency where the authority which designated the parking place has so empowered the chief officer of police. A constable acting under the instruction of the chief officer of police may suspend a designated parking place for up to seven days to mitigate congestion and obstruction of traffic or in exceptional circumstances.

Disabled Persons   ROAD TRAFFIC REGULATION ACT 1984 S 117.

Restriction of parking orders under Ss 1, 6, 9, 35, 45, or 46 of the Road Traffic Regulation Act 1984 shall provide for an exemption for a disabled person's vehicle displaying in the relevant position a disabled person's badge and, where the period of prohibition is more than 3 hours, an orange parking disk with the time at which parking began marked. Wrongful use of a disabled person's badge is an offence.

PART 6

SUPPLEMENT FOR SCOTLAND

A NOTE TO OFFICERS SERVING IN SCOTTISH POLICE FORCES

The original intention of the *Traffic Officer's Companion* was to provide operational officers serving in English and Welsh police forces with a handy guide book on Road Traffic legislation.

The book has been very successful and has proved itself to be a valuable asset to operational police officers in England and Wales. In discussions with Police Review Publishing I was invited to adapt Gordon Wilson's works in order that officers in Scottish forces could benefit from his skills.

As a result I have prepared the enclosed supplement for officers in the Scottish police forces. This supplement deals not only with Traffic legislation which is only applicable to Scotland but also contains additional legislation common in Scotland.

In keeping with Gordon Wilson's works, the relevant legislation has been subjected to practical interpretation. It should not, therefore be regarded as a definitive work of reference and specific technical details may require further research. On no account should it be used for study purposes by candidates sitting the Police (Scotland) Promotion Examinations

Unless stated otherwise the text in the main part of this book is applicable to Scotland.

John Pilkington LLB BA
Former Inspector Strathclyde Police

MEANING OF THE TERM 'ROAD'
SECTION 151 ROADS (SCOTLAND) ACT 1984

Definition of 'road'

Any way (other than a waterway) over which there is a public right of passage (by whatever means and whether subject to a toll or not) and includes the road's verge and any bridge (whether permanent or temporary) over which, or tunnel through which, the road passes, and any reference to a road includes a part thereof.

Unless stated otherwise, officers in Scotland should use the above definition of a road as they work through this book.

The term 'public road' as defined for the Vehicle Excise and Registration Act 1994 has the same meaning as is applied by the Roads (Scotland) Act 1984, and means a road which a Roads Authority has a duty to maintain.

CONTROL OF BUILDERS' SKIPS ON ROADS

SECTION 85 ROADS (SCOTLAND) ACT 1984

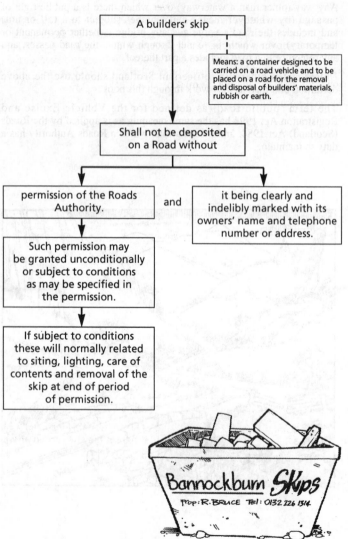

A builders' skip

Means: a container designed to be carried on a road vehicle and to be placed on a road for the removal and disposal of builders' materials, rubbish or earth.

Shall not be deposited on a Road without

permission of the Roads Authority.

and

it being clearly and indelibly marked with its owners' name and telephone number or address.

Such permission may be granted unconditionally or subject to conditions as may be specified in the permission.

If subject to conditions these will normally related to siting, lighting, care of contents and removal of the skip at end of period of permission.

Bannockburn *Skips*

Prop: R. BRUCE Tel: 0132 226 1314

Offence S 85(3)

For the owner of the skip who uses it, or causes or permits it to be used on a road in contravention of Section 85.

Defence S 85(4)

It is a defence, (except in relation to the offence of not having owner's name etc, on the skip), to prove another person undertook the responsibility of complying with the permission/condition contravened, and that the offence was committed without the consent or connivance of the owner; and that other person may be charged with and convicted of the contravention as if he were the owner.

REMOVAL OF SKIP etc
SECTION 86

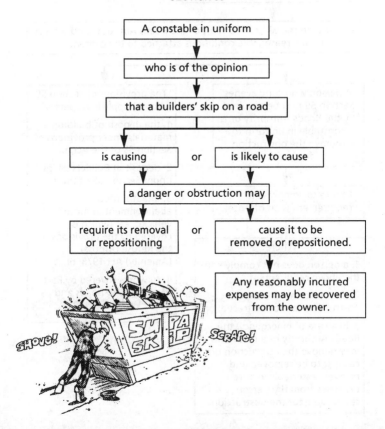

CONTROL OF OBSTRUCTIONS ON ROADS

SECTION 59 ROADS (SCOTLAND) ACT 1984

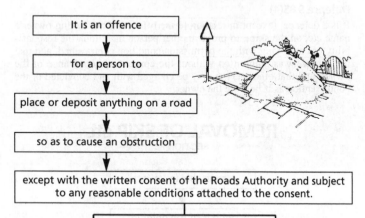

It is an offence

for a person to

place or deposit anything on a road

so as to cause an obstruction

except with the written consent of the Roads Authority and subject to any reasonable conditions attached to the consent.

A person who contravenes Section 59 may be required by the Roads Authority or a constable in uniform to remove the obstruction forthwith.

Failure to comply with this requirement is an offence.

Where:

1. a person does not comply with the above requirement;

2. the person who caused the obstruction cannot be traced; or

3. in a case of emergency, the Roads Authority or a constable may remove the obstruction or cause it to be removed and recover reasonably incurred expenses from the person responsible for the obstruction

The provisions of Section 59 do not apply in respect of:

1. the deposit of building materials under provisions of Section 58 of the Act; or

2. deposit of Builders' Skips under Section 85 of the Act;

3. unauthorised abandonment of motor vehicles, etc (which is covered by the provisions of the Refuse Disposal (Amenity) Act 1978; or

4. to works covered by Part IV of the New Roads and Street Works Act 1991.

RESTRICTION ON PLACING BRIDGES, ETC OVER ROADS

SECTION 90 ROADS (SCOTLAND) ACT 1984

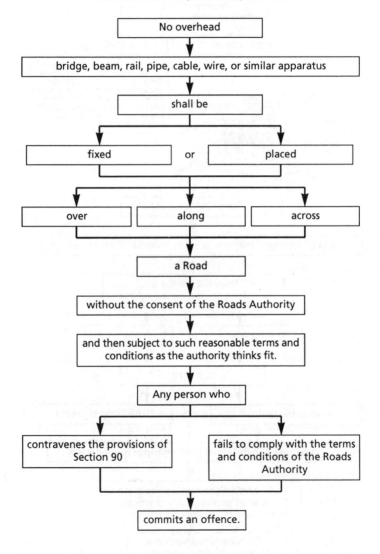

No overhead

bridge, beam, rail, pipe, cable, wire, or similar apparatus

shall be

fixed   or   placed

over   along   across

a Road

without the consent of the Roads Authority

and then subject to such reasonable terms and conditions as the authority thinks fit.

Any person who

contravenes the provisions of Section 90

fails to comply with the terms and conditions of the Roads Authority

commits an offence.

DEPOSIT OF MUD etc ON ROAD
SECTION 95 ROADS (SCOTLAND) ACT 1984

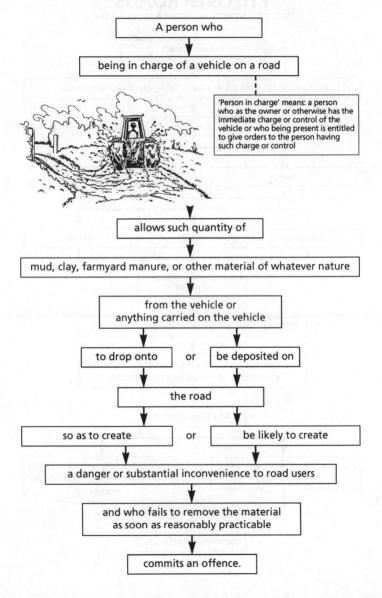

A person who

↓

being in charge of a vehicle on a road

'Person in charge' means: a person who as the owner or otherwise has the immediate charge or control of the vehicle or who being present is entitled to give orders to the person having such charge or control

↓

allows such quantity of

↓

mud, clay, farmyard manure, or other material of whatever nature

↓

from the vehicle or
anything carried on the vehicle

↓

to drop onto   or   be deposited on

↓

the road

↓

so as to create   or   be likely to create

↓

a danger or substantial inconvenience to road users

↓

and who fails to remove the material
as soon as reasonably practicable

↓

commits an offence.

DAMAGE TO ROADS
SECTION 100 ROADS (SCOTLAND) ACT 1984

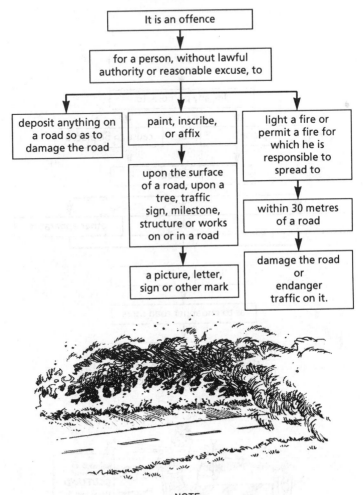

```
It is an offence
        │
for a person, without lawful
authority or reasonable excuse, to
   │           │              │
```

| deposit anything on a road so as to damage the road | paint, inscribe, or affix | light a fire or permit a fire for which he is responsible to spread to |

```
                    │                          │
        upon the surface of a road,     within 30 metres
        upon a tree, traffic sign,        of a road
        milestone, structure or works           │
        on or in a road                          │
                    │                  damage the road
        a picture, letter, sign or           or
        other mark                        endanger
                                        traffic on it.
```

NOTE

A farmer who culpably and recklessly endangered the public, by neglecting to ensure that no danger was caused to persons on a public road from a fire – he had set to straw in his field, which spread to vegetation at the side of the road and smoke obscured visibility, causing a collision – was found guilty of the common law crime of Culpable and Reckless Fire-Raising.

PLACING ROPES ETC IN ROAD
SECTION 101 ROADS (SCOTLAND) ACT 1984

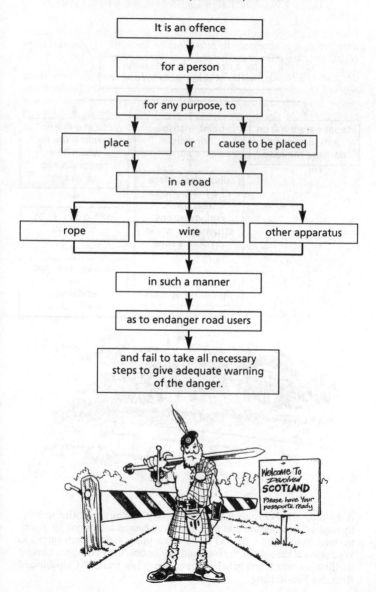

It is an offence

↓

for a person

↓

for any purpose, to

↓

place   or   cause to be placed

↓

in a road

↓

rope | wire | other apparatus

↓

in such a manner

↓

as to endanger road users

↓

and fail to take all necessary steps to give adequate warning of the danger.

Welcome To ~~Devolved~~ SCOTLAND
Please have your passports ready

AIDING AND ABETTING – ROAD TRAFFIC OFFENCES IN SCOTLAND

In order to charge a person with aiding and abetting the commission of an offence, it is necessary to prove that he knew of the circumstances constituting the offence and helped in its commission.

Section 119 Road Traffic Regulation Act, 1984 contains provisions relating to aiding and abetting certain Traffic offences in Scotland and provides that 'a person who aids, abets, counsels, procures or incites any other person to commit an offence against the provisions of the Road Traffic Regulation Act, 1984 and any regulations made under that Act, shall be guilty of an offence and shall be liable, on conviction, to the same punishment as might be imposed on conviction of the first mentioned offence.

Care has to be taken when dealing with other Traffic offences outwith the scope of the Road Traffic Regulation Act, 1984. Where such offences employ the words **use**, **cause** or **permit**, then an accessory to the offence should be prosecuted for **causing and permitting** the offence rather than **aiding and abetting**. If, however, there is a clear case of a person having aided and abetted a Traffic offence not covered by the Road Traffic Regulation Act 1984, the offender should be charged with a contravention of Section 293 Criminal Procedure (Scotland) Act 1995 and shall be liable to the same penalties as the original offender.

TAKING MOTOR VEHICLES WITHOUT AUTHORITY (STATUTORY CLANDESTINE POSSESSION)

SECTION 178 ROAD TRAFFIC ACT 1988

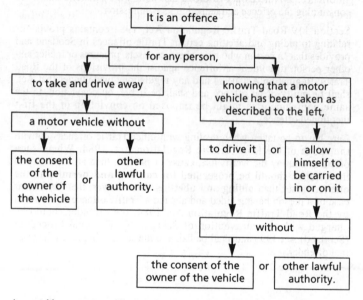

A constable may arrest without warrant any person he reasonably suspects of having committed or having attempted to commit this offence.

An offence under Section 178 may only be committed in respect of motor vehicles (ie, mechanically propelled vehicles intended or adapted for use on the roads). A person who takes and drives away a mechanically propelled vehicle (not intended or adopted for use on the roads) without the consent of owner, etc would commit theft or clandestine possession.

Note 1: An accused who proves he acted in the reasonable belief that he had lawful authority or that the owner of the motor vehicle would, in the circumstances, have given consent if he had been asked for it, shall not be convicted.

Note 2: Section 178 is generally intended to deal with cases where motor vehicles are taken, driven away and then abandoned. If, however, the vehicle were abandoned in a place where it is unlikely to be found, the offender may be held to committed theft, rather than an contravention of Section 178.

Note 3: Where the police trace the vehicle, while still in the possession of the person(s) who took and drove it away without authority, it normal to charge the offender(s) with theft, rather than a contravention of Section 178. However, the final decision as to the charge rests with the Procurator Fiscal.

CARELESS DRIVING – CASE LAW
re USE OF TELEPHONES IN VEHICLES

As a result of telephones being fitted to vehicles, a body of Scots Case Law has grown up relating to the use of telephones in moving vehicles and the offence of careless driving under Section 3 of the Road Traffic Act, 1988.

There are three main cases to consider:

1. *McPhail v Haddow 1990 S.C.C.R 339*

   In this case, the accused was charged with careless driving for using a portable telephone while driving. The court held that, in the absence of any lack of control over the vehicle or any danger to others, there was no evidence of careless driving.

2. *Rae v Friel 1992 S.C.C.R 688*

   In this case the accused was charged with careless driving for travelling in excess of 70 mph on a motorway while holding a telephone in one hand and overtaking five other vehicles in two overtaking manoeuvres. He had only one hand on the steering wheel during these manoeuvres.

   The court held the important feature was that the accused overtook five vehicles, and that if any of the had happened suddenly to move out into the overtaking lane an emergency would have been created to which the accused would not have been able to react appropriately – as a result the accused was convicted of careless driving.

3. *Stock v Carmichael 1993 S.C.C.R 136*

   In this case, there was no overtaking manoeuvre, but evidence was led that the driver was not aware of a police vehicle alongside him and that the use of the telephone, except in an emergency, was a breach of the Highway Code.

   The court held the driver was guilty of careless driving in this case but stressed that each case depends on its own facts and circumstances.

POWER OF ARREST IN SCOTLAND FOR DANGEROUS OR CARELESS DRIVING OR CYCLING

SECTION 167 ROAD TRAFFIC ACT 1988

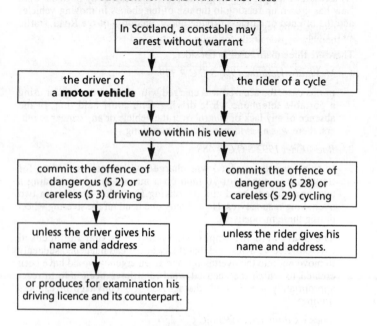

> In Scotland, a constable may arrest without warrant

the driver of **a motor vehicle**	the rider of a cycle

who within his view

commits the offence of dangerous (S 2) or careless (S 3) driving	commits the offence of dangerous (S 28) or careless (S 29) cycling

unless the driver gives his name and address	unless the rider gives his name and address.

or produces for examination his driving licence and its counterpart.

NOTE

Although Section 2 and 3 offences may be committed in any mechanically propelled vehicle, the powers provided under Section 167 in respect of Sections 2 and 3 can only be used against the driver of a **motor vehicle** (ie a mechanically propelled vehicle intended or adapted for use on the roads).

Refusal to provide name and address etc

Section 169 Road Traffic Act 1988 provides that if the driver of a mechanically propelled vehicle, who is alleged to have committed an offence under Section 2 or 3 RTA 1988, or the rider of a cycle who is alleged to have committed an offence under Section 28 or 29 RTA 1988, refuses – on being required by **any person** having reasonable grounds for so requiring – to give his name or address, or gives a false name or address is guilty of an offence.

NOTE: Section 169 applies throughout Great Britain

PEDAL CYCLES

1. Dangerous cycling

SECTION 28 ROAD TRAFFIC ACT 1988

It is an offence for a person to ride a cycle dangerously on a roads.

A person is to be regarded as riding a cycle dangerously if (and only if):
a) the way he rides falls for below what would be expected of a competent and careful cyclist; and
b) it would be obvious to a competent and careful cyclist that riding in that way would be dangerous.

The term 'dangerous' refers to danger either of injury to any person or of serious damage to property.

2. Careless and inconsiderate cycling

SECTION 29 ROAD TRAFFIC ACT 1988

It is an offence for a person to ride a cycle on a road without due care and attention, or without reasonable consideration for other persons using the road.

PEDAL CYCLES (cont)

3. Cycling when under the influence of drink or drugs

Section 30 Road Traffic Act, 1988

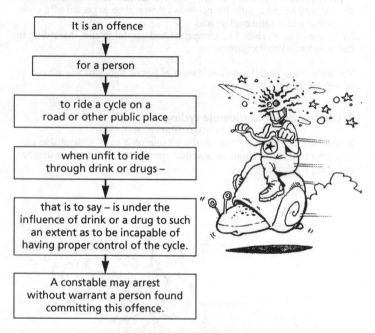

It is an offence

↓

for a person

↓

to ride a cycle on a
road or other public place

↓

when unfit to ride
through drink or drugs –

↓

that is to say – is under the
influence of drink or a drug to such
an extent as to be incapable of
having proper control of the cycle.

↓

A constable may arrest
without warrant a person found
committing this offence.

NOTE

Under the provisions of Section 294 Criminal Procedure (Scotland) Act, 1995 any person who **attempts** to ride a cycle on a road or other public place when unfit to ride through drink or drugs also commits an offence under Section 30 of the Road Traffic Act, 1988.

The police have no power to require a cyclist suspected of contravening Section 30 to provide specimens of breath, blood or urine. However, the cyclist may be requested to provide such specimens and/or undergo a medical examination and tests provided he is informed that he is entitled to refuse and, that if he agrees, the results may be used in evidence.

DUTY TO GIVE INFORMATION AS TO DRIVER
SECTION 172 ROAD TRAFFIC ACT 1988

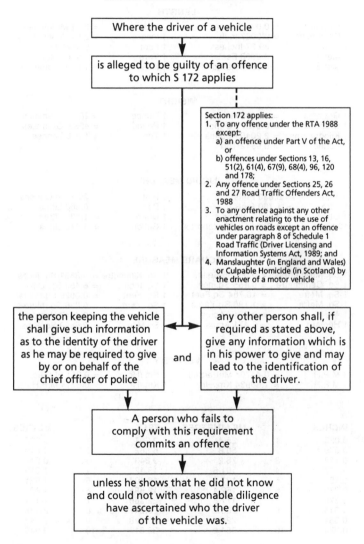

Where the driver of a vehicle

is alleged to be guilty of an offence to which S 172 applies

Section 172 applies:
1. To any offence under the RTA 1988 except:
   a) an offence under Part V of the Act, or
   b) offences under Sections 13, 16, 51(2), 61(4), 67(9), 68(4), 96, 120 and 178;
2. Any offence under Sections 25, 26 and 27 Road Traffic Offenders Act, 1988
3. To any offence against any other enactment relating to the use of vehicles on roads except an offence under paragraph 8 of Schedule 1 Road Traffic (Driver Licensing and Information Systems Act, 1989; and
4. Manslaughter (in England and Wales) or Culpable Homicide (in Scotland) by the driver of a motor vehicle

the person keeping the vehicle shall give such information as to the identity of the driver as he may be required to give by or on behalf of the chief officer of police

and

any other person shall, if required as stated above, give any information which is in his power to give and may lead to the identification of the driver.

A person who fails to comply with this requirement commits an offence

unless he shows that he did not know and could not with reasonable diligence have ascertained who the driver of the vehicle was.

CONVERSION TABLES

LENGTH

1 Millimetre	= 0.03937 Inch	1 Inch	= 25.4 Millimetres
1 Centimetre	= 0.3937 Inch	1 Inch	= 2.54 Centimetres
1 Metre	= 39.37 Inches	1 Foot	= 0.3048 Metre
1 Metre	= 3.2808 Feet	1 Yard	= 0.9144 Metre
1 Metre	= 1.0936 Yards	1 Mile	= 1.609 Kilometres

WEIGHT

1 Gramme	= 15.432 Grains	1 Ounce	= 28.35 Grammes
1 Gramme	= 0.03527 Ounce	1 Pound	= 453.6 Grammes
1 Kilogramme	= 2.2046 Pounds	1 Ton	= 1.016 Tonnes
1 Tonne	= 0.9842 Ton		

LIQUID MEASURE

½ Litre	= 0.880 Pints	1 Pint	= 20 Fluid Ounces
1 Litre	= 1.760 Pints	1 Pint	= 0.568 Litres
1 Litre	= 0.220 Gallons	1 Quart	= 1.136 Litres
10 Litres	= 2 Galls 1½ Pts (approx)	1 Gallon	= 4.546 Litres

SQUARE MEASURE

1 Sq. Millimetre	= 0.00155 Sq.in.	1 Sq. Kilometre	= 0.3861 Sq. Miles
1 Sq. Centimetre	= 0.155 Sq.inch	1 Sq. Inch	= 6.452 Sq. Cms
1 Sq. Metre	= 10.764 Sq.Feet	1 Sq. Foot	= 0.0929 Sq.Metres
1 Sq. Metre	= 1.196 Sq.Yards	1 Sq. Yard	= 0.836 Sq. Metres
1 Are	= 0.0247 Acres	1 Acre	= 0.4047 Hectare
1 Hectare	= 2.471 Acres	1 Sq.Mile	= 2.5899 Sq. Kms

VELOCITY

1 M.P.H.	= 0.44704 Metre/Sec.	1 Km./Hr.	= 0.911 Ft./Sec.
1 M.P.H.	= 1.60934 Km./Hr.	1 Km./Hr.	= 0.6214 M.P.H.

INCHES		MILLIMETRES	FEET		METRES
0.039	1	25.4	3.281	1	0.305
0.079	2	50.8	6.562	2	0.610
0.118	3	76.2	9.843	3	0.914
0.157	4	101.6	13.123	4	1.219
0.197	5	127.0	16.404	5	1.524
0.236	6	152.4	19.685	6	1.829
0.276	7	177.8	22.966	7	2.134
0.315	8	203.2	26.247	8	2.438
0.354	9	228.6	29.528	9	2.743
0.394	10	254.0	32.81	10	3.048

YARDS		METRES	SQ. FT.		SQ. METRES
1.094	1	0.914	10.764	1	0.093
2.187	2	1.829	21.528	2	0.186
3.281	3	2.743	32.292	3	0.279
4.375	4	3.658	43.056	4	0.372
5.468	5	4.572	58.819	5	0.456
6.562	6	5.486	64.583	6	0.557
7.655	7	6.401	75.347	7	0.650
8.749	8	7.315	86.111	8	0.743
9.842	9	8.223	96.875	9	0.836
10. 936	10	9.114	107.640	10	0.929

OUNCES		GRAMMES	POUNDS		KILOGRAMMES
0.035	1	28.350	2.205	1	0.454
0.071	2	56.699	4.409	2	0.9072
0.106	3	85.049	6.614	3	1.361
0.141	4	113.398	8.819	4	1.814
0.176	5	141.748	11.023	5	2.268
0.212	6	170.097	13.228	6	2.722
0.247	7	198.447	15.432	7	3.175
0.282	8	226.796	17.637	8	3.629
0.317	9	255.146	19.842	9	4.082
0.353	10	283.500	22.046	10	4.536

PINTS		LITRES	GALLONS		LITRES
1.761	1	0.568	0.22	1	4.55
3.521	2	1.136	0.44	2	9.09
5.282	3	1.704	0.66	3	13.64
7.043	4	2.272	0.88	4	18.18
8.804	5	2.840	1.10	5	22.73
10.564	6	3.408	1.32	6	27.28
12.325	7	3.976	1.54	7	31.82
14.086	8	4.544	1.76	8	36.37
15.847	9	5.112	1.98	9	40.91
17.600	10	5.680	2.20	10	45.46

MILES		KILOMETRES	MILES		KILOMETRES
0.31	$^1/_2$	0.8	3.42	$5^1/_2$	8.8
0.62	1	1.6	3.73	6	9.7
0.93	$1^1/_2$	2.4	4.04	$6^1/_2$	10.5
1.24	2	3.2	4.35	7	11.3
1.55	$2^1/_2$	4.0	4.66	$7^1/_2$	12.0
1.86	3	4.8	4.97	8	12.9
2.17	$3^1/_2$	5.6	5.28	$8^1/_2$	13.7
2.49	4	6.4	5.59	9	14.5
2.80	$4^1/_2$	7.2	5.90	$9^1/_2$	15.3
3.11	5	8.0	6.21	10	16.1

INDEX

Forgery etc of records 181

G

General arrest conditions
226
Glass 47
Goods vehicle
definition 3
operators' licences
88-91
plating 97-100
tests 97, 100
Grass cutting machines
51

H

Hackney carriages 108
roof signs 108
Hazard lights 144
Hazard warning
labels 207-210
panels 207-210
signs (diamonds)
209-210
Hazchem code 111
Headlamps 126-127
definition 114
Heavy locomotive
definition 3
Heavy motor car
definition 3
Hedge trimmers 51
Height
maximum 10
travelling 23-24
HGV
documentation list 72
Horn 36
Hours of darkness
definition 114
Hours of work 166-168
definitions 169
general 156-159
selector 157
records 170-173

I

Indicators, direction
136-137
Insecure load 30
Instruction, driving 236
Insurance 87
European Community
vehicles 87
foreign vehicles 87, 110
penalties 239
International freight
permit 110
Invalid carriage,
definition 5
registration mark 96

speed limits 198

L

Lamps, *see* Lights
Large goods vehicles,
definition 5
licence 82
Length, maximum 6-7
Light locomotive
definition 3
Lights
bicycle 115
cleanliness 114
colour 124
daytime 121
direction indicators
136-137
end-outline marker 148
flashing 125
fog, front 143
fog, rear 141
front 128-129
hazard 144
headlamps 126-127
maintenance 114
masking 121
motor cycle 115
movement 125
obligatory 114-119
obligatory,
exemptions 114-119
obligatory, use 122-123
obstruction of 123
position 114, 128-131
projecting loads 154
rear 130-131
reflectors
132-135, 147-153
registration plate 144
reversing 142
side marker 146-147
stop 138-139
towing 120
using 122-123
warning beacons 124
Living van 28
Load
abnormal 58-61
insecure 30
projecting, lights 154

M

Maintenance vehicles 52
Manufacturer's plate
11, 98
Marker lamps
end-outline 148
side 146-147
Markers
projection 155
reflective, rear 149-153

side 155
Mascots 69
Medium-sized goods
vehicle, definition 4
Military vehicles 50
Minibuses, PSV, as 107
Ministry plate 11, 98
Mirrors
fitting 46
requirement 45
use 46
Moped
definition 5
plates 101
Motor car, definition 2
Motor cycle
crash helmets 233
definition 5
driving licence 73
footrests 70
lamps 115
noise 31
plates 101
registration mark 95
sidestands 69
silencer 31
trailer 27
training certificate 81
Motor tractor
definition 3
Motor vehicle
categories
75-76, 160-165
definition 2
Motorways 234
speed limits 198-200

N

Noise 31
excessive 69
Notice of intended
prosecution 232
Notional gross weight 22

O

Obligatory lights 114-119
exemptions 114-119
Obstruction 246-247, 250
Offences 237-239
aiding and abetting
in Scotland 251
Opening doors 70
Operator's licence 88-91
exemptions 89-90
types 88
Overhang 8

P

Parking
darkness in 69
disabled person 240